TWISTED

A MINNEAPOLIS TORNADO MEMOIR

Marie Porter

Photography by Michael Porter

Celebration Generation

Twisted: A Minneapolis Tornado Memoir

First Edition, May 22, 2012

ISBN-13: 978-0-9846040-9-8
ISBN-10: 0-9846040-9-X

Celebration Generation
P.O. Box 41844
Plymouth, MN USA
55441

www.celebrationgeneration.com

Acknowledgments

There are so many people that we need to thank...I'm dreading the idea that I could possibly forget someone!

First off, I would like to thank my best friend, my husband Porter. I have no idea how I would have gotten through this without him, in so many ways. From emotional support through the ordeal, to him being so skilled with the rebuild, to his undying support for this book - he was amazing.

Thank you SO very much to friends - new and old - who volunteered many hours of hard labor to help dig us out from this mess: Peter Gamache, Tara Q, Jessica McMillan, Jennifer Fairchild, Todd Murray, Carrie Iwan, Otha Lohse, Jeanne & John Rubbo, Heather & Mark Sauntry, David Waldorf, the Smith family, Tom, and anyone I may have forgotten. (Forgive me, it was a high stress time!). Aside from the desperately needed physical help, you guys really helped keep us sane. We hope to be able to repay the favors some day!

Thank you, so very much, to everyone who generously donated towards our repairs. With such a huge gulf between what insurance would cover, and the actual damages... you guys were amazing. We are so touched by the generosity not only from friends, but from complete strangers. Thank you, Anime Twin Cities, Mark &Heather Sauntry, Barb Andersen, Karen Cyson, Jeanne & John Rubbo, Jason Wynia, Barbara Ploegstra Hunt, Carrie Iwan , David Medinets, Helen Shin, Sheila Smith, Brent Black, Christopher MacAllister, Shawn Colton, Jason Glaser, Charlene Russell, Dave Benhart, Charlotte Nickerson, Shawn Bakken, Amy Rea, Tom Hogan, Ray Porter, Sarah Elizabeth, Alicia LaMunion and various employees at Boston Scientific - Maple Grove.

Thank you to everyone who bought my cook books as a result of the tornado, and spread the word. We're not used to accepting charity, so it was nice to have some help in earning our way out of this mess. I hope you loved the books!

Thank you so much to Tracy of Iron River Construction. You walked in to SUCH a mess- both literally and figuratively - and took such great care of us. Also, big thanks to Jim Leighton for the recommendation!

Thank you to the geek communities - both local and otherwise - as well as to friends and followers on social media. Thank you for putting up with me through this whole roller coaster, for help finding contacts, resources, referrals, & information, and for your continued support.

HUGE thanks to the people behind the North Minneapolis Post Tornado Watch page. "Rock stars" doesn't even begin to describe you guys. Your tireless work to make sure that those of us affected by the tornado were kept up to date on resources and information was awe inspiring. Peter Kerre, Mandi Studler, Genesia Williams, Shane Williams, and Anthony Newby - you guys are awesome.

Thank you FEMA, for your quick response to the tornado, and honestly trying to help us. While we may not have qualified for individual assistance, I want you to know that some of us appreciate your efforts, and your obviously caring & concerned employees on the ground here. It's nice to know that part of the government was looking out for us, even when our local government was NOT.

Finally, I should - grudgingly - thank the City of Minneapolis. If it weren't for their blazing incompetence - making everything FAR more stressful and convoluted than it ever needed to be - I wouldn't have been fired up enough to write this book. On the same note, I suppose thanks is also due to opportunistic vultures and poorly behaved contractors. You all made this such an ... *interesting*... experience

Table of Contents

Preface

I'll never forget my first real exposure to life in a tornado zone.

I'd moved to Minnesota a few months before, in the middle of February. Having been born and raised in Canada, there was so much that was new to me... and so much that no one had bothered to tell me.

I was gassing up my car in Maple Grove, on a sunny and warm spring day in 2006, when the air raid sirens went off. I had absolutely NO idea what one was supposed to do in the event of an act of war, and freaked out.

While frantically dialing my husband at work and ducking, I tried to remember what I'd seen in those old movie clips. History class, about wars that had happened many decades before, kids in school - what did they do? Was that "duck and cover"? I know it's not "stop, drop, and roll" - we'd learned THAT one! Was I supposed to get under my car? Who paid attention to what they did in air raid drills in these old movies? It was Canada, and I'd never lived anywhere where that would be a real consideration.

I'd never been so scared in my life. It's one thing for something like this to happen... but to be completely unprepared and left floundering? THAT is what scared me more than anything. I'd had no cultural exposure to this, and I was missing any "air raid drill" training that kids that grew up here probably were receiving.

My husband picked up the phone, and I was so glad he was around to do so, as he worked in a huge building in the area - for all I know, it could be a target for this apparent air raid.

I'm sure I sounded like a madwoman, asking what the HELL I'm supposed to do when air raid sirens go off.

He laughed. Hard.

As he explained that those sirens weren't for air raids, they were for weather, I finally noticed that no one else was scared, they all milled about their business on this sunny afternoon. Not only was the siren NOT about an act of war, it was a regular, scheduled thing. This was the first Wednesday of the month, it was 1:00pm, of COURSE there was supposed to be a siren going off. Of course.

Of course, that would have been nice to know ahead of time! I'd never lived anywhere that had any sort of weather that required sirens to announce it, and I'd only ever heard of that sort of siren in the context of old war movies.

While my husband thought he was giving me good news - allaying my shock that I apparently lived in a place that had to be concerned about air raids - he was actually giving me terrifying news. Oh shit, I'd moved somewhere where tornadoes are frequent enough, they have sirens set up to warn about them.

I had never considered tornadoes as a concern, moving to Minnesota. Had he lived in Oklahoma or Kansas, he would have had a much harder time getting me to move. I may never have been exposed to tornadoes, but they scared the shit out of me - in theory. I'd handled floods. I'd handled never ending blizzards, and 5-6 yards of snow over the course of a week or two - snow drifts higher than the houses. I'd walked down Bourbon street during a tropical storm, not that long before Katrina.

Tornadoes, though? I don't DO tornadoes.

"Don't worry", my husband said. "They never hit in the city. You're safe!"

7

Our New Beginning

Racing towards our Minneapolis home, I'd never been so scared in my life.

Normally, I'd consider myself to be calm under stress… maybe even thrive on it. When having conversations that no couple should ever have to have, as our world was coming down around us though? Not so much. On May 22, 2011 our lives changed. Violently.

A few months earlier, we'd been renting-to-own a home in a nearby suburb. The rent was crippling us, and it was impossible to save up for a down payment. It was a world of hurt for us, but we loved the house, and tried to stick it out.

When the foreclosed house next door sold for 1/3 of what we were contracted to pay, though… we decided to look into buying a foreclosed home.

I still laugh when I think about how lucky we were, in buying this new house. Within minutes of finding out the selling price of the neighbor's house, we were scanning listings online.

I came upon one listing that grabbed my attention. To this day, I don't know what it was that caused me to take notice. It was a fairly average older house, one of many in our price range. The exterior was not the nicest color, but the inside looked "ok". There wasn't a ton of room… there wasn't any real particular advantage to this house at all.

Instinct is a funny thing. I just had a feeling that THIS was our house. We wanted to see it right away, super excited about the possibility of owning our own home. So, just after 8pm that night, we drove out to look at it, in the dark.

It was a house. It was dark, and completely in snow. Just a regular old house, nothing really spectacular… but I was still feeling like this was "the one". I arranged to meet a realtor at the house the next day.

Honestly, the tour almost ended immediately. The kitchen was awful - seriously the worst kitchen I'd ever seen in my life. It was tiny, had awful cabinetry up one side, a weird, super tall sink unit (that was very trashy looking), and it was shaped like a ... stealth bomber.

I felt sort of guilty about wasting the realtor's time, so I toured the rest of the house. The two bedrooms on the main floor would make great offices for us. The bathroom was awful, though. The living and dining rooms had gorgeous dark wood trim, but the walls were in crappy shape.

I headed up the stairs to the converted attic, which was the main bedroom. Huh. Some moron had sprayed popcorn finish all over the walls and ceiling, and then painted it an ugly yellow color. Never seen anything like THAT before!

From the top of the stairs, I scanned the room, with its unfinished floor. That amount of space would be nice... I could picture hanging out on the mini deck on the other side of a patio door... I think I was trying to convince myself that my initial instinct wasn't horribly wrong.

Then I noticed a weird little alcove off the far end of the room, behind the stairs. Unlike the bizarre yellow popcorn walls, it was nicely finished in cedar. It looked new... what the hell? Was that a .. THERE IS A JACUZZI IN THE BEDROOM? Maybe I'm simple, but the idea of buying a house for $45k, that had a Jacuzzi alcove in the bedroom? That's enough reason to make everything else work. I have NO idea why that Jacuzzi was neither mentioned nor photographed in any of the real estate listings for the house, but I loved it.

I had my husband drop what he was doing at work, and come view the house.

On first glance, he thought it was a cute older house, and immediately fell in love with the woodwork. Aside from the gorgeous dark wood trim that I loved, the hardwood floors throughout were in excellent condition, and the doors were all solid wood.

He's a handy guy, so started looking for potential deal breakers. He checked out the foundation, looked for any sort of major repairs that would be needed. Not as concerned about the cosmetic issues, he wanted to ensure we were buying a sound home.

Having already researched the crime statistics that morning - North Minneapolis having a reputation as a bit of a bad neighborhood - he gave his seal of approval, and we put in an offer immediately. One month later, the house was OURS.

For him, the bedroom was a huge selling point. While his calculations on crime and population density had us facing the average of getting broken in to once every 5 years, he loved the idea of the bedroom as an "oasis". No matter what may be going on outside, this would be our fortress of solitude, vaulted above the street below.

We hired dry wallers and painters to come in and fix the place up. The popcorn finish was scraped from the bedroom wall and all of the ceilings, with "knock down" texture added. New carpet was installed in the bedroom. The walls on the main floor were repaired and painted. I made custom curtains for the entire house. Aside from the kitchen and bathroom, the interior of the house was gorgeous when we moved in, in March 2011.

For budget and scope reasons, we decided to wait until the summer to start discussing what we were going to have to do in the kitchen and bathroom. They just required too much work, to try and wrap our heads around at the time. With the rest of the house done so beautifully, though... we could wait.

We were so very happy with our purchase, and with the work that had been done so far. This house was our freedom! It was the end to paying exorbitant amounts of rent, with no long term gain from it. It was OURS, and we loved it.

That's not to say that it was perfect, of course. With our new purchase came a list of things that the city wanted us to do to renovate it. Most items were small... replace the outlet covers, put a new railing on the stairs to the basement. The big, labor intensive, and expensive to-do was to add railings to our sizeable deck, which would have to wait until the snow melted.

We had plenty to keep us occupied for the next 3 months. The decision to move, home purchase, and actual move had all happened so fast, nothing had been properly packed. We picked away at unpacking the many boxes, and trying to get things where they were supposed to be.

10

We tackled some of the interior fixes that needed to be done. We brewed up a few batches of wine in our new "brew room". We thoroughly enjoyed our new "oasis" bedroom... soaking in the Jacuzzi, watching movies, and snuggling with our 4 cats. Life was good!

As spring arrived, the melting snow provided us with another unexpected surprise from the house.

Carrying groceries in from the car, I noticed an ugly, wrinkled little mass on the ground. I wasn't sure what it was, but damn - there were quite a few of them. I was hoping that it wasn't some sort of weird fungus, when I saw that one of them was cracked open. It looked like... yes, it was a walnut. A walnut!

I can't even tell you how excited I was to find out that the huge, gorgeous old tree in our back yard was a black walnut tree. I'd never had a walnut tree before, but I'd heard of other people locally who owned them - and I was a little jealous.

The discovery sent me into a flurry of research. What do you do with the walnuts? How do you shell them, dry them... what would I make with them? The ideas flew. I'd actually just read an article about making Nocino liqueur, and Italian walnut liqueur.

In addition to the happiness that the find brought me, it also brought a bit of negative information. I learned that black walnut trees render the soil beneath them - for a large radius - toxic. Not many plants would grow in our back yard, as a result.

"Oh well", I thought. We may not be able to have a garden out there like we'd hoped, but we had WALNUTS! I was so very excited for the possibilities.

As the end of May - and our repair deadlines - approached, we planned for the completion of the deck railings. We did the math, selected the necessary wood and hardware, and placed an order for everything we needed. My husband cleared some room in the garage - which was impassable, with unpacked boxes from our move. I worked on unpacking my office, to allow for us to bring in the final piece of my matched set of office furniture, a shiny purple hardwood credenza.

11

Knowing we'd need to rent a truck to haul the wood, I juggled logistics to handle a few other errands at the same time, maximizing that investment. I'm a logistics person, and when May 22nd came around, we were prepared with a game plan. It was going to be a long day of hard work, but I'd choreographed the day beautifully, and we were READY for the day.

As it was to be a long day, we rented our moving truck early.

Sweaty, covered in water and dirt, hauling decking at Menards. #HomeOwnership #DamnItFeelsGoodToBeAGangster #YesISaidSterNotSta - Twitter, Sun May 22 15:40:53 UTC

We first picked up the lumber, then headed to the city impound lot, for a tree - something we had been looking forward to for a few months. The city had a "tree trust" program, where residents could purchase a tree of their choice for just $25. We'd chosen to pick up a Honey Crisp apple tree, and were looking forward to the addition to our backyard. A walnut tree AND an apple tree! Think of the possibilities!

The next stop was to visit our former home, to move the remaining items from the garage and shed. As one of the items was a large, heavy commercial Hobart mixer, the moving truck would come in handy.

It was miserable work that morning. It was hot and humid in the morning, which had made pulling the lumber order a sweaty and arduous task. By the time we got to the impound lot for our new tree, the sky had darkened and was starting to drizzle. We picked a 10' tall apple tree that was in full bloom, and scrambled back into the truck to avoid the weather.

As we arrived at our former home, the sky had opened up completely, and was pouring rain. We trudged through the mud and water puddles to collect the last few pieces of yard equipment, our grill, and garden tools.

Soaked to the bone, we dropped my mixer off at my father in law's house, where we would have to store in until we could find a buyer. After chatting a while, we headed home, to unload the tree, the lumber, and the last of the items from our former house.

Back in the moving van, heading towards the rental agency, we patted ourselves on the back for a good job done. We had busted our asses, and managed to finish the entire list of tasks early! Exhausted but happy, we decided to grab some lunch, and then spend the rest of the day alternating between watching movies and soaking in the Jacuzzi. Not only did our sore muscles need the rest and soaking, we figured we'd earned the rest of the day to relax. With all of the moving, unpacking, and renovating leading up to that day, the idea of an afternoon off was deliciously indulgent.

We returned the truck, and went to a nearby Arby's for lunch. It felt good to get off our feet, it was such a relief to be done for the day, and we happily discussed movie options for the afternoon.

It was raining pretty hard by then, so we talked about opening the curtain above the Jacuzzi, laying back and watching the rain through the skylight above. Maybe there'd be lightning to watch... oh, it all sounded so relaxing and blissful.

... and then the sirens went off.

Running in to Hell

From that initial "air raid siren" incident, I never did acclimatize to the whole idea of tornadoes, or weather sirens. Rather than getting better over time, things had managed to get worse. On two occasions in the weeks leading up to May 22, we'd been out driving when tornado sirens went off. Rather than "We've never seen one", or "Nothing has happened!", my mind processed it as "we're going to get it, sooner or later", and every false alarm was just hurling us closer to ... whatever vague idea I had about what it would be like to encounter a tornado. I was terrified.

The anxiety I'd started developing about tornadoes had reached a point where I could NOT handle being away from the house, out in the open, with sirens going off. We packed up the remains of our meal and headed home, where I would feel safe.

It had gone almost black outside at that point, despite being the early afternoon. The rain was sheeting down like I'd never seen before - not in that tropical storm in New Orleans, not in several years living on the east coast. Visibility was pretty much zero.

We had only driven a block or two when my phone rang. The rain was so loud, I could barely make out what the caller was saying. It took a few tries before I finally made it out - she was calling from the alarm company, our system was reporting that there was a fire in our basement.

A fire. Something I've never had to deal with. My mind raced - the cats. I didn't even consider property damage, I was so focused on getting the cats out safely. We didn't yet know our neighbors, and no one had a key to our house. The fire department had been called, and we raced to get home.

While my husband took some small degree of comfort in "It's a basement fire, we should have a half hour buffer to save them!", I tried to calm and distract myself by posting a few quick blurbs to my twitter account.

Omg!!! Trying to get home through this monster storm, just got a call that our fire alarm is going off! SO SCARED for the cats. - Twitter, Sun May 22 19:21:36 UTC

14

I've never had to deal with a fire. I am freaking out from the tornado sirens, everyone is driving like an idiot and I am scared for cats - Twitter, Sun May 22 19:30:52 UTC

The weather was not helping. The rain had somehow managed to get worse, the roads were flooding, and everyone was driving like maniacs. Looking back, maybe they'd received similar calls? I couldn't even think straight, all we knew was that we had to get home fast. What would normally be a 20 minute drive home felt like an eternity.

I called the alarm company back almost as soon as I'd hung up. In our hysteria, we'd forgotten to mention that we have a keyless door, and could provide the code. The operator would relay the information to the fire department.

Within a few minutes, they called back with some horrifying information - the roads were impassable, the fire department would not be coming, we were on our own.

I still have no idea how we made it home safely. We weren't driving safely, and the conversation we were having.. No one should ever have to have that conversation. It was a mix of steeling ourselves for what we would be coming home to, formulating a plan to get the cats out, and trying to figure out what items, if any, we'd need to save in order to rebuild our lives. We had no idea how bad the fire was, what we'd be coming home to. I'd certainly never been in a position to run into a burning building for ANY reason, much less to find 4 animals that were likely VERY scared, who were good at hiding.

About a mile from our house, we were stopped by a roadblock. We turned north, and encountered a tree across the road. We turned down another street, and there was another tree in the way. It was all very surreal. Loads of HUGE trees, uprooted like they were mere weeds. I was hyperventilating, Porter was trying to calm me down, and it seemed like a nightmare. I've never been so scared and upset in my life. Every new street we tried to turn down, there were massive trees blocking the road. I've never seen anything like it in my life.

After navigating the new maze for what seemed like hours, we managed to get about 3 blocks from our home. We got out, and sprinted in the general direction of our house, completely disoriented by the chaos around us.

Trees everywhere.

A roof on the street. Garages smashed in, people everywhere, being careful to avoid the masses of downed power lines. All we could think of was our cats, and the fire that had been reported. I've never been so scared in my life.

Between leaving the car and arriving at the house, the memories are fuzzy. Both Porter and I agree that we came out of the back alley across from our house, cutting through someone's yard - but neither one of us remember actually entering the alley, or any part or running through the alley. SO bizarre, how we're both missing the same few minutes of memory - I wonder if we'll ever get them back? I remember running through that yard, and past the people who lived there, who were visibly stunned at everything around us. I remember apologizing for cutting through their yard, which - in hindsight - must have seemed completely ridiculous.

The Obstacle Course to Get Home

When we finally got to the house, there was no immediate evidence of a fire. As Porter ran to the basement to check for a fire, I started to search for the cats.

We were so scared for them. We were calling for them, and there was no response from any of them. We have incredibly vocal cats, they respond to their names... hell, most of them even come when called.

After a quick search through the house, we started a second, more detailed pass. We looked everywhere, pulling debris and unpacked boxes aside. Porter started to look for blood, I was trying to figure out if they could have gotten out.

While there had been no fire, we was plenty of other damage. There were trees sticking in our 2nd floor bedroom wall, we had to duck under a toppled tree to get in our front door... another of the trees in the front yard was leaning on our neighbor's house, ripped right out of the ground.

It was impossible to get to our back yard. Both sides of our yard were completely impassible, having been filled more than waist deep random debris, just packed in there - trees, fencing, roofing, part of someone's deck... the railings from the neighbor's upper deck ...

Reaching the back yard through the house wasn't any better. The small porch just outside of the kitchen had been smashed in, with broken glass and branches everywhere.

Our black walnut tree had broken off - so I thought - and had smashed in our deck, and was leaning against our house. It wouldn't be til days later that I'd find out that the tree - over 100 years old - had actually been ripped from the ground, landed on one part of our roof (smashing it in), and BOUNCED off to land on another section. I can't even imagine...

I remember looking out over all that destruction, how impassable it all was, and thinking that if the cats had gotten out of the house, we would NEVER be able to find them.

It took an hour or so, but we did eventually find all of the cats.

We had NO idea what to do, so we were putting them in the bathroom as we found them. The scope and gravity of the situation hadn't even begun to process.

We found Jame - "The Princess" in the front entryway, crammed between the side of the couch, and a wall. I set her up with food and cat litter in the bathroom, and then just lost it. I'd done a once-over of the house, and just couldn't handle it. I sat on the front steps and just... screamed. Completely useless, completely inconsolable. I started learning right then - though it wasn't something I'd ever considered before, Aspergers and tornadoes just do NOT mix.

My husband was more functional than I was at the moment, and continued to look for the cats while I had my meltdown. Somehow, Tweak - "The Fatass" - had managed to cram himself under the couch. I have no idea how he managed it. This is a BIG cat, and there is not much clearance under that couch - he must have just dove under there.

Some time after Tweak was safely sequestered in the bathroom, Rat - "The Ninja" came strolling out from nowhere, all nonchalant. Very "Hey dad, what's up?". Into the bathroom with her, as we tried to find Turbo - "The Baby". Turbo was only about 6 months old, and it wasn't looking good. We combed over areas we'd already searched, and finally found her under my office desk, hidden behind all of the moving boxes that ended up in and around the desk.

With the cats - all shaken up, but otherwise ok and uninjured - safely in the bathroom, we finally surveyed the damage. It's so weird how we could be searching the house for the cats, but not actually process what had happened around us. Not fully.

I had been vaguely aware of water in the kitchen while searching, but it hadn't stuck out as a glaring abnormality. With the cats safely sequestered... wow. The kitchen ceiling had been smashed in, water was pouring in, and the kitchen floor was sort of caving in, in the middle. There was water everywhere. We hadn't done the dishes before leaving that morning, and there was a cookie sheet of baked goods sitting on the stove... ALL sopping wet now.

Looking out to the backyard... it just looked like a land fill. The yard had just been filled up with crap from everywhere, along with our tree. Trees, roof materials... a lot of random crap. Plant matter was plastered against the house like it had been sprayed on as a finishing texture.

Upstairs, there was a crack along the walls/ceiling seam, all along the south end of the house. The tornado had ripped the roof up and dropped it back down.

The patio door had been completely smashed in, its glass scattered all across our brand new carpet. The mini deck was full of tree branches and random debris.

To the left of the patio door - right at the top of the stairs - a tree had pierced the wall. It had entered in a downward trajectory, coming to rest in the cat litter box. That it landed in the litter box like that? It made a hilarious photograph, and it likely saved our hardwood floor up there... but at the time, it was a scary sight. No one should ever have to see a tree - probably 5" in diameter! - sticking in their wall like that. I hope the cats were nowhere near their litter box when it happened!

Cats are all ok. The house is not. There is a tree in our bedroom. Likely a write off. Our new house. Devastation is incomprehensible - Twitter, Sun May 22 22:02:31 UTC

We were suddenly aware of how weird everything felt - not even so much the visuals, but the complete lack of noise. There were no birds chirping. Without electricity, neither our air conditioner - nor anyone elses- was running. All of the minute "noise pollution" that we never even notice was just non existent. My husband likened it to being at a loud nightclub with music, having it all get shut off instantly, and everyone just quiet in shock. On top of that, it had gotten very humid.

I felt like the walls - and all this destruction - were closing in on me. Suddenly, our "oasis" felt very claustrophobic. I had to get out. I went back out to the front steps for some fresh air, and finally got a clear look at my surroundings

Outside, I realized that I was crying and shaking. I thought I was going to have a total nervous breakdown. I looked out over my street, and it was just... surreal. It was like something out of a disaster movie, but so much worse. Our street had been completely canopied by many VERY old trees, they were now almost all flattened. Ripped out of the ground, roots and all, like they were NOTHING.

Picture that for a moment. Completely open sky. Not only did many houses get their roofs damaged / torn off, the whole neighborhood lost its "roof".

I noticed that my beloved car was hidden under a large tree that had landed on it... and it was far from alone in that sense. Every car on the street - and probably for blocks around - were destroyed. A car across the street had a large section of tree sticking out of its windshield, many were just flattened.

There were trees in the streets, trees blocking the sidewalks, and trees laying on top of houses. 3 houses down, one tree had landed on another, inverted. Truly bizarre sight! There were power lines everywhere, garages flattened - at least one garage was just no longer there. Just gone! There were distraught people were EVERYWHERE, wandering around in shock. No one knew what to do.

At this point, "fight or flight" was starting to kick in. Unfortunately, it manifested as "flight" for me, and "fight" for my husband.

I just wanted to get the hell out of there, get away from the chaos, and be able to think. I couldn't THINK with all of this destruction around me. I'd never been exposed to such a disaster before, I had NO experience to draw on - not even tangentially, from knowing anyone who'd gone through it - and it all seemed so... catastrophic. There were so many issues to consider, and so many things that would need to be dealt with right away - I couldn't even wrap my head around it. I'm a planner. With decent conditions, I can think/plan my way around anything, and I was confident that a temporary change of venue would be the best for us.

My husband, on the other hand, had other ideas.

Porter described it as him being more like a horse. A horse will apparently run back into a burning barn, seeing it as its "safe place", even when surrounded by imminent danger like that. The house was my husband's "comfort area", and where he wanted to be. He's a "fixer", and wanted to start cleaning up and getting back to normal.

Security was also a concern in his mind. Any area devastated by a natural disaster is a prime target for looting. Even before news channels were reporting looting in the area, he was feeling the "stay and protect my house" urge.

Looting and protection of our stuff was the furthest thing from my mind, as I was more fixated on basic needs. We obviously would not be staying in our house that night, nor for a long time to come. Hell, I didn't even know if the house was safe to BE in, much less live in!

We needed to get the cats situated somewhere, we needed a game plan. We needed to figure out where we would be retiring that evening, when all was said and done.

As reasonable as both sides sound on paper, we didn't handle it reasonably. We stood in our livingroom, making vaguely coherent arguments while screaming, crying. I was in hysterics. He was mad that I wanted to leave. I had "my" two cats in a very small carrier, and was threatening to get in the car and drive all the way to Canada, not looking back. He was trying to grab the cat carrier from me, blocking the door... it was the ugliest fight we've ever had. I couldn't believe that he was being so stubborn and unreasonable. It all felt like the end of the world.

Somehow, between threats and screaming, we finally managed to come to a compromise - we'd take the cats to his father's house, briefly regroup, and then return to start cleaning up.

The first logistical decision to be made was HOW to get the cats out. We had one small cat carrier that would hold two cats relatively comfortably, or we could *stuff* all four in. After some debate, we decided to take two, let them loose in the car, and return to the house for the other two. After calling and leaving a message for our insurance company, we were good to go.

21

As we left the house, we did arm the alarm - having it run on battery power. We had no idea how long the battery would last, but felt better knowing that it was still working.

We carried the cats for the three blocks back to the car, much more keenly aware of our surroundings this time around. There were a LOT of downed power lines and other hazards everywhere, and even just carrying the two cats in that carrier was proving difficult. One of us would climb over a downed tree, the other would pass the carrier over, and then follow in climbing over.

By the time we go back to the car, we decided against going back for the other two right away. We would head to my father in law's house, get the first two cats situated, and then return.

As my husband drove, I was finally able to plug in my now-dead phone, and catch up on twitter. I was worried about having freaked people out with my last tweet, unable to update on the situation at all.

My feed was flooded with inquiries, offers of help, and well wishing. My user name, Celebr8nGenr8n had become a trending topic in the time that had passed since my earlier tweet.

As my husband drove, I read off the replies we'd received, trying to calm down so I could get to a place where I could think straight. There were too many comments to reply to, too many questions to answer, I was so overwhelmed. I made a bit of a joke, but it didn't do much to help my mood - I just went right back to the mental images of what we were driving away from.

We had JUST finished the bedroom. Oh God. I can't even.. everything is destroyed. It looks like something out of a movie... surreal.- Twitter, Sun May 22 22:10:03 UTC 2011

By the time we were halfway to my father in law's house, I managed to snap out of it a bit, enough to be moderately functional. The main concern for me was figuring out where we'd be staying that night. With four cats, finding a hotel that would take us would be tricky. As we drove, I made some calls... turning up empty-handed.

We arrived at Ray's house, and got the cats situated in a bedroom. The news was on, and every channel was reporting the tornado damage. We watched the coverage and discussed options, while I tried to keep up on the news and information coming to me from my followers on Twitter.

At father on laws house now, trying to regroup and figure out what the hell to do now. Completely losing my shit.- Twitter, Sun May 22 22:29:02 UTC 2011

Upside: I'll bet this puts an end to my husband joking about my tornadoes. Not a phobia if one destroys your house. More like intuition. - Twitter, Sun May 22 22:32:27 UTC 2011

So many beautiful old trees completely lost. Our gorgeous, super old black walnut that I was so excited for is lost. Trees everywhere. - Twitter, Sun May 22 22:35:37 UTC 2011

Our house was just shown on channel 5. Oh my God. This is insane. That white car under a tree? That's mine. Surreal. - Twitter, Sun May 22 22:37:24 UTC 2011

Less than half an hour after arriving at Ray's house, we were back on the road. We would get to the house, I would take the other two cats to my Ray's house, leaving my husband at the house to start cleanup. Once the remaining cats were situated, I would return, help with cleanup, and we would stay at Ray's place that night. With rum. We would need a LOT of rum to deal with this.

That was the plan, anyway.

There is not enough booze in the world, to deal with seeing a tree in your bedroom. Heading back now to start on clean up. - Twitter, Sun May 22 22:55:29 UTC 2011

Trying to get to house now. Many roads impassable. This is insane. Looks like a war zone. - Twitter, Sun May 22 23:15:50 UTC 2011

We would be there for two and a half hours that evening.

Our Street

Neighbors surveying the damage

So many trees lost

Surreal

My car. Never did figure out whose yard the tree came from!

Side of our yard and the porch

Our Deck

Brand new apple tree, in front of 100+ year old walnut tree

I... was not thinking right. I look back at my actions that day, and I can't explain how I was thinking. When we arrived back at the house, I noticed these bottled Sobe drinks we'd picked up on sale, still in the paper grocery bags. Very wet grocery bags, with broken glass everywhere. For some reason - with my roof destroyed, my car under a tree, no electricity, no idea if our house was a goner...- I was stuck by the "waste" of this... oh, probably $30... in drinks. That were bottled. That would be fine if we moved them, these drinks that didn't require refrigeration or anything.

So, to not "waste" them, I picked them out of the wet bags and broken glass, loaded them into a big blue IKEA bag and walked up and down my street, handing them to neighbors. I think, for some reason, I thought that they'd end up having to be thrown out if not consumed RIGHT THEN AND THERE. I still can't wrap my head around whatever logic I thought I was following at that point. We had a fridge/freezer full of hundreds of dollars of meats and fish that I could have been freaking out about at the time, but instead, I was hyper focused on these stupid drinks.

Looking back, I wish I'd thought to offer up our freezer contents to friends. Later on, when it came time to empty our freezer... it was painful to throw everything out. Ugh. On the upside, as I was handing out those drinks, I'm sure it helped someone. Knowing how fried my own thought processes were that day, I bet that hydration wasn't at the top of anyone's list of priorities.

Shortly after we arrived back at our house, our friends Heather and Mark showed up, along with their son. They had brought granola bars, dried mangoes, and bottles of water with them, knowing that we probably weren't even thinking of food and drink. They were right.

Heather and I sat out on the front steps, her providing an ear, while I alternated between tearing ranting and stunned silence. Heather's son is autistic, so she had a pretty good idea of what we were going through at this point. At some point, the eerie silence had erupted into cacophony, with chain saws all around, shouting, and a swarm of helicopters in the sky. It was all a LOT to deal with - it would have been a lot for anyone to deal with, really... but several trips through the war zone had already left me extremely overstimulated. Between that, all of the "change" all around us, the noise... it was a perfect storm brewing, ripe for the mother of all Aspergers meltdowns. She was so patient, kind, and understanding... and it really helped me keep things in check.

Every once in a while, we were interrupted by various men in suits... looking to sell us remodeling services. The number of times this happened that first afternoon was actually stunning. With all of the reports of impassable roads, police roadblocks set up - truly, we weren't even sure that Heather and Mark would be able to make it through the roadblocks, even with very specific people to come help - we were blown away that so many salespeople were streaming through.

After the first few instances, my Irish Canadian temper started taking over. We hadn't even been given a chance to process what happened, what was still happening, and what we needed to do - and here were these smarmy salespeople, infringing on our space. It just didn't sit well with me.

After I'd truly had enough with "The Vultures" - as we'd come to term them - I started taking a much more direct approach. When one salesperson started up my walk ...

Him: "Good afternoon! Are you the homeowner?"

Me: "If you're here to sell me something, I will punch you right in the face."

Him: "Uh... never mind, good bye!"

As soon as the salesman left, Mark turned to me and said "That is the LEAST Minnesotan thing I've ever seen in my life!". I had to laugh.

With Mark's help, we arranged to hire someone to put up some secure tarp on our wide open roof. I packed a suitcase - mostly clothes and alcohol! - to get us through a few days, and we finally decided to call it a night. With no electricity, our ability to do much of anything was becoming severely limited by the setting of the sun.

As we walked towards the car, we saw a sight we just weren't prepared for. A vehicle pulled up into a tight intersection, and a bunch of people got out, carrying massive amounts of lawn signs under their arms. It was like... a clown car. These people proceeded to start putting up their remodeling business signs on any little bit of available land, just littering the place.

Let me try and explain the scene a bit better.

The roads were such that - for the streets you could actually get down at all - the pathways for vehicles were very narrow. There were trees and random debris everywhere. Even the main cross streets were like this, most of them impassable... and this company had just pulled up and parked, without any consideration for anyone that may be coming through with a more honorable, entitled, or urgent purpose. The size of even one car was *significant*, given the obstruction in the roads.

So then, rather than getting out en masse and offering to help people, these vultures were swarming the area with dollar signs in their eyes. Rather than pick up debris, or even ask home owners if they'd like a sign in whatever tiny piece of their yard that may have been visible under all of that rubble, they just spread those signs like they were marking their territory. Such disregard for the devastation around them. We saw RED.

As we approached our car, my husband kicked a sign, and just sent it flying. As he later explained:

"I tried to kick very hard- to really make a point. I am no jock, so I really gave it all I had, in an attempt to send it flying. The shape of the sign meant that it was quite stable, like a paper airplane. Even my non-athletic kick really sent it flying away. My foot was left aching, as the bottom of the sign where I kicked was rather thin Refusing to acknowledge the pain, I walked on as if it was no problem at all"

Again, I just can't even begin to describe how pissed off we were, that these people were doing this just hours after the tornado. Who thinks like that? Who looks at this sort of disaster on TV, and gets all excited about the profits they can make? Who rounds up as many people as they can, on a Sunday afternoon, to just litter the neighborhood with advertising?

Similarly, I can't even express how shocked we were when one of the company reps ran up to my husband and told him off for kicking the sign. I just can't even imagine how bereft of basic humanity a person would have to be to not only engage in that profiteering behavior in the first place, but to also have the lack of integrity to go up to a victim of the disaster and tell them off like that?

I lost it.

As this pathetic creature wagged his finger at my husband, I screeched at him. I'm sure that the entire neighborhood heard me shriek "We just lost our HOUSE, you vultures!" at him - perhaps not my proudest moment, but... really.

Alpha Exteriors ... you should be ashamed of yourselves. You are the lowest form of humanity.

If your business is that desperate for income that you would conduct yourself in such a skeezy, disgusting manner as to descend upon the area THAT quickly, with that many people... you could have done it a LOT more honorably. Why not dress all of those people in company branded t shirts and send them in to help clear debris? I'm sure that more than a few people would have appreciated it, and asked for business cards.

That is how decent people would do it, anyway. Instead, you're forever immortalized in our photos, arm loads of signs in tow... a loathsome pack of weasels, completely lacking souls.

Leaving for tonight. If some salesperson gets the tar beaten out of them tomorrow, and a 'violent' immigrant deported as a result, well... - Twitter Mon May 23 01:59:54 UTC 2011

Just a few hours after the tornado

Thoroughly exhausted, we headed towards Ray's house. It's only about 25 minutes away - under normal circumstances - but between the debris, randomly parked cars, other hazards, and the degree to which we were worn out... it felt like forever. We realized that - although it was getting quite late - we hadn't really eaten since right before the tornado. While the dried mango and other goodies were much appreciated, we just hadn't been in the mood to eat while Heather and Mark were there, and we were now regretting that.

Additionally, we realized that I'd managed to forget to pack our toothbrushes and toothpaste. Yes, I packed the rum, and forgot toothbrushes. Awesome.

After a quick stop at a pharmacy for the toiletries, we decided to pick up something to eat at White Castle. I tell ya... "Harold and Kumar"'s journey to White Castle had *nothing* on us that night. I can only imagine how we looked to the other people there. Dirty, disheveled, tear streaked, exhausted.

As we waited for our food, we called Stephan, the owner of Dakota Painting and Drywall. He was the small business owner we'd dealt with for our initial wall fixes and painting when we bought the house. As he'd been the one to apply the ceiling finish, we wanted to hire him again, for as seamless of a repair as possible.

When we were done telling him what happened, I felt so much better. He was such a calming presence, very sweet and kind. After our conversation was the first time I started to feel like "We can handle this!", and that everything would be ok.

Just talked to the awesome dry waller that did our initial reno, he'll take care of us, as soon as the insurance company bothers to call.- Twitter, Mon May 23 03:08:42 UTC 2011

... And with that taken care of, I'll be free to unleash all KINDS of crazy on the profiteering vultures tomorrow.- Twitter, Mon May 23 03:10:20 UTC 2011

We ate our meal and headed back to my father in law's house to get settled in for the night. We were only starting to get an idea of the enormity of the road ahead, but we'd dealt with as much as we could for one day.

I was trending in Minneapolis earlier, and welcome new followers, but feel bad that first impression is looking like a complete psychopath!- Twitter, Mon May 23 03:54:24 UTC 2011

So hey, anyone that thinks I was being a big wuss freaking out over storm/tornadoes last week or the week before ....- Twitter, Mon May 23 04:05:39 UTC 2011

Also, we are holed up at inlaw's house. Have cats locked in bedroom w/ us due to dog. They've come out from under bed, purring & exploring - Twitter, Mon May 23 04:08:30 UTC 2011

We appreciate all of the well wishes and offers to help. Will regroup tonight, start replying tomorrow. - Twitter, Mon May 23 04:10:04 UTC 2011

I think I'm done with crying. Now alternating between numbness and anger. Should be a MACHINE tomorrow, so that's good.- Twitter, Mon May 23 04:12:50 UTC 2011

Going to bed. Hoping that insurance company & construction people can save the house - hope to find out tomorrow. - Twitter, Mon May 23 04:54:16 UTC 2011

Was too upset to even get into booze tonight, lol. Anyway, gonna try to get some sleep. - Twitter, Mon May 23 04:59:01 UTC 2011

The room was hot, the bed was lumpy, but we had each other, the four cats, and a vague idea of what would need to be done the next day.

Aftermath and Cleanup

Waking up the morning after the tornado, I was sort of expecting that none of it had happened. I tend to have epic, extremely detailed dreams - it really wouldn't have surprised me to wake up in my own bed, with an intact roof overhead.

Unfortunately, that wasn't the case.

As we got dressed, we were still struggling to make sense of what had happened, and where we were to go from there. There was just SO much work to be done. I may be a logistics nerd, but the whole scene was incredibly overwhelming, even to me.

We knew for sure was that we had to expect the worst when it came to the insurance, and we were sort of dreading the call from the adjuster. Between "high risk" under-value insurance being our only option when we bought the house, and only being with the company for 3 months... we were NOT expecting good news.

We were also keenly aware of the fact that there was no way we'd be able to do any of this alone. Where does one even start, with that kind of damage? It wasn't anything we had ever been exposed to, nothing we'd ever considered, and really... there's only so much that two people can do. We both had fairly non-physical, usually sedentary jobs... and were utterly unprepared for hauling all of that debris alone.

With news coverage of the tornado playing in the background, we formulated a quick plan for the day. We knew that we'd need some supplies - garbage bags, work gloves, bottled water - as well as hats, sun screen, and breakfast.

We'd need volunteers. We needed advice. I needed to vent... so I went to the one place I could satisfy all of those needs... Twitter!

For those offering to help, we can definitely use extra hands/minds. Call me at 612 XXX XXXX when you are willing/available. - Twitter, Mon May 23 12:51:11 UTC 2011   I went through 10 years of PTSD after my car accident, with mild/infrequent issues now. SO glad I wasn't there during the storm. - Twitter, Mon May 23 12:52:53 UTC 2011

But I worry for the future. Tornado sirens go off so often, and I'll never forget the visuals. Will I ever feel safe here again? - Twitter, Mon May 23 12:54:05 UTC 2011

Ok hivemind! Headed back to house. Any recommendations for supplies we should pick up? Anything else to keep in mind? - Twitter, Mon May 23 13:26:21 UTC 2011

Twitter came through for us. We learned that most of the roads in the area were still impassable, and that road blocks were being set up. We juggled incoming messages with contact information for people who were willing and able to volunteer - when they were each available, and what they were able to do. The tears had dried up the night before, and now we were down to business.

It was so much to process, all at once. What we needed to do, who was coming when, where we would be staying that night... and trying to draw upon ANY past experiences we may have had, that could potentially prepare us for the weeks and months to come.

My whole life, I've been surrounded by crazy weather conditions, but actually being through a disaster was a new one. I was born during as massive flood in my home town of Winnipeg, and I lived there during the great flood of 1997. I lived in Newfoundland during a series of blizzards in... 2000?.. that dropped something like 6 meters of snow. It was insane. Never before - and never since! - had I seen snow drifts reaching/extending ABOVE roofs! A trip to New Orleans in 2005 was bookended with tropical storms, and Katrina hit not that long after I returned home.

I started to wonder if there was some sort of natural disaster punch-card club. If I made it through an earthquake, would I collect the whole set? Haha!

As my husband ran in to pick up breakfast en-route, I received an message from one of my cake friends in Toronto. She was suggesting that I get a hold of a friend of hers at CBC, who was looking for Canadians living in the tornado zones. I fired off a quick message to say who I was, what our situation was, and that sure - I was willing to talk about it.

Technology, gotta love it. To this day, I have no idea how we would have made it through the whole thing, without the use of the internet, smart phones, etc.

We had to get creative with how we approached our house. We were about a mile from a main highway, and several exits into our area were apparently closed. Also, our initial drive into the war zone the day before was still fresh in our minds, and we had little desire to zigzag around streets still completely blocked by trees.

As we drew near, we were shocked at just how NORMAL things looked, just a few blocks away. Almost like nothing had happened at all, only eerily still. The buildings were fine, the trees were still standing... not even so much as a branch out of place.

Then we came to it - massive destruction. It was amazing, just how clean the line seemed to be between "untouched by the tornado", and houses with almost no roof left. Between a street fully canopied with full trees, and just wide open sky, no tree canopy at all. I had to wonder how disturbing that had to be for the people living on either side of the border - to have been only one house away from safety... or one house away from losing everything.

As I was considering the implications that must have on relationship dynamics between neighbors, we pulled up to a "safe" parking spot a block away from the house - the closest we could get. The phone rang, and I held back in the car to discuss the tornado with CBC while my husband started bringing supplies to the house. It was honestly sort of comforting to hear that Toronto accent!

As we had yet to hear from the insurance company, we weren't quite sure what all we could - or should - be doing. We wanted to get started on the cleanup and repair. We wanted to prevent any further damage to the home - and protect it against the possibility of theft - but did not want to jeopardize anything as far as our insurance payout would go.

We knew we would be working with far less money than what was needed, as it was!

Early on, we determined that getting my car cut out from under the tree that had landed on it should definitely be a priority. The car wasn't covered by insurance, so that wasn't an issue... and with city crews expected to start cleanup soon, we wanted to do as much as we could. With as much damage in the area as there was, we knew they wouldn't be super concerned about not causing further damage to the car.

As Porter carefully and strategically cut the branches that covered and surrounded my car, a bit of hope began to emerge. While we're worried that the car would be a car would be a complete write off - it was a HUGE tree - the situation had looked a lot worse than it actually was. Both windshields would need to be replaced, along with one side mirror and one of the doors. Not cheap, but definitely cheaper than replacing the car!

Once Porter was finished with my car and had moved on to getting ready to start clearing debris from the yard, I busied myself with cleaning up the mess from the shattered back windshield. The idea was that we would clean it up as best we could, affix a tarp, and tow it out of the area ASAP to be professionally cleaned out.

As I carefully dusted broken glass from the back end of the car - indoors and out - I could hear a vehicle approach and slow down. I'd sort of expected it to be someone asking if they could help, and I couldn't be further from the truth. Well, in my mind anyway - apparently the driver and I had very different ideas on the subject.

You see, as I was thrilled that my car - that I loved - had *just* proven to be salvageable, this jackass leaned out of his pickup window and offered me $100 for it as a "junker"... and then told me it would be doing me a favor. It was a company vehicle, the first of many drive-by vultures who were looking to make money off the damaged vehicles, preying on the confusion, despair, and desperation in the area.

Oh, I was mad.

Some asshole drove by, leaned out, handed a flyer, said he'd "do us a favor" and offer $100 for my otherwise-great shape car. I hate people. - Twitter, Mon May 23 19:18:40 UTC 2011

The vultures and helicopters are getting to me. Enough of a warzone as is. - Twitter, Mon May 23 19:19:41 UTC 2011

We aren't totally desperate, and are resourceful. Others can't say the same. Pisses me off that people are preying on those in need. - Twitter, Mon May 23 19:21:10 UTC 2011

You know, there wasn't enough room on our street to park the "able bodied" car we had. There were crews trying to get through to work on tree removal and restore electricity to the area. Legitimate volunteers were getting turned away by at the roadblocks, being told that no one who didn't live in the area would be allowed through... yet SO many of these profiteering vultures were driving up and down the area. It blew my mind.

While I was still fuming over the insulting $100 offer, some unfortunate telemarketer called my business cell phone. Now, this is not going to get a great response from me on the BEST of days... but this was not the best of days. I ended up screaming at them - and I quote - "I just lost my home in a tornado and do NOT FEEL LIKE BEING SOLICITED FOR SEO HELP!"

Honestly, it felt kind of good. I may need to employ that as a tactic for future unsolicited calls!

Having a bit of a giggle at the idea of using that tactic on future sales calls, I managed to calm down a bit before my CBC interview. A good thing, I suppose... I'd had NO idea what I was going to say, how I was going to respond to whatever questions they had for me.

Well.. I ended up cracking a joke about all of our new skylights, and saying "Tornadoes are BULLSHIT"... in a live interview. Several times. They told me that I was "handling it like a Canadian", but I still feel bad for sounding like a crazy person.

Realizing that tornadoes turn me into a big douchebag. - Twitter, Mon May 23 20:17:50 UTC 2011

With hip injuries, two bad knees, and serious fascia problems preventing me from being much of a help with hauling, I busied myself by taking care of logistics.

I've always been a logistics nerd - I can plan anything out. I'm great at seeing the big picture, planning for various possibilities, and I pride myself on my logic and efficiency.

In the midst of tornado aftermath? It was definitely a scenario I'd never pictured, prepared for, or had any sort of concept with. Also, it was difficult to plan for so many needs, so many things that needed to be done - WHILE things needed to be happening - while my head was so muddled. It definitely gave my problem solving abilities a workout!

First, there was the matter of juggling volunteers. Who was coming, when, who was bringing what, what sorts of abilities and skills were being represented, when?

What would we need to accommodate them? Contractor bags, of course... but what else would they need, to safely help out? Work gloves. Dust masks. Did we need any supplementary equipment, and if so, when/how were we obtaining it?

Did we need any supplementary labor? I love our friends, but - realistically - we're all geeks and nerds. The people coming to help us were computer programmers, engineers, etc. Great people, quick learners, and kept us sane... but were we missing anything? Was there any particular brand of brawn, or experience that we should add to the group?

Down that path, what were we doing with the walnut tree? It was HUGE. I'd never had to deal with any tree removal - ever. Even for Christmas trees, as I've always been a "fake tree" kinda person. I didn't even benefit from whatever help that the experience of putting a used-up fresh Christmas tree on the curb could have provided!

The tree falling was a huge tragedy for us. Out of everything that happened, it was the biggest waste, and the only thing that was truly irreplaceable. It was a tragedy that we couldn't spend a lot of time mourning - the tree would need to be removed in order for the power company to get in and restore our electricity. We needed to make decisions and arrangements FAST.

Logistically... that was a big tree. That was a big tree that was going to take some serious equipment to cut up, and some serious labor to remove. Where it went from there, I had no idea. From murmurs I'd started hearing on twitter, the city would pick up the trees and shred them to mulch.

The idea of this tree being mulched broke my heart. There had to be some way to "save" it, to use the wood. That was a LOT of wood though. I'd heard that black walnut was expensive wood, maybe I could find a mill to buy it. I'd have to figure that out QUICKLY, as I had no idea what was involved with selling a downed tree to a mill, what we'd have to do/ not do to the tree to prepare it, etc. I thought that this would be a great way to help pay for the tornado repairs.

I communicated the idea to Twitter, and several people looked into the possibilities for me - what was involved, what mills locally would buy wood, how much money we'd be looking at, etc. Oh, hive mind... I love you. Thank you so much for all of the help.

We soon realized that selling the wood wasn't really an option. Because it was in the city, no mill wanted it - too much risk of there being nails, etc in it. My brilliant idea of being PAID for the wood, rather than having to pay for its removal went right down the drain.

Then, I had a better idea...

Reconsidering "Sell the black walnut tree" idea. Tossing around possibility of milling it for our new kitchen cabinets - Twitter, Mon May 23 22:21:28 UTC 2011

I don't know. It's too great an asset to lose. It would be horrible for it to end as mulch. Reminder of tornado, though? - Twitter, Mon May 23 22:24:57 UTC 2011

My tweeps loved the idea. Comments flooded in, telling me that doing so would mean I "won over Mother Nature", etc. Add "figure out what the deal is with milling wood" to the to do list.

After a fair amount of research by my tweeps, and a few calls, I determined that having the wood milled was going to be our most cost efficient way to deal with it, by far.

Truly, we could get a 120 year old tree's worth of premium wood, for not a whole lot more than it would cost to have it cut down and removed by a tree company or the city. Also, it would do double duty by covering a cost we already anticipated - the lumber for the new kitchen.

It wasn't a hard sell to my husband, whose only concerns were logistics-related: How, who, and where. Could we actually pull it off?

I decided it was worth a try. Social media provided a reference to a local mill, I called for the details on what to do with the wood, and we were all set. Well... mostly, anyway. Like I said - a bunch of geeks and nerds. Not a logger amongst us.

Craigslist to the rescue! I posted an ad to look for logging help, and soon received a handful of replies.

"Hi. I have a chainsaw, logging chains, a full size 4x4 and experience as a logger/tree guy. I can start tomorrow for $18 an hour cash. This is half my normal rate for this type of work".

Done and done. We hired Chris, and arranged for him to show up the next day - May 24, two days after the tornado. He was confident that he could handle getting the tree prepped for the mill... HUGE weight off our chests.

Finally, beyond volunteer and tree logistics, there were the more basic concerns of shelter and money. Money was something that I couldn't even wrap my head around yet, so busy with everything else. Shelter, on the other hand, was an immediate concern.

We were pretty sure that our insurance wouldn't cover a hotel stay, given how woefully under insured we already were.

Though we'd been given information about shelters being set up, that wasn't really an option for us, either. Don't get me wrong, we are both VERY functional with our Aspergers, having each had an entire lifetime to figure out how we tick, how to handle things, etc.

Again, though... never been exposed to a natural disaster. We were both teetering on the edge of completely losing it. Aside from the stress of what had happened a day earlier, there was the matter of over stimulation.

Between the chain saws and the helicopters, people coming and going... NOTHING where it was supposed to be, changes of plans, a change of where "home" would have to be, etc.. yeah.

With our friends, it was all good. Most of them have at least one toe dipped in the Aspie pool, if not either full out Aspergers themselves, or married to/related to someone with Aspergers. They got it, and worked towards keeping us calm and in control of ourselves.

The idea of going to a shelter, however? No. If we were going to have to stay somewhere other than our own house, it would have to be somewhere we could be alone, somewhere we could decompress, etc. We needed recovery time each night, to be able to handle the monumental amount of work and planning that each day would be bringing.

Staying in a shelter - a change of venue, feeling very temporary, and with SO many strangers (and the noise that would come with it!)... we'd be up all night, completely stressed out. As a result, we'd be tired, cranky, and useless in the daytime. We'd be miserable to be around, and didn't want to subject our friends and volunteers to that. Additionally, with the amount of stress everyone in the area was in... NO ONE in any shelter needed to have one or both of us having a complete meltdown in their midst. It was just better for everyone if we found an different option.

We did receive many offers of guest rooms from friends - and complete strangers! - on Twitter and Facebook. As grateful as we were for those offers, though, we had to decline, for the same reasons as the shelter - at least for the first little while. We needed to establish some sort of routine, a new "normal", and really didn't want to put anyone out, or risk ruining any friendships by subjecting anyone to, well, us.

Added "find cheap hotel room" to the logistics to do list!

As I busied myself with logistical and labor concerns, friends started to show up. It felt like the cavalry had arrived, and we were able to breathe a little sigh of relief at not being on our own for this.

As we saw it, there were a couple of different "first priority" items to take care of.

42

For one, it was impossible to get to the back yard, from either side of the house. Both side yards were piled with random debris - trees, someone else's fencing, various bits of homes from around the area.

I guess if I'd ever had to picture what would happen to a house in a tornado, I would have pictured it basically to be smashed, with one's own house debris more or less in the same area. I have no idea why I would have pictured it this way - I do have a fairly good grasp on physics, after all - I guess it's just not something that ever crossed my mind.

In reality, I have no idea where everything came from. It wasn't all from either our house or the neighbor's, there was a fair amount of debris of unidentifiable origin in there. This wasn't just the case for our side yards, of course. The tree that was laying on may car? We have NO idea where it came from. We'd also heard that the sign from a local gas station ended up something like 1 mile away from where it was ripped up. Insane.

The funny thing about all of this? Two houses down, we have some neighbors that had a whole bunch of random stuff in their yard, prior to the tornado. Of this, the most creepy and bizarre was a GIANT clown's head. I have no idea what it was, never thought to ask - we assumed it was part of a big parade float or something.

Anyway, we noticed that it was missing after the tornado, we have no idea where it landed. The idea of someone emerging from their house after the tornado, and being faced with a gigantic, creepy clown head, though? Hilarious!

I'm honestly sort of surprised that we didn't hear of its fate - people were sharing stories about the tornado online, and in the media. I think my favorite was hearing about the guy who was napping on the second floor of his house when the tornado hit... and woke up still on his mattress, only it was on his front lawn.

I think it sounds like a myth, but if it's not... could you imagine?

Anyway, I digress. Yes, loads of random crap in the side yards of our house, which made it impossible to get to the back yard. Because so much of our repair needs - and high priority issues- were in the back yard, being able to get through the side yards were a high priority.

Getting the tree cut up and removed was also a huge priority. We needed to get the tree out of there in order for the utility lines to our house to be re-strung, and to be able to deal with the damage to the house and deck.

Another high priority item for us were the three Arborvitae trees out front - we thought that there was a chance that we could save them. All three had been uprooted, but more or less stayed in place: 1 was leaning against our neighbor's house, another was leaning sideways, against the roof above our door, and the other was freestanding at a 45 degree angle.

So as couple of our friends went through the house and out the back door to start cutting branches off the walnut tree, a couple others started work on clearing the side yards, while Porter and I tried to save the trees.

You know, arborvitae trees are a lot heavier than they look. They may be tall and skinny, but trying to haul those suckers back into place takes some serious muscle! We wrestled them back into place, and Porter used rope to secure them to each other, to our railings - any way he could. We packed the soil back into place around the roots and hoped for the best.

It didn't end up working. The trees weren't going to stand on their own again, and started dying - we had to cut them down a week or so later. It was sad - not only the fact that we ended up losing them, but just... that our efforts were for nothing. It's like ... we had a LITTLE control, and then had it ripped away from us.

Inside the house, yet another volunteer - Tara - worked on getting rid of all of the broken glass and debris from where our bedroom patio door was smashed in. We were sure that the carpet was a complete goner - I've got weird issues about the idea of having anything puncture my foot, and the idea of broken glass throughout the carpet really creeped me out.

Tara, on the other hand, was pretty sure that we could save it. I was surprised at how good it looked when she was done, but was still horrified at the idea of teeny shards of glass getting stuck in my foot, weeks or months after the fact.

By the end of the day, the debris was cleared from the side yards, and many of the smaller branches had been cut off the tree. It was a long, long day, but SO productive. We were shocked at how big the pile of debris out front was, after only one day.

The next day was more of the same - cutting tree branches, clearing debris from the back yard, hauling it to the front yard.

That was the first day of us having additional, professional help: Chris, the logger we found on Craigslist. He was there to oversee the processing of the large portion of the tree, and most of the labor and cutting involved along with that. It was so nice to have someone with experience involved!

Found a logger to process the walnut tree. Gonna have the "Log Driver's Waltz" in my head for days. #ItPleasesGirlsCompletely - Twitter, Tue May 24 03:59:03 UTC 2011

Additionally, that was also the day that our insurance company finally got back to us. Yep. We'd left a voice mail on the day of the tornado - Sunday - and didn't hear back from them until Tuesday. When they said that they would have someone out on Thursday afternoon - 4 full days after the tornado - I almost hit the roof.

Luckily, they were perfectly understanding about our need to clean up, etc... so they agreed to just let us take photos of any mess/damage that we were working on.

As useless as I was for the more physical aspects of the cleanup, I had plenty to keep me busy. The news that we'd been hit by a tornado ended up resulting in a bunch of cookbook sales through my website. Luckily, my cases of cookbooks had not been in one of the rooms with water pouring in, so I was able to fulfil the orders. This ended up being one of the most surreal events throughout the cleanup process, for me.

The house was very dark inside. We had no idea when we'd be getting electricity back, so we were keeping our curtains - all VERY heavy and light-blocking - closed, to keep the house as cool as possible, for as long as we could. As a result, the only place I could really prepare the orders was outside.

The patio table was located and hoisted up onto what remained of the deck, which had now been cleared of debris. It was more or less safe to walk on this section, as long as one was careful not to step in any of the spots where flying tree debris had blasted through the deck surface.

So, that's where I signed and packaged my books... Out there on my destroyed deck, a big black walnut still laying across the other side of the deck, where it was being dismantled. Surrounded by the sounds of chainsaws and helicopters, in the middle of a disaster zone. It was so WEIRD.

Were it not for all of the destruction and flurry of activity all around me, it would have been nice. It was a gorgeous day, and could have been a really nice change from doing so in my office.

Signing/packing cookbooks outside-no electricity! It's actually kinda nice... PS: buy my books! WWW.TheSpiritedbaker.com #NeedANewRoof #NoMi - Twitter, Tue May 24 23:01:46 UTC 2011

As weird as it felt to be doing so, it was important to me that I got the orders out in a timely manner. Not only was it the right thing to do, but I could see the possibility of errors being an issue for me, if I were to let them pile up. I think that people appreciated the effort, also.

RT @flash119: How much does @Celebr8nGenr8n kick ass?? Despite a tornado ravaged home, she got my cookbook order out the same day! - Twitter, Wed May 25 15:27:44 UTC 2011

The rest of my time tended to be divided up between running to the store for supplies - bottled water, snacks, blade replacements, etc... as well as trips to the post office to mail cookbooks, and picking up meals for the volunteers. Beyond that, I was busy trying to secure contractors for the repairs we'd need.

The meals were an interesting challenge. Without electricity, most places that we knew of in the area were closed. Beyond that, most places that had electricity and were open did not deliver to our area, and/or weren't open for lunch, etc. Trying to figure out what was available and when was a bit of a challenge, with my dying cell phone battery and spotty coverage.

Securing contractors was a huge headache. We didn't want to hire anyone that came to our door, as we didn't appreciate the fact that these people were so quick to try and profit from our bad situation... but it seemed like no one else actually wanted the business. More on that in another chapter!

It was so great to be surrounded by friends throughout the whole cleanup. The circumstances sucked, but they made it oddly pleasant. Many of our friends didn't know each other, despite all being part of the same geek communities. There were a lot of great conversations, joking around, smiles, and laughing. It all really served to minimize the pain of what had happened.

One of my favorite memories from the cleanup was of our friend Todd. Todd was a friend that we'd met through Convergence, a great guy who was known as "The Predator". Nope, not someone you'd see on a crime special - he's someone who's insanely talented at costuming, and known for dressing up as "The Predator" from the horror movie series.

Todd singing a high pitched, tornado-themed version of Rebecca Black's "Friday", while clearing debris? Absolutely priceless!

By the end of that second day of hauling, it was getting impossible to reply to all of the emails, Facebook, and twitter messages that were checking in on us, asking what we needed, and/or offering to help. So, the following day - May 25th - I dropped Porter off at the house to continue work on hauling debris, while I went to find electricity for my laptop.

I felt guilty, sitting there in an air conditioned coffee shop, while Porter and our friends were busting their asses to dig us out from that mess, but there was not much I could do from the house, without electricity... but it needed to be done.

I don't even remember how long it took to reply to all of those messages. I ended up coming up with a few canned responses, as many of the questions were asking the same things. I felt bad for sending such impersonal replies, but it's the only way I could keep up - as soon as I replied to one message, there were two new ones waiting for me!

So, I decided to write a blog entry to address it all. I titled it "... And then a tree went through our bedroom wall..."

I can't even imagine what other people were thinking, in the coffee show that morning. I had to have looked dirty, disheveled, and completely worn out. I sat there with my brightly colored fruit smoothie, and started banging out an account of what had happened a couple days earlier.

47

I'm sure I had to have been shaking as I typed out enough details to answer the vast majority of the questions we were being asked: Where were we when it happened, are the cats ok, what happened to the house, do we need anything.

"Do we need anything". That was the question that I was having the hardest time with. I hated the idea of asking for help. I've never been in the position of needing to accept charity. I was used to being on the other end of things, and was having a hard time accepting the gravity of our situation. It's amazing, the disconnect that can happen between fact and perception. I could see, on paper, that things were extremely bleak for us... but it felt like if I actually asked for the help that we would need, THAT would somehow be the tipping point to making the numbers on paper become reality.

Logically, I knew we were screwed. We'd looked at our insurance papers, and knew we'd come up tens of thousands of dollars short, even before the adjuster came to look at the house. At this point, it was obvious that it wasn't a matter of IF we'd be short, but how MUCH we'd be short by.

We've both been quick to help out any way we could, when we've known someone in need... so we also knew how helpless it can feel to be watching this sort of thing from afar. Right before the tornado happened, I was starting to organize to send books to a town where the library burnt down in a huge wildfire. A year after the tornado, I can still remember how horrified I was to watch that on the news, and how helpless I felt. Even with gathering the books to send... horrible.

So, I tried to rationalize it that others probably feel the same way, and that's why they're offering. I tried to look at it as a debt of karma... that us having to accept charity was a loan of sorts, and that we'd be obligated to "pay it off" by paying it forward whenever and however we could. I looked at it as though we were taking on this loan that we did have the ability to repay, even if not financially. I sucked up my pride and addressed the question of what we needed:

"There are SO many people that are much worse off than us – people who had NO insurance, and people whose homes were destroyed beyond repair – that we have decided NOT to make use of the Red Cross / city / etc disaster relief offerings. I'd like to see that sort of public type money going first to those who really, really need it. We had some insurance, and we're resourceful... so we wouldn't feel right getting aid like that.

However, there's no way we're going to come close to covering our financial costs. So, if you're interested in helping out financially, here are a few ways to.

1 – My preferred means of helping us – order my cookbooks! I'd rather earn the money than accept much charity. The Spirited Baker and Evil Cake Overlord can both be ordered directly from me – my cases of books were unharmed! Also,I coded a new page this morning, which allows people to order from anywhere in the world now! Click here if you're ordering the books from outside of the USA.

2 – Per request, I set up a "donation" link through Paypal, for those who prefer the more direct approach:

I have plans to come up with some nice thank-you gifts for those donating through Paypal, so we don't feel so awful about setting up this option. It'll just be a while before we get that together, so please have patience!

As for non-financial needs, here is what we've come up with so far:

- It would be great if we could get massage certificates for our volunteers. This has been insanely grueling work, and they're not pros. They're going to HURT later, and I'd love to be able to ease some of that discomfort!

- Restaurant coupons. If you have any Groupon type vouchers, Entertainment coupons, or anything like that, that you're willing to part with, that'll help us with our month or so of non-covered-by-insurance forced "vacation". Without a kitchen / house/electricity, these kind of costs are going to cripple us.

- Suggestions. We could use some suggestions on where to get good decking material cheaply (Cedar), where to get the car fixed cheaply, and who – if even possible – we can hire to clean he upstairs carpet. It's not ripped or stained, but all that broken glass is a HUGE concern. We're really hoping the glass can be safely removed from the carpet, rather than having to replace it or have to wear shoes up there forever.

- Spread the word. I would LOVE to get the book more out there, and EARN our way through this. If you know food or liquor/lifestyle/etc bloggers, media, book store owners... please put in a good word. I can't afford to give away a bunch of review hard copies, but I have digital copies

of both books. Any book publicity or bookstores/gift shops willing to carry the book would be awesome."

... and that was that. I hit enter, and hoped for the best. By "best", I was hoping to sell a bunch of books. I knew that my cookbooks were great, and that anyone buying them were getting a great value. With book sales, I wouldn't feel so.. Ashamed, I guess. Guilty about having to ask.

Friends, tweeps, the extended geek community online, friends of friends... people were so helpful in getting the word out, once the blog entry went up. My Facebook wall lit up with people posting a link to the entry, encouraging people to buy my cookbooks - usually with positive comments about the books themselves, or the quality of my baking. I was so touched!

The book sales did pick up, to the point where I sold out of my first cookbook within a couple of days, and had to order another print. That kind of shocked me, but it sure felt good to go to reprint! Gotta say, I've never seen "get hit by a tornado" in any "How to promote your book" type article!

The Insurance Situation

The insurance adjuster showed up on Thursday May 26, four days after the tornado.

As many people online were reporting on their own experiences with insurance adjusters - many of whom were out within a couple days - we had plenty to be worried about. The four days gave us ample opportunity to hear all kinds of horror stories about how insurance companies were using the age of the houses against the insured, marking all values as low as possible, and paying out as little as possible. Knowing that we were already severely under-insured, we were definitely fearing the worst.

As it turned out, we had a total of $90,000 in coverage - to cover house, garage, and personal property. As we suspected, we had no insurance coverage for living expenses while we were unable to live in the house.

The first thing that he looked at was damage to the house itself, which we had a cap of $75,000 on. On the upside, the adjuster wasn't nitpicking damage. He wrote off the carpet, saying that there was NO way we'd get the glass out. He wrote off the roof, the deck, the porch.

"You have $75k insurance limit? I can see more than $75k in damage ON MY FIRST GLANCE". OMG. #NoMi #TornadosAreBullshit #NervousBreakdown - Twitter, Thu May 26 15:57:05 UTC 2011

As suspected, we blew way past our insurance coverage... just on the stuff that they actually would cover. Between the house, the garage, and personal property, they estimated our damages at around $120,000.

Beyond that damage, there were several things not covered.

As we already knew, my car was not covered for that sort of damage. The costs of hotel and eating out weren't covered in this total. Additionally, our policy didn't cover landscaping, or items like trees - and a 100+ year old black walnut being pulled out of the ground does *massive* damage to a yard.

As well, there were a couple surprises that we didn't discover until after our claim had been paid off. Given that we blew past our coverage ceiling anyway, it's not that it mattered as far as the payout goes, anyway.

First of all, we missed the fact that a window in our bathroom had dislodged by about 1". As we weren't living in the house, we weren't taking showers there - and it was easy to miss. Unfortunately, it caused water damage behind our shower, and the whole thing needed to be ripped out.

Secondly - and this was a huge issue throughout our neighborhood, given the ages of the homes: Insurance would cover what was actually broken, or actually needed replacement. Sounds obvious, and not a problem, right?

Well, the thing is that with our homes being as old as they are, the electrical and plumbing behind the walls - in a lot of cases here - aren't up to code, but were grandfathered in to the current requirements. Again, not a problem...

However, when one of these homes - in our case, our kitchen - suffered damages that required a wall to come out, homeowners are required to bring everything behind the wall up to the current code. What this means is that while insurance will pay for your wall to be replaced, you could be on your own as far as the extra burden goes.

51

This may be common knowledge to everyone but us, but in case it's not: Not all policies are like this. Like I mentioned earlier, our options were severely limited when we bought our house as an unoccupied foreclosure property, so this coverage wasn't even an option for our policy. Even if it had been, it wouldn't have made a difference for us, as it would be included in the limits we had.

Some policies have it built in, some have it optional... but what you're looking for is called "Law and Ordinance Coverage". From talking to people in the months following the tornado, it sounds like a lot of people were missing that coverage on their policy... and paid dearly for it.

If there's one thing that you take from our experience, it's that you should look at your policy and make sure you have adequate insurance coverage: A high enough ceiling, coverage for living expenses should your home be rendered unlivable, and this law and ordinance coverage.

As an aside... every time I type "law and ordinance", I hear the DUN DUN sound from Law and Order.

Anyway... we received a check for the full amount of our insurance coverage, something like 2 weeks after the tornado. This was in stark contrast to all of the stories of people who were fighting for their insurance money even months after the fact. I guess there's an upside to being horrifically under insured?

Overall, our dealings with insurance were a complete non-issue, once the adjuster came out. They wrote us a check and cut us loose - literally. Fun fact about maxing out your insurance policy: They cancel your policy completely, and you have to have a new one written.

Insurance is a bizarre thing. While we had desperately searched for ANYONE to cover our house when it was a completely intact, unoccupied foreclosure... it was far less hassle to get insurance on our newly-written off house. Not only that, it was far better coverage: higher limit, living expense coverage in case this ever happens again, etc. We had the new insurance in place before we had the roof replaced... so bizarre.

A few months later, the City of Minneapolis Tax Assessor's office also wrote our house off. I mean, completely wrote it off, valuing our house as being worth nothing. Literally, $0 value on it. Kinda took our breath away. Don't get me wrong, the property tax relief that came with that was sorely needed, but.. Damn.

Continued Cleanup

Regardless of what the adjuster had said about the carpet upstairs, we decided that it would be worth the effort and investment to try and save it. We had a small amount of insurance money to cover an insane amount of expenses, we needed to be as careful as we could about every expense.

On the suggestion of one local friend, we called a small, locally owned carpet cleaning company. She was sure that they could get all of the glass out, the company was sure that they could get it all out.. it was worth a try. I mean with a glowing recommendation like: "I have a guy who does my carpets - he's seriously awesome. His name is Eugene Owens, J and J Carpet. Phone is 952 261 3324. He's the only one we'll have do our carpets."... it was definitely worth a shot!

So, amid all of the debris removal going on at our house - and all of the disaster cleanup going on throughout the neighborhood, the company showed up to try and save our carpet. We didn't even have electricity yet! I still remember how weird it was to not have to worry about the front door being open, with our cats gone, and no electricity for wasted air conditioning to be an issue.

Miraculously, they saved the carpet - I have no idea how they did it. Just looking at the carpet, after they left, you'd never have known that we'd been hit by a tornado. (The "seam" where the roof was pulled up and dropped down, the tree sticking out of the wall, and the smashed-in patio door covered with a tarp were another story, though! It looked brand new, and saved us a ton of money in the process.

Even beyond the financial situation, it would have been awful to have to replace the carpet - it had been installed less than 3 months before the tornado! Aside from that, it would have been a logistical nightmare to replace the carpet - the couch, bed, end tables, coffee table, night stands, and dressers would have had to be moved downstairs.

Not only is that a huge pain, with our narrow, steep hallway ... where would they go? All of the rooms downstairs were barely passable as it was, with narrow paths left between piles of ... stuff. HUGE sigh of relief to have the carpet dealt with!

With the carpet cleaned, we were able to start the rest of the cleanup in the bedroom. We wanted to have it as cleaned up as possible, to make it easier for all of the repair work that would need to be done up there.

... What a mess. I can't even imagine the force it took to wreak that kind of havoc on every surface up there.

Our top floor is pretty much a bedroom suite, consisting of two open rooms, side by side. Only a small edge of wall separates the two rooms, which stretch in a line from the patio door that was blown in.

If looking at the patio door from inside the room, there is a small bar fridge just inside and to the right of the door, against the wall. Somehow, debris had managed to get wedged behind it. Perpendicular to the patio door, on the far side of the room, more debris had gotten wedged between the back of the couch and the front wall of the house. Our bed - in the room furthest from the door - was full of broken glass and random debris. We had JUST bought new bedding a week or so before!

The debris consisted of leaves, plant material, and.. random shit. We picked up a piece of vinyl tile... we don't have any of this in our whole house. We had random bits of other people's houses splattered across the two rooms. Surreal. 10 months later, it inspired me to write my first haiku since.. Grade 5?

Vinyl tile, not ours
Where the fuck did it come from?
Clean up treasure hunt

Random plant matter was plastered to every vertical surface, as well as in the fur of our plush, battery operated "Tribble". It was cute, and would shake and "purr" if nudged. We'd gotten it from ThinkGeek - I had a laugh as I tweeted to them about it:

The trouble with Tribbles... is figuring out how to get #NoMi tornado debris out of fur! Suggestions, @thinkgeek? - *Twitter Sun May 29 17:45:02 UTC 2011*

While we had a good laugh at the ridiculousness of combing crap out of "Tribble fur", it paled in comparison to the mental image of this thing trembling and cooing as the tornado was busting our door in, and trashing our room! Hilarious!

Other aspects of the cleanup were far less funny. Cleaning out the kitchen was particularly heartbreaking.

When we bought our new house, our fancy new fridge, and were celebrating all of the freedom that came from no longer paying exorbitant rent, we treated ourselves to a freezer full of really nice meats... 5 lbs of the most gorgeous Atlantic cod I'd ever seen. A striploin roast. Gorgeous, high quality chicken breasts. It had been a huge splurge for us.

Our fridge was similarly well stocked. As foodies, we have an appreciation for unique, artisan items... which was reflected in our fridge. Locally made sauces, jams, etc - all opened -... an amazing collection of cheese. We had to throw out everything from the fridge and freezer. . Absolutely heartbreaking.

Things went from bad to worse when we opened one of the cupboard doors and were greeted with an overpowering smell of wet wood and rot.

We hadn't been a fan of the cabinetry, and knew that we'd need - at the very least - to get some more, once we got around to redoing the kitchen. In the wake of finding out just how under insured we were, we thought we could get by with them for a while. They were functional, we could just replace the ceiling and fixing the floor around them. Maybe they'd have to temporarily come up, who knew... but we weren't anticipating them being a write off.

My Car, The Badass

Beyond all of the other logistics I was dealing with that first week, there was the issue of my car. With all of the able-bodied people busily working on debris hauling and tree dismembering, I was charged with getting my car dealt with.

Although Porter had cut my car out from underneath the tree branches that covered and surrounded it in an effort to prevent further damage to the car from city crews, it didn't actually stop them from doing just that. After watching helplessly as city crew repeatedly rammed the tree into my car, it was quite apparent that we would need to get the car out of the area, in order to repair it.

I'm still pissed off about that. We had a bright blue tarp affixed across the back windshield, I would have thought that would have been a clear sign that we were planning to save the car. If they weren't able to get a good grasp of the tree with their machinery, in order to pull it away from my car - shouldn't they have manually worked with it, maybe taken off a few more of the branches if needed?

As a result of the city workers, my car was now ALSO sporting a smashed rear quarter panel, along with weird crumpling along the tops of the driver side doors. While we'd been able to open the rear driver's side door in order to affix the tarp, it was now smashed to the point that the door was unable to open. Additionally, the action of smashing the tree up against my car had ground the tarp into the car, leaving huge blue stains.

Assholes.

I didn't end up finding out that I could have filed a reimbursement complaint against the city for that, until it was too late. Apparently a huge natural disaster is not a good enough excuse to extend the deadline. The damage that the city caused remains on my car to this day, because it would cost more to fix it, than it would to just replace the car.

I don't have the heart to replace it... I'm sure this is going to sound silly, but I feel like I owe it to the car to keep it. Like, that it was badass enough to survive a tornado, when many others hadn't... I don't know. I don't have a tendency to anthropomorphize inanimate objects, but I loved that car, and loved it even more after we pulled the tree off it. I feel like it was a fighter, and ... I don't know. I feel like I owe it the honor of NOT getting rid of it.

I feel like I'm the only one that'll be capable of loving that car, not only *despite* that damage, but partially *because* of it. Rather than seeing it as ugly damage, I see it as almost a badge of honor, that this car is a badass survivor.

56

We are just fixing the car bare-bones. Replacing doors/mirrors w/used ones, replacing windshields. Ignoring dents/cosmetic. #NoMi #Grateful - Twitter, Fri May 27 23:39:08 UTC 2011

5 days after the tornado, Porter crawled in through the passenger side and drove my car up onto Peter's tow dolly, so Peter could drive it to my father in law's place in the suburbs. The car would be stored in his garage until we could get it fixed, protecting it from the elements. I was so happy to see it drive up onto the platform of the tow dolly - it DROVE! I think that's when it really sunk in that my car would be ok.

Chris, our logging guy, knew a guy who owned a wrecking yard. He offered to arrange for the replacement doors, and would install them himself about a week later.

The afternoon that he was to come over and replace the doors, he told me he'd be leaving in about 20 minutes... and that's the last we heard from him. He never showed up. Phone calls and emails over the following week went unanswered, and we were very worried. This was the guy who always showed up early to work on our tree and deck dismantling/hauling, and the hardest worker I'd ever met. He'd taken such great care of us in the week and a half that we'd been working with him, this seemed so out of character for him.

Worried that he'd gotten in a car accident on the way over, we kept an eye out on the news, hoping for SOME sort of infomation that he was ok.

A few days later, another friend stepped up to help us out with the door. We went to purchase doors and windows from a couple of different wrecking yards, and he set about replacing them.

We discovered that the rear quarter panel was too smashed up to be able to replace the rear door, but were able to replace the front door and window. I was thrilled to see my car being put back together - the housing and transportation situation, post tornado, had been killing us.

I hired out the windshield replacement to a company that would come to us - the car wasn't legal to drive in the state it was in. $400 later, and the car was almost legal to drive - all we needed was a replacement side mirror, which we had to order online, having been unable to find at the wrecking yards.

The only other issue was cleanup of the interior. While we were sure that the detailing company we'd used in the past would be able to clean up all of the broken glass, the mold smell was another issue. The smell seemed to be concentrated in the trunk, but permeated the interior of the car as well.

June 16th - three and a half weeks after the tornado - we had the car professionally cleaned out. The idea that all of the cost and replacement so far could have been for nothing, should the mold issue be permanent? Scared the shit out of me. After a day of stress and worrying, the car was returned - and it looked like we were in the clear!

Cautiously optimistic - looks like my car survived! Waiting for Lysol smell to dissipate before celebrating. - Twitter, Thu Jun 16 22:07:08 UTC 2011

A week later, the replacement mirror arrived - and with it, my freedom. June 22, one month to the day that the tornado hit, my car was fixed and cleaned and legal to drive.

About a month after Chris disappeared, the mystery was solved. He emailed to explain that he'd spent the month in jail, due to a DUI. I can't even begin to tell you how disappointed I was... I don't think I ever even replied to his email. Drunk drivers have caused a lot of pain and loss for both Porter and me, and I was completely distraught that this guy - who we'd come to like and respect - had managed to get a DUI on the way to help us. Early in the afternoon, at that!

The fact that he'd been good to us was a huge part of the reason I couldn't reply to him. I don't know that I would have been capable of not telling him off, had I replied. I figured that sparing him the rage that I have towards drunk drivers was... merciful? I don't know, I just felt like I owed him that.

Deck and Porch Removal

Once the bulk of the tornado debris and tree were dealt with, we were able to focus on getting the deck and porch dismantled and hauled out. They were smashed beyond repair, completely written off by the insurance company, and would need to come out so that we could figure out what we were doing with our "new" back yard. It was hard to picture what we'd be doing with the new deck, when the whole backyard was SUCH a mess.

So, on May 26th - four days after the tornado - the whole thing was dismantled and hauled out. It amazing to look at the time line of events now, almost a year later. The cleanup didn't start until the 23rd... just remembering how much crap was dumped in our back and side yards, and remembering how "clear" it was, the morning of the 26th. Beyond remarkable, the progress that was made in just two short days!

The day started out on the right foot - we got our electricity back! Yes!

At 8am, I posted our daily labor needs/invite to Facebook:

Getting ready to head back to the house for the day. Big push to get the deck dismantled and hauled this am! If you want to come by, help out, and have some fun (I'm not kidding!), call me at 612 XXX-XXXX

I meant it - fun. A crowd of geeks pretty much guarantees a good time. Geeks with power tools? Even more so! A local friend replied, confirming as much:

"Sledgehammers, crowbars, and power tools are all a ton of fun, people. Remember that they are the favorite thing of most any kid."

Another friend - in Ottawa, Canada - replied to ask why no one he knows ever goes through a natural disaster when he's around, adding "It's not fair...". He wasn't kidding, either!

Porter and Chris used their power saws to cut up the remains of the deck, while Tara, Todd, and Pat would haul it all out. The deck had flanked - and covered - a stairwell down to the basement. As the wood planks that formed the deck were removed, a couple of things became obvious to us.

For one... wow, whoever built the deck definitely wasn't building it with safety in mind. Some of the beams were simply resting on top of posts, not actually attached at all. In once case, the beam was only *barely* resting on a post, having gotten knocked almost completely off the side of it. While the wood was premium cedar, this thing had not been built to last.

Additionally, we saw that when a previous owner had dug out the stairwell, they'd simply deposited the unearthed soil and clay onto either side of the stairwell, then built the deck over top. Once the deck was completely hauled out, they looked like two gigantic ant hills.

Deck is gone. Porch is coming down now. Backyard just.. destroyed. I can't even.... just.... this is surreal. #NoMi - Twitter, Thu May 26 20:30:43 UTC 2011

After the deck was dismantled and removed, attention was turned toward the remains of the porch. Much like the deck, we quickly realized that the porch was plagued with construction issues. Two large windows were resting on the top edges of vertical plywood planks, they had not even been framed in. Over time, the plywood walls had gotten wet, softened, and started compressing. As a result, the windows themselves were sagging at weird angles, with gaps at the tops.

Behind the drywall of the ceiling was a layer of clear plastic, which contained insulation... and thousands of huge ants. Swarms of them, nesting there in the porch ceiling - I think every one of the guys involved were completely grossed out. The decision was made to cut a slit in the plastic, a little off to the side of the concentration of ants, stick a Shop Vac in there, and suck them all out.

I'm so glad I was nowhere near when this was going down. Ugh!

After the hoard of ants was dealt with, the ceiling and walls came out, leaving the floor. I have to wonder if "floor" actually needs quotation marks around it... it was more like several layers of building materials, loosely forming a horizontal surface. "Floor" seems a bit generous.

The cheap wood flooring was pulled up, revealing a layer of Astroturf. The wood floor had been laid down right over top the turf... what the hell?

The turf was pulled up to reveal several layers of particle board, which had become wet and started turning to mulch over the years. It was becoming obvious that the porch was attached to the house as a bit of an afterthought, definitely thrown together.

Once all of that was pulled out, all that remained was a small section of deck, which precariously straddled the stairway below... balanced atop poorly laid retaining wall bricks by just a couple of beams. It was pretty scary - and entirely unsafe! - but the decision was made to leave it in place, to not render the back door unusable. Once we were ready to put in the new deck, we'd remove that last bit of decking.

This beam was the only thing between the and ground 10 feet below it!

Around the same time that the deck and porch were dismantled, the power company came to collect their transformer that had fallen through the roof of our garage.

Porter had checked in on it the day after the tornado, worried about what could be leaking from it, all over our garage. With us having just moved in at that point, the garage was just crammed full, yet to be organized... Who knows what damage could have resulted from the transformer falling through the roof? I'm just glad that it didn't catch fire!

It ended up being stopped by the rafters and plywood up in the ceiling, rather than crashing through to everything on the ground below - a tiller and various other metal stuff.

Once the crew pulled it up through the hole it had punched in the garage ceiling, the oil poured out of the transformer, all over our garage interior. The crews were nice enough to wipe everything off, and thankfully it didn't actually damage anything. Lucky, because all of the lumber we'd picked up the morning of the tornado was still in the garage!

With the deck and porch out of there, we were almost ready to start rebuilding... aside from the matter of the clay piles from under the deck. Peter once again came to our rescue, using various tools of his former trade - landscaping - to level the ground. Several dump truck loads of dirt and clay were scooped out and brought to a land fill site, leaving us with an incredibly bare yard. We had NO idea what we were going to rebuild in its place, but at least we now had a blank canvas to work with!

As for the lumber for our now-non existent deck, Menards kindly allowed us to return it.

Finding our Roofer

Since the tornado, I've completely lost track at how many times I've caught myself being completely shocked at how long something has taken to do, or how difficult a particular task was. With reality shows showing an entire house being built in a couple weeks, or a kitchen renovation being completed in a week... I guess I had some skewed ideas of what to expect.

The who issue with finding a roofer, though, still baffles me to this day. Especially with the way the economy has hit the construction industry, I was shocked at how hard it was to even get a roofing company in to quote the job!

It started with a roofer that our drywall/painting guy referred to us. After waiting a week to ever hear about when he could start, we finally gave up. We scoured the internet, looking up licensed roofing companies, making endless calls. Many wouldn't return messages, or would come up with excuses. When we finally found one to sign a contract with, they ended up walking out on it before even getting started. More on all of that nonsense in another chapter...

Anyway, when our contracted roofer walked out on us, I was devastated. It was almost two weeks after the tornado, we were scared out of our minds about potential water damage from our smashed-up roof, and I was just so tired of the bullshit. I couldn't understand why it was so difficult to just find someone who wanted the job, could do the job, and wouldn't try to screw us in the process. I was so beaten down by trying to find a roofer, that I was pretty much ready to just walk away from the whole thing.

Among a few recommendations that started flowing in from friends came a glowing reference for a local roofing company - Iron River Construction. The message was from someone who'd worked with them on his roof twice, both due to hail damage. At the end of the message, he noted that - as a bonus - it's a female owned business.

Now, I've never been one to judge a person's ability to do a job by what they're carrying between their legs... but it did sell me this time. After all of the bullshit I'd been encountering from the other construction companies - including enduring verbal abuse from the one that we contracted - I was just sure that this one would have to be different.

We called the main number from our hotel room, at the end of a long day of work. As it was a Saturday, I was expecting to reach a voice mail, having to wait until Monday to hear from them.

Not so! The call was answered by Melissa, whose cheerful, friendly demeanor was such a welcome change from the bleakness we were dealing with up to that point. She was truly a ray of sunshine.

Melissa was positive that they would be able to help us, and very reassuring on the phone. I can't remember if I cried, or was fighting to NOT cry, but the whole thing had overwhelmed me. We made an appointment for a consultation and quote two days later, on Monday. In closing, Melissa instructed me to get myself a cocktail and go hang out in the pool's hot tub.

I liked the way she thought!

I think I found the ONE!! Just talked to a roofer that was recommended, she sounds AWESOME. I like the way she thinks. Woo! - Twitter, Sat Jun 04 23:51:08 UTC 2011

Leading up to the consultation, I was really rooting for this to be THE ONE. They seemed honest and principled, and like they were going to be thorough. After all of the drama we'd gone through for the 2 weeks leading up to this point... I'm sure that there were a lot of fingers crossed on our behalf that day

Today we find out if we have a roofer contracted, and get a final total & check from the insurance company. Cross fingers for us! #NoMi - Twitter, Mon Jun 06 11:11:57 UTC 2011

.. don't be surprised if I have a total meltdown today, between insurance & roofer hiring. Getting to end of rope - Twitter, Mon Jun 06 13:42:52 UTC 2011

I'll never forget standing in our back yard with Tracy, the owner of Iron River. As she surveyed the damage, a rooster from a few houses down crowed. Tracy remarked that the scene reminded her very much of Haiti, post earthquake. She would know - she'd gone down after the earthquake to do volunteer work on rebuilding a school in a small rural village.

Haiti. Damn. With the tree cut up and neatly piled in a corner, the deck and porch dismantled, and all of the debris removed... I'd been thinking it looked pretty good, at that point!

The insurance adjuster showed up, and talked with Tracy about the damages. Notes were written, and... that was that. Tracy left, saying she'd get back to us with a quote.

She did, and we hired Iron River... what a RELIEF to finally have it taken care of! The first priority was for them to replace the roof, of course... but we were also hiring them to replace the walls, ceiling, and floor in the kitchen, the patio door and deck upstairs, as well as all of the windows in the house

We have a roofer!!!! Wooooo!!! #NoMi - Twitter, Wed Jun 08 16:24:04 UTC 2011

That night, we celebrated.

Tree Drama

Once we had made the decision to mill our fallen black walnut tree, and figured out what would need to be done to prepare it for milling - I thought that everything beyond that point would be the easy part. So much had gone into even just determining what to do with the tree in the first place, then all of the research and phone calls to find a mill, and what they would need from us - it had seemed like that was the bulk of it.

I still can't believe how WRONG I was. I'm still blown away by just how much was actually involved with moving ONE tree.

By two days after the tornado, we had been absolutely set in the idea that milling was what we wanted to do. In addition to being the most cost effective way of dealing with the loss of the tree - by being able to use the wood to rebuild the kitchen - we were really excited about this unplanned upgrade for the kitchen. We'd initially wanted walnut cabinetry when we first bought the house and discussed kitchen renovation... but quickly realized that it was out of our budget.

If it weren't for that excitement, we probably would have thrown in the towel sooner. If definitely would have been easier to cut the tree into smaller, manageable chunks and just hauled them out to the boulevard, than to spend 7 weeks trying to get the tree to the mill!

By the end of Thursday May 26th - only 4 days after the tornado - Chris had the entire tree cut up into 8-10 foot long lengths, per the request of the mill that would be dealing with it. Contrary to the warnings we'd been receiving that it could be full of rot, the logs were gorgeous, high quality specimens... beautiful wood, no rot, and each log was very, very straight - the best possible result that we could have hoped for!

We sorted the wood, and moved it all to where it needed to be - the logs that were too small to mill went to one side of the yard, til we could figure out what we wanted to do with them. The bulk of the root ball was dragged up the alley, for the tree debris removal crews to pick up, and the wood that would be going to the mill was moved over to the very back of the yard, so it could easily be accessed from the alley.

I figured that I could simply call a company to come in, pack the logs onto a truck, and deliver them to the mill. Apparently, I seriously underestimated the work involved with this.

For an entire month after the tree was prepared to be milled, I was getting nowhere. Companies would refuse the job for being too small, or because they couldn't get their equipment into our alley. The companies that sounded interested in the job over the phone either wouldn't show up for the quote (happened several times!), would show up and realize it was beyond their capabilities, or would quote exorbitant rates.

As time wore on, I had to get more flexible with what I was looking for. Hell, I'd be ok with renting a truck myself, and just hiring general laborers to move it onto the truck bed... but no dice.

So then I looked into having a portable sawmill service come to us, process the wood down, with the idea that we could rent a truck and move the planks ourselves.

Well, most companies were unavailable, for many of the same reasons we couldn't find someone to haul it out - too small of a job, too narrow of a lane, etc.

My phone apparently has more computing power than it took to land people on the moon in '69, but getting a tree out of yard is IMPOSSIBLE - Twitter, Mon Jun 27 21:29:00 UTC 2011

As more time passed, we started to worry that we were going to lose the wood. It was rainy, there were all sorts of bird and other criters who had lost their homes in the tornado as well... there was a good chance that something bad would happen to the logs.

I may be a logistics person, but even *I* am blown away with the amount of BS dealing with the tree. Was easier to get a whole new roof done - Twitter, Mon Jun 27 21:17:58 UTC 2011

On July 11th, my luck turned around. I complained to Tracy - owner of Iron River, the company that was handling our major repairs - about the problems I was having with the tree removal. Tracy's idea was to hire one of her roofing crews - a team of about 10 guys - to lift the logs into their dump truck and drive it to the mill for us.

In other news, after 7 WEEKS... looks like we finally have someone to haul the logs out of our yard, to the mill!! Fingers crossed! - Twitter, Mon Jul 11 18:36:50 UTC 2011

Finally! Things were starting to look up! We made plans for her crew to show up the next day, after finishing up with another roofing job. Because of the hours - and the distance to - the mill, the logs would have to leave our house no later than 4pm. They would take it in their truck, I would drive my car, meeting up with them to deal with the mill company.

Tree guys are late. Augh. Please please please be the day that I have someone competent actually take care of our walnut tree! #EnoughDrama - Twitter, Tue Jul 12 15:59:32 UTC 2011

The weren't able to come out that day. We rescheduled for the next day

Another day.... another day that the tree is still in our yard. Sigh. Completely ridiculous, how much time I've invested in saving the thing - Twitter, Wed Jul 13 21:12:02 UTC 2011

... they ended up not being able to make it.

I was pretty much losing my mind over it all. To be SO close to finally having it all off my plate, only to be met with these delays? Very frustrating.

That third day - Thursday - they were supposed to show up before their other jobs, arriving at my place by 11am. Things were getting desperate - we had booked a HUGE delivery for Saturday. With all of the bricks for building the patio, all of the wood for rebuilding the deck, the new patio furniture, etc set to arrive, we needed the logs OUT of there.

11pm, no show.

Several hours later... still no roofing crew.

3rd day in a row where the tree is "for sure" going to be hauled out of the yard and taken to the mill. Was supposed to be before 11am..- Twitter, Thu Jul 14 18:48:04 UTC 2011

By new estimate, I was told they'd be there by 3pm... Then at 3:25, I was told that they were 10 minutes away. I'll let my tweets from that day tell the rest of the story:

3: 24 - IF the guys show up by their latest estimate, they have about 25 minutes to load 4 huge logs into a trailer. NOT liking those odds. Drama.:(

3:31 - Whatever happens, I am losing my shit at 4 pm. I hope it's because 7 weeks of tree BS is finally over, and not because it's NOT over.

67

3:40 - 10 guys. 4 big logs. One is ~2000 lbs. 20 minutes to do it. I am freaking out.

3:50 - Omg there is movement. Only 10 minutes to work with and they have none in the trailer yet though. Augh!!

3:53 - This is the closest I've come to having the tree issue finally off my plate in 7 WEEKS of dealing with it. So close... but 7 minutes left!

3:56 - Obviously, my worry that the valuable logs were at risk of being stolen if left in the yard was a SERIOUS miscalculation.

3:58 - It's IN! OMG the 2000 lb log is in the trailer, along with one of the smaller ones! OMG this nightmare shitfest is almost OVER!!!!!

4:01 - Third log is in!!! That's the weird shaped, 2nd most difficult/heavy one! One more! A few minutes late, maybe we can make it up on the hwy.

5:04 - At the mill. Tree is 5 miles behind me. Starting to feel a little relieved. Will be better when it's dropped off.

5:55 - It's OVER. The tree is safely at the mill. 5000 lbs off my back!

6:08 - Decided that finally getting the tree dealt with is justification for an evening "off" -too many 16 hour days lately. Gonna watch Dr Who.

There are no words to describe the relief the next morning, waking up to the knowledge that I no longer had 5000 lbs of tree to deal with!

That relief was short lived - a few days later, the mill called to let us know that they would be unable to work with one of the sections that we had hauled there, as the shape was odd. They asked if we wanted to keep it (of course we did!), letting us know that we would need to come pick it up ASAP if we did.

So, we rented a pickup truck, drove the hour back to the mill, had them load it in for us, and brought it back to the house. Man, for two people to work with, that thing was a bitch to get out of the truck! I have monster quads - with only a small amount of training time, I can leg press almost 1000 lbs - but I couldn't even get the damn thing to budge. We tried using lumber as levers. Nothing was working.

Finally, we tied a strap to both the tree and one of the metal fence posts that still remained upright, and drove the truck away. THAT finally did the trick, ending up with the tree standing perfectly upright in our driveway!

As luck would have it, a local guy with a portable sawmill service had emailed me the day after we'd hauled the wood to the mill, saying that he could do it for us... so we called him up to handle this log, along with some of the smaller ones we had left.

Because of their schedule, it was mid October before they were able to mill it:

On a happy note, last of our black walnut gets milled today, at our house. The guy is gonna have fun with it, give us unique cuts. Excited! - Twitter, Mon Oct 10 20:59:00 UTC 2011

The tree guys are here! So excited! Still sucks that we lost our black walnut tree, but SO happy we're saving as much of the wood as we can! - Twitter, Mon Oct 10 22:19:00 UTC 2011

A few days later we rented a pickup truck again, loaded it up with the remaining wood, and I drove it out to the mill to add to our order.

Once at the mill, I ended up having to unload it all by myself. I was sick as a dog that day, but was desperate to just get it all off our plate... so I pushed through. I think I managed to pull every muscle in my torso AND legs in doing so, was overheated and out of breath.. but damn did it EVER feel good to be done with it.

We figured that the wood from the first load was enough to cover the kitchen rebuild needs, so this was all "extra", that we could have fun with. The wood from the smaller, last-remaining batch turned out to be especially beautiful, so we can't wait to build things out of it.

We won't receive our wood until months after this book comes out, but when it does... I'm thinking a gorgeous new table and hope chest. I think it'll be a good idea to make some items that can come with us wherever we go, with the idea of them eventually becoming heirloom items. Lasting symbols of resilience!

REBUILDING OUR LIFE

Life as a Tornado Refugee

It's amazing how unstable one's life can become, just for not being able to get "living expenses" coverage on their home insurance!

For several weeks following the tornado, we were in and out of various hotels, spending only 2-3 nights in each. The last night we spent in any given hotel, we'd search online for the cheapest hotel in the area starting the next day. We'd book as many consecutive days as we could at that rate, and that was that. In the mornings, I would drive Porter to work before packing up our hotel room, checking out, and heading to the house to get some work done.

Late every afternoon, I'd check into the new hotel, get everything situated, then go pick Porter up from work. We'd find something to eat, then head back to the house to get a little bit of work done, if possible.

Every day - evenings on weekdays, mornings on weekend - we'd go visit the cats. Porter's dad had graciously agreed to put them up in his spare bedroom, as not many hotels would allow any cats at all, nevermind four of them. Also, most hotels require you to be in the room with pets at all times - which obviously wasn't going to work, as we were racing to clean up and rebuild everything.

The cats seemed fairly happy, if not sort of lonely. They were so used to getting near constant attention and affection, now they were down to maybe half an hour daily - it really sucked. They were closed away in a single bedroom, as Ray owned a dog... things could have been ugly if they got out.

Daisy was a source of entertainment for the cats though - whenever she'd go outside, she would run back and forth in front of the guest bedroom window, and four cats would be lined up, four heads following her side to side path in unison.

They were definitely glad to see us on our short daily visits. We'd feed them, change their water and cat litter, and snuggle them like crazy.
It was killing me that Turbo - my baby - was growing up pretty much

without us, and in such a temporary situation. She got so BIG during her stint as a tornado refugee!

None of us could wait until the situation was rectified, and we tried to push up our move-back date any way we could.

While it wasn't liveable overnight, we tried to spend as much time as we could at the house during the days... even on days when work was hampered by weather. By May 20th, we managed to get our bedroom mostly "daytime livable" - All of the debris cleaned out, the walls and carpet cleaned up, our bedding laundered, etc. Aside from the hole in the wall where the tree had some in - now covered with a contractor bag taped in place - and our tarp-covered patio door, we didn't have any big reminders of the tornado in there, and we were able to sort of ignore it. All of the real damage was done in the one half of our bedroom - including the seam where the roof had been ripped up, and all of the nail punches from it being dropped down a bit off from where it started.

The other half of our bedroom - including our bed, Jacuzzi, and TV - were fine after we cleaned it all up. We were SO happy to have at least that - When we originally moved in to the house, we referred to our bedroom as our "Fortress of Solitude". It was our own personal refuge away from everyone and everything, and it was perfect. To have it smashed up in the tornado felt personal... a violent violation of our privacy. Getting the bedroom cleaned up to "daytime livable" went a long way to giving us some sort of feeling of... center. We may have been in and out of the hotels, but we had our own bedroom to hang out in when things got too overwhelming, even if only for a few hours at a time.

A few weeks after the tornado, our friends Heather and Mark granted us a bit of a reprieve from hotels- they were departing on their honeymoon, and asked if we'd be up for house sitting, taking care of their two cats while they were gone. I don't remember if it was a week or 10 days, but it was a much longer stint than the 2-3 nights we were spending at each hotel. The first night, we stopped by a liquor store for some drinks to celebrate, and decided to watch the Harry Potter movies - Mark and Heather had the whole set, most of our friends loved the movies, but we'd never seen them.

We settled in, and immediately discovered that one of her two cats was completely psychotic. I mean... batshit crazy.

71

Heather had made comments about him being antisocial before, which I took to mean as "He won't be coming to you for snuggles"... fine. This was something completely different - he was stalking us, and lashing out with a flurry of paws and claws. When we'd try to walk towards the washroom, he would situate himself in the middle of the hallway... crouching down, hunching up, and basically daring us to try and pass him. If we got too close, he would attack.

This was completely bizarre to both of us. My husband is... the cat whisperer. Cats LOVE him, follow him everywhere, etc. I'm the same way, but to a slightly lesser degree. When we met, Porter was shocked that his antisocial cat - who loved HIM, but couldn't stand other people - let me pet her. He was sure she'd rip my face off for trying.

Yet, here was this cat that hated us, and was doing his best to get us OUT of his house. He'd run up and attack our legs, and sliced my arm up one time I bent down to pick something up off the ground. I still have NO idea where he came from, when that happened!

We quickly decided to retreat to the basement, where the guest bed was. In the morning, he'd be crouched just outside of the door to the main floor, again daring us to try and pass him, this vicious little ball of fur.

After just two or three nights, we decided that this was total bullshit, that we were tired of bullshit, and that we were going to move home - huge holes in our wall or not. Partially functional bathroom, nonfunctional kitchen be damned - "Crazy Cat" was the last straw.

So, we moved home. It didn't feel quite right, not having the cats there with us - but we wanted the contractors to be finished the main work before bringing them back. All of that banging would scare the shit out of them, and they'd been traumatized enough.

The first night back in our own house, one of my fears came to fruition - having holes punched in the walls and a big section of roof missing for that long had invited every manner of creepy crawly into our house. I am VEHEMENTLY anti-bug, so this was all sorts of NOT cool.

I was unable to sleep that night, so at 4 am, I decided to go down to my office and try to get some writing done. I flicked on the light and SCREAMED.

Something big darted out and ran across the floor. It was about the size of a large mouse, but didn't move like a mouse. It sort of zig zagged - and completely scared the shit out of me. I'm not the best at handling sudden movements as it is... but couple it with the size of that thing? I didn't know what it was, but there was NO possibility that would have been even remotely acceptable. Mouse, frog (from the way it moved weird)... I didn't know. The scream was completely reflex.

Porter came FLYING down the stairs, out of a solid slumber. The same guy who takes at least 30 minutes to get out of bed, and is slow moving when he finally does.... I'm not entirely sure that he made contact with more than a small handful of the steps on his way down. I thought he was going to KILL me for screaming at that hour.

That is, he'd have killed me if he was anything less than the awesome person I married. He asked what happened, obviously very worried for me - I pointed and tried to choke out the words to describe what I'd just seen. He went after it and killed it - it turned out to be the biggest house centipede either of us had ever seen. He didn't even get the slightest bit upset at me! I'm still impressed by that!

That wasn't the first creepy-crawly that we had to deal with after the tornado. Mice got in on our main floor. We had the cats locked upstairs during the renovations for their own safety, so they were useless. The mice were super ballsy - it's almost like they knew that there were no cats to deal with them. One popped out from across the hallway, darted towards me, and stared me DOWN. Ugh. It took a few weeks of mousetraps and poison to get rid of them.

Ants. There were ants EVERYWHERE, mostly in our bedroom. I have to wonder if a nest got picked up and thrown into our house, it's the only way to explain the numbers. Gross... a few weeks of ant bait took care of it, but... ew. Everywhere, even in our bed. It was really awful.

The gigantic mutant spider - I've never seen anything like it. I went down to the washroom one morning, and it was there in the tub, probably the size of the palm of my hand. It had hairy legs... the thing was massive. I'm a recovering arachnophobe. I'm not full out phobic anymore, but I really, really hate spiders, and they still freak me out... and this thing was SO massive, it was mesmerizing. I stayed back, of course... but I couldn't help but marvel at it for a minute. You know, before getting Porter to kill it.

He took a photo, and we later found out that it was likely a wolf spider - and that not only bite, they jump. That'll be the last time I hesitate to have a spider killed, I'm getting the shivers just writing about the idea of one jumping at me. Moving right along...

I lost track of how many times we went to Menards in the months following the tornado - At times it was daily, sometimes it was twice in a day. I'm all for efficiency, and put every effort in to plan each shopping trip as well as possible, but we were constantly being caught off guard on things. We'd buy the stuff for a certain project, get started, and run into something unexpected and weird. We'd buy too much or too few of something, or not quite the right thing, or just change our mind part way. For certain projects, we'd need to buy the stuff to get part way, assess from there, and maybe end up buying something else to proceed.

Also, there were so many decisions to make, it got overwhelming. We'd get partway through a shopping list and just start veering into overstimulation - and have to cut it short. It's hard to make decisions when you're overstimulated, and we tried to be careful to avoid that when possible.

Additionally - especially with regards to the kitchen - there were plenty of times where we thought we had some time to make a decision, and then all of a sudden had a new, shorter deadline forced on us. It wasn't just "hurry up and wait", it was "Hurry up... wait... OMG PICK WHAT KIND OF MICROWAVE YOU WANT RIGHT NOW OR THE WORLD WILL END". The kitchen foreman may have been slightly less ridiculous than that, but not by much!

This was my first summer away from the wedding industry. When the bulk of your business is wedding cake, you lose weekends entirely... and this was a big part of the reason why I quit. I was working myself into the ground, and didn't feel like I had a chance to live, myself. In was constantly in a state of rushing around, working on the next order, etc.

This summer was supposed to be relaxing. I was supposed to rediscover weekends, which would be lazily spent hanging out with my husband. I was honestly excited to know what it felt like to go into a weekend with no plans at all, to be able to sleep in... it all sounded wonderful.

We'd talked of doing spontaneous road trips to small towns nearby, just to check out whatever random tourist monument was the pride of the town. "Largest ball of twine" and whatnot... completely ridiculous, and completely different from the nonstop stress of the wedding business.

Instead, our road trips all led to Menards. I'm surprised that the staff there didn't know us by name, even if many of them knew us by sight! Seriously, Menards needs to start some kind of VIP program. If you're in there daily, dropping thousands of dollars... there should be someone to greet you by putting a fruity cocktail in your hand, and offering up a foot massage.

Ah, one can dream. Sure would have made it a lot less annoying to go there many dozen times!

As it turned out, those road trips probably wouldn't have happened that summer, on account of weather. We were hit with the most ridiculous heat wave that I've ever been through, which pretty much confined me indoors. An excessive heat warning was issued on June 4th, and seemed to stay with us for the entire summer.

On July 19, the heat index reached a record high of 119... The humidity and heat in Minnesota was higher than in the AMAZON that day.... and that same day, we got 1" diameter hail. The next day, I observed:

"It is 9 degrees cooler in JAMAICA right now, than it is in Minneapolis. 12 degrees cooler in Brazil. 5 degrees cooler in Orlando. 16 degrees cooler in Maui. Seriously, WTF MN?!" - Facebook, July 20 2011

I felt awful for the people whose roofs were still tarped up, yet to have roof replacement work start. Heat, downpours, crazy hail, strong winds - it was a hellish summer. It got so bad that the main highway through Minneapolis - 94 - was actually buckling from the heat! At least two lanes experienced "pavement failure", right near downtown. TOTAL nightmare for driving.

The heat let up only slightly. We were still dining outside into December, and never really did get a winter that year. By March 2012, I wasn't sure that we were going to even get a spring - the temperatures were excessively high. On St Patrick's day, temperatures reached 80 degrees, and we spent much of the day outside. SO bizarre.

Temperatures finally cooled back down to normal - maybe cooler than normal - in April 2012. Between the lack of a winter, the extended heat wave in March, and the temperature dive in April... I worry about what the 2012 tornado season will look like.

Roof

The wild temperatures and weather conditions definitely kept us stressed out, in the wait for a new roof.

While waiting for the roofer we'd been referred to, our big task was to pick out the shingles. Before that point, I'd never even noticed that shingles even came in more than one color. I guess it makes sense, I just had never bothered to pay attention to roof colors, or given it ANY thought, whatsoever.

Well, choosing the shingles was the easiest decision of the entire remodel, and far less annoying than I had imagined. We looked at the wall display of different colors, I pointed to the one I liked, stated "I like that one the best", Porter replied "So do I", and that was that. Damn shame that the rest of the choices weren't so easy!

The winning choice was "Harbor blue", a mix of tiny blue and black dots. We obtained a small piece of it as a sample - not just for the roofers, but also to decide on paint colors for the stucco, trim, and bricks.

After a couple of false starts - our original roofer flaking out, and second one - that we'd actually contracted with! - trying to raise the total price, then walking out of the contract - we had finally hired a company that seemed far more on the ball, and willing to work. On Monday June 13th, the work began on our roof replacement.

OMG! I think I hear someone on my roof! Are the roof repair noises FINALLY coming from my own house!? - Twitter, Mon Jun 13 12:27:54 UTC 2011

YES YES YES!!!! They are tarping my roof! 3 weeks after #NoMi, and we are FINALLY getting this show on the road!!! - Mon Jun 13 12:29:26 UTC 2011

Is it wrong that I want to pour a glass of wine and go up to my bedroom and just listen to the roofers, like you'd enjoy a good rainstorm? - Twitter, Mon Jun 13 13:05:19 UTC 2011

Within a couple days, we had our new roof. Two, actually - the house and the garage. They were incredibly cute roofs - and now they matched! Up til that point, they'd been two different colors - a fact that I didn't notice until my husband pointed it out to me, post-tornado.

WE HAVE A ROOF!!!! They're starting on laying the shingles now! No more holes! No more tarp! WE HAVE A ROOF!!! - Twitter, Tue Jun 14 12:46:02 UTC 2011

While we were relieved to finally have a new roof, it didn't come without a bit of aggravation - the roofers had managed to scrape up the skylight above our Jacuzzi, and trample the hops that Porter had planted shortly before the tornado.

The construction company replaced the skylight without any sort of fight whatsoever - we were so grateful for that. Accidents happen, but it's rare for people - or company to take responsibility without some sort of drama over it. While we were disheartened to have to deal with more post-tornado damage, it was kind of nice to have THAT level of reassurance that we had definitely chosen wisely in hiring them.

Would have been nice if the City of Minneapolis had shown that sort of integrity when it came to their cleanup crew smashing my car up, rather than hiding behind a complaint deadline!

Bedroom

With the roof completed, we were able to get the repairs done in our bedroom - an important step in getting the cats home. While we knew that it could be months before it would be safe for the cats to roam around the first floor, we knew that we could sequester them upstairs until that point. That is, after the repairs were done up there.

On June 15th, we had Stephan come by to see the damage to the walls and ceiling in there, and plan to fix it. Stephan's company - Dakota Painting and Drywall - had been so wonderful to work with when we first bought our house - fixing and repainting the walls, redoing the texture on the ceilings - that it was a no-brainer to hire them for these repairs.

As always, he was super upbeat. He was positive that they could get it fixed, and that the cosmetic stuff isn't actually as awful as it looked. Also, it was the first time they'd seen the house since they had finished up, just before we moved in. He hadn't seen it with furniture, drapes, and everything we did after his crew had finished. Amongst all the destruction, it felt kind of good for the pats on the back and raves over what we'd done with the place. It was nice to have their cheerful, positive energy around the house again.

On June 17, the last *big* hole in our house was repaired - the smashed in patio door. All that would remain after that was the two holes where the trees came through. How surreal is that thought? "We'll still have the holes in the walls from the trees, though".

The day started off with some bad news - some asshole had stolen building materials from our yard, the night before. Seriously, what kind of low life do you have to be to steal building materials from a smashed house after a natural disaster? I don't think that we were actually on the hook for the cost associated with it, but the news really pissed me off.

I have NO idea what the fuck is wrong with some people.

The patio door was replaced with no issue. It was nice to not have just a blue tarp separating us from the elements, but the view wasn't much better with the door in place. Through our new glass sliding door, we could now see not only the destroyed mini deck just beyond the door, but the sea of tarps and tornado damage still left in the neighborhood. We had no idea, back then, that we would still be looking at some of those tarps almost a year later!

On June 20th, part of that was taken care of. Pete and Jeff from Iron River, who came by to replace the mini deck.

I was sick in bed with a nasty bout of allergies or something, but was excited to see the old deck go. Even before the tornado, the deck hadn't been much to look at. It was very small - a fact that wouldn't change - but was very dark, closed in, and boxy feeling. It looked like a weathered old shipping crate. The new design would feel bigger and more open, featuring turned spindles rather than a solid wall. It would be bright new cedar, and it would be a great change from the smashed up deck we were left with, post-tornado.

I just have to say, I loved working with Iron River. We would have been happy with just having contractors who did the job well, without screwing us over in the process. Hell, by 2 weeks after the tornado, I would have probably taken "did an ok job and did not screw us TOO much...". These guys though? Above and beyond that. Nice, honest, easy to work with, and even sort of fun to have around.

Pete actually offered to go get me some chicken soup when he saw that I wasn't feeling well! I didn't take him up on the offer, but I was very touched at the consideration he showed that day. I'd recommend them to anyone!

That didn't scare Pete away from scaring the crap out of me, though. I could barely stand to watch him, once he'd gotten the deck stripped down to just the support beams. I was so nervous, it didn't seem safe - I'd hate to see him fall!

Between Pete, Steve, and Jeff, the deck seemed to be finished in record time, with no mishaps - and it was gorgeous!

On June 27th, work began on the rest of the damage to the bedroom - the tree hole in the wall, the nail punch damage to the ceiling, the seam along the tops of the walls, where the roof was pulled up. Additionally, they would be refinishing the drywall around the second, small skylight - which had been damaged in the tornado and since replaced.

All that's separated our bedroom from the outside - ~1' diameter hole! - for the past 5 weeks has been a garbage bag duct-taped to the wall.- Twitter, Mon Jun 27 13:47:10 UTC 2011

Which, admittedly, was not as bad as the 4 weeks where the entire patio door in our bedroom was open, and had a tarp taped up over it... - Twitter, Mon Jun 27 13:49:26 UTC 2011

Or the 3 weeks where a good deal of our roof was missing, w/ tarp put up over THAT. Man, now I feel like I'm nitpicking over the tree hole!- Twitter, Mon Jun 27 13:50:32 UTC 2011

They got the repairs done in no time - I think it may have been a total of two days, for all of it! Aside from the brand-new look of the patio door and the deck just beyond it, no one would ever have guessed that this room had a tornado go right over it, just over a month earlier. It was beautiful, and it was OURS again.

On July 4th, the cats moved back home. Not only was our "Fortress of Solitude" completely repaired, our family was finally back together.

Kitchen

Of all of the damage to the house - and the repairs needed to fix them - the kitchen was by FAR the most stressful, long, drawn-out nightmare of the lot. I'm guessing it was Murphy's Law once again marking its territory all over my life.

At the time the tornado hit, I had just started work on what would be my third cookbook. With the damage to the kitchen, that project ended up back burnered indefinitely. Not only did I have no idea when I would get my kitchen back, I had no idea when I would have TIME to work on it. With Porter working full time outside of the house, the brunt of planning, logistics, and dealing with contractors fell into my lap.

At first, we thought it was be just a matter of fixing the ceiling and floor, both damaged by the water and debris coming through where the tree bounced off our roof. (What a completely bizarre thing to have to type!). Several days after the tornado, however, we realized that the cabinetry also sustained major water damage, and the entire kitchen would need to be gutted - a complete loss.

On the plus side, however... we WERE starting with the world's ugliest, least functional kitchen ever. It had one counter which was super narrow, and had one row of cupboards - immediately over that counter, and excessively low, rendering the counter almost useless. There was a free standing sink cabinet - which looked to be almost falling apart - and a completely lackluster sink.

That was it, the whole kitchen. The walls had some cracking, the roof had ugly popcorn finish, and there was only 1 dinky little light in the whole room. It really did need a complete overhaul, so I guess it's good that the tornado forced our hand on that - who knows how long we would have been stuck with it in that condition.

One major challenge for the design was the shape - between a short hallway towards the dining room - with a stairway leading down to the basement from it - and a weird little breakfast nook area, our kitchen was "stealth bomber" shaped. The bizarre shape and relatively small size made planning for new cabinetry a challenge - it was incredibly difficult to design a coherent and efficient kitchen around the constraints we were faced with.

We wanted to focus on the roof before tackling the kitchen, for obvious reasons... but as the kitchen floor started sagging badly from the water damage, we had to bump it up in priority. The last thing we wanted was an unexpected "skylight" to the basement!

So, we hired contractors to deal with the ceiling, floor, and walls for us. Once the basic structure was fixed, our painting and drywall guys would paint the walls and put texture on the new ceiling.

Because of the way grandfathered code works in the area, we were obligated to have the HVAC, plumbing and electrical behind those walls replaced, bringing them up to current codes. Good enough, right?

Well, that meant that we needed to actually design the layout of the kitchen before they could start work, as the electrical and plumbing plans would be based around the cabinetry layout.

Now, I've been all about design, my whole life. When I was a fashion designer, I easily drafted patterns from scratch, usually fairly freehand. I've been in floral, cake, fashion, and graphic design, I have a great grasp on geometry and balance... hell, my spatial reasoning is in the 99th+ percentile. I should have been able to design that kitchen easily!

Not so much. It took about a week of frustration in messing around with photoshop, photos, to-scale paper cutouts, and graph paper before I threw in the towel. Anything I came up with had at least one element that was just gross, and didn't work.

Compromises had to be made with the space, and usually resulted in less-than-efficient use of whatever. I'm pretty sure that I've never felt like more of a failure in my life, than when I had to admit defeat on kitchen design.

As luck would have it, there was a group purchasing deal on kitchen design consultations waiting for me in my email the next morning. I haven't decided if that was fate rubbing my nose in it, or just plain taking pity on me. Either way, we purchased it in the hopes that a professional wouldn't be as stumped by it as we were.

June 13th - The morning that the roofers started - our kitchen designer showed up to measure, take photos, and get an idea of what she was working with. She would render it all up in AutoCAD and present the possibilities to us a few days later.

Well, my poor bruised ego felt a bit better when we went to her showroom to see the results on June 16th. She expressed frustration with it as well, having had a very difficult time coming up with a workable design. Everything basically came down to the weird middle section of the kitchen - the same section that I was having issues with. The difference between her and I was that she managed to come up with a very simple solution that fixed everything I was having problems with - the inclusion of a triangle shaped cabinet piece to join that middle part up to the cabinetry in the soon-to-be-former breakfast nook. (We were planning to have the wall ripped out to minimize the separation of that area from the rest of the kitchen).

That was one hell of a "EUREKA!" moment for me. Kind of ridiculous that we had to hire someone to point out that one little angle could fix everything I was having issues with. I felt like such a dolt, but at least we had a finished set of plans to submit to the construction foreman!

When we arrived home from the design consult, we were informed that the reason our floor was sagging so badly was because one of the main beams (joists?) under the kitchen wasn't actually supported by anything. The construction guys would install a floor jack in the basement, and were confident that it'd solve the problem. The actual structure of the floor wasn't damaged, and we didn't need to replace all THAT much. They'd be ripping things out down to the sub floor, replacing that, and leveling it if needed.

Beyond that, both exterior facing walls would need new insulation, and both windows needed to be reframed in order to replace them. Loads of work, but nowhere near as bad as having to rip the whole floor our down to the studs!

We were looking forward to getting construction started - it'd be nice to have some sort of kitchen back, even if it was just going to be our appliances in an empty room. It may have been only 3 weeks since the tornado, but we were already completely sick of the eating-out situation. It really sucks to be perfectly capable, personally, of cooking really great food, and not having somewhere to do it. We were so, so sick of fast food, yet couldn't afford to go somewhere decent for all of our meals.

In preparation for the demolition, we had to go through the kitchen and sort through everything. Damaged stuff was thrown away, items that we didn't think we'd be using any more got donated, and the rest was packed.

Stuff that we could use in the relatively short term - when we got basic use of our kitchen back - was packed into open boxes for storage in the living room. Anything that wouldn't be useful until we had our complete kitchen back - cabinets and all - was packed into sealed boxes and hauled upstairs to be stored in the newly-repaired crawl space under the roof.

Almost done packing the kitchen to prepare for tomorrow's demolition. We JUST packed our old kitchen and unpacked here 3 months ago! #TooSoon - Twitter, Sun Jun 19 02:15:44 UTC 2011

Finishing up last of kitchen packing before demolition today. Sash!'s "Move Mania" comes on radio. Ugh. Too appropriate. :(#NoMi - Twitter, Sun Jun 19 15:23:47 UTC 2011

In an effort to speed up the process - and save money - we decided to demolish the kitchen ourselves. We tested negative for lead, and were ready to go! On June 19th, I officially lost the rest of what had been my kitchen.

Before Todd and Tara arrived to help destroy the place, we busied ourselves by taking the doors off the cabinets. You know, I never knew how easy it would be to get help with hard physical labor... but I learned that there is usually SOMEONE who is all over the idea of swinging a sledgehammer and busting shit up!

We taped plastic up between the kitchen and the rest of the house, opened the back door, and they went to it. I had to bow out on account of a horrible case of allergies from the dust - my eyes were pouring so bad, I could barely see.

They, on the other hand, sounded like they were having a BLAST with ripping out the walls and ceiling. I listened to the festivities from the next room, and couldn't help feeling left out. So... I busied myself with tweeting snark about it all.

It was probably better that I couldn't participate - three nerds and geeks armed with pry bars and sledge hammers in one small room is probably not the safest situation by itself, never mind adding a fourth!

I have the best of both worlds in my husband. Man who is not only brilliant, but really handy. He's really into the demolition - kinda HOT! - Twitter, Sun Jun 19 16:47:51 UTC 2011

I think the brains shut down as soon as the tools came out. Visions of accidentally launched projectiles injuring someone...- Twitter, Sun Jun 19 18:59:55 UTC 2011

My bet is on this one - my husband - being the first ER trip of the day. - Twitter, Sun Jun 19 19:03:00 UTC 2011

Any bets on what first injury is? Stab-type (nails, etc). Bludeoning with flying cabinetry? Electrocution? Anyone's game, given past 20 mins - Twitter, Sun Jun 19 19:17:31 UTC 2011

My guess that hubby would go flying backward off the step stool and drag the cabinets down on him did not happen, though it seemed likely - Twitter, Sun Jun 19 19:19:59 UTC 2011

Awesome. Tons of mouse droppings under the cabinet, too much testosterone flowing for them to listen to my requests to spray before moving.- Twitter, Sun Jun 19 19:41:55 UTC 2011

So now I'm trying to remember how long hantavirus can be an issue in mouse shit, now that they've stirred it all up.- Twitter, Sun Jun 19 19:43:32 UTC 2011

Well, cabinets weren't enough to satiate their manly urges. They decided to rip out the ceiling and walls. Plaster, not drywall. Oh boy.- Twitter, Sun Jun 19 20:46:15 UTC 2011

Oh the year was 1778, how I wish I was in Sherbrooke now...- Twitter, Sun Jun 19 20:47:43 UTC 2011

Pretty surreal to be sitting in our newly renovated (3 months!), nicely done livingroom.. looking at a sink ON TOP of a dishwasher... / .... and then looking through the clear plastic over the doorway, to see the carnage in the kitchen. Damn. Those walls were OLD. - Twitter, Sun Jun 19 21:00:27 UTC 2011

When all was said and done, we learned that the walls had pretty much no insulation. The newspaper that had been packed into the walls as insulation WAY back when had turned to mulch and fallen down to the bottom of the wall cavity.

While the kitchen foreman had given us an estimate of 10 days to finish the project, the start of it had been delayed. Rather than his crew coming on Monday June 20th to finish the demo (the breakfast nook wall/header), he pushed it back a few days, starting them on Thursday the 23. In the meantime - June 22 - we were told for the first time that we would actually have to purchase the microwave/range hood before they got started. That night, we did more "emergency shopping" - it would have been nice to have more notice. I mean, we'd had them contracted for a over a week by then!

The professional demolition was like nothing I'd ever experienced before - taking the kitchen nook's wall and header out *completely* shook the house. Scared the crap out of me!

Kitchen remodeler now saying Wednesday start. Far cry from last Monday! I'm wondering when his "10 working days" starts/ed. Upsetting. #NoMi - Twitter, Tue Jun 28 03:02:30 UTC 2011

By June 30th, the kitchen had sat untouched for a week, with no work having been done on it since the wall and header had been ripped out. Any time we were told work would start, the foreman would end us bumping us in priority for other jobs - even though we had a signed contract with a signed timeline!

That day, the most recent excuse was that his HVAC guys were too busy - on a day that they were supposedly booked to work on our kitchen - because it was hot outside. Awesome. If that was going to bump us, we may not get the work done for months!

We seriously discussed our options, coming very close to the point of canceling our contract with them. We were SO sick of being bumped in priority, it had already been 6 weeks without a kitchen. I talked to the owner of the company, discussing our desire to get out of the contract and hire someone else. The owner understood, agreeing to give us a new foreman.

That never happened, and things started to get ugly. In addition to our "6 weeks without a kitchen" and "being bumped for more 'important' jobs" frustration, there was a state strike looming - if we didn't get things finished and have the electrical inspected and signed off on by then, we would be stuck until it was over.

Stuck with our awful kitchen contractor, things continued to be utter shit. I have no idea why someone with NO organizational or communication skills at all would take a job as a foreman. Or be given one, really... he came off as a skeezy used car salesman... and we trusted him about as much as we'd trust one of them, too!

2 major communication issues in as many days... a WEEK after we wanted him off the job for myriad issues. I'm seriously losing my mind. - Twitter, Wed Jul 06 19:05:09 UTC 2011

I'm about 1 dropped contractor drama away from a straight jacket & padded room. White is NOT my color, either - Twitter, Wed Jul 06 20:03:12 UTC 2011

Man, there is a war brewing. Over our KITCHEN. Hoping things don't get TOO ugly.- Twitter, Wed Jul 06 21:50:23 UTC 2011

The drywallers were finally supposed to put in the walls and ceiling on July 7th... and then we failed our insulation inspection.

They finally started on July 7th.

"WE HAVE WALLS AGAIN!! The dry wallers just finished hanging the sheetrock. SO excited to not see "down to the studs" in there. after a few weeks of that." - Facebook, July 8, 2011

"WOOOO!!!! If everyone keeps their shit on schedule, we have a new kitchen floor on Thursday, the walls painted and the ceiling textured on Friday, I tile this weekend AND THEN WE HAVE THE BASE OF A KITCHEN!!!! It'll just be appliances and a really ghetto sink until Porter makes the cabinets, BUT STILL!!" - Facebook, July 12, 2011

In case you're keeping track, July 12 is 22 days after they were supposed to start their "10 day project".

Picking up our paint and tile for the kitchen that day was probably the only thing that kept me happy enough to not throttle someone. It finally felt like we were getting somewhere!

WOO! Our kitchen walls should be painted, ceiling finished by Friday night! I'll tile this weekend, then we'll have a skeleton kitchen back!- Twitter, Tue Jul 12 19:37:59 UTC 2011

July 16th was the day that the kitchen finally got painted... and it looked great! With the ceiling and walls finished, all we needed to do was tile the floor and have another inspection so that the outlets and lights could go in.... then we'd finally have a room with appliances in it, for the first time in over a month. Unlike the rest of the kitchen redo, that part went off without a hitch.

Words cannot properly express just how thrilled we were to be finished with that foreman. I was certain that I was going to be getting myself deported over the escalating nonsense.

On July 16th, I tiled the kitchen floor all by myself... that was a first for me! We had picked out some gorgeous textured vinyl tiles. I'd never seen vinyl tiles that legitimately looked nice, but these sure did - almost like real stone.
The colors in it looked great against a slice of our walnut tree, and I couldn't wait to see the finished product!

July 20th - a full month after the contractor work began in our kitchen - we finally had lights and working electrical outlets in there. We were ecstatic!

We have no counters or cabinets, but my kitchen now has electricity!!
Embarrassed that the first meal I'm cooking in it is a frozen pizza :/ -
Twitter, Wed Jul 20 22:56:06 UTC 2011

The next day, we had more foreman drama to deal with. For some completely unknown reason, the kitchen foreman had told his plumber that he would be handling our bathroom remodel. I think my Facebook status expressed my feelings on that perfectly:

"SO fucking sick of dealing with the guy in charge of our kitchen remodel. They're DONE, aside from electrical inspection. Right? So now his plumber thinks they're handling our BATHROOM for some reason, and I'm supposed to screw around with calling HIM up? NO! Fucking call him yourself, YOU are the broken communication, and have been SINCE THE BEGINNING!!!" - Facebook,   July 21, 2011

The very final bit of foreman drama came over a week later, and it was over the window inspection. We had no idea that we even needed the windows inspected... and he gave us two hours notice about it. Awesome - I immediately had to rearrange my plans for the day as a result. That was the day I was actually supposed to go get our deck permit, and I had to put it off another day, as a result.

That 3 hour window for inspection? Just ended. No inspector yet. AWESOME. Guess I'm not applying for my deck permit today after all :/ - Twitter, Thu Jul 28 18:04:40 UTC 2011

Sigh. At least we were done with him... and more or less done with the kitchen for the next few months.

The next few months were spent working on pretty much everything BUT the kitchen. We bought some portable shelving units to hold groceries and disposable plates/cutlery/cups, and. I was finally able to cook!

My makeshift counter space started as a 6' long, fold out banquet table, eventually replacing it with a rolling kitchen cart with additional "counter" available as a flip-up leaf. After months of living without a kitchen, that felt downright luxurious!

With a moderately functional kitchen, it became sort of easy to procrastinate on the cabinet building. Having a basement that was completely crammed with random crap - both from when we moved in, and from post-tornado storage needs - didn't help the situation. That's where he'd be building the cabinetry, after all.

While picking away at organizing the basement, we started to discuss options for the kitchen back splash. We figured that we should probably get that figured out before building the cabinets, just in case we needed to make a slight adjustment on the space between the uppers and lowers as a result of backsplash design.

We'd watched enough DIY tv to know that we didn't really want a glass tile back splash, fearing that the current trendiness of it would render it completely dated in a few years. The problem was... what then? Pretty much everything available was either ugly, inappropriate for our overall kitchen design, or exorbitantly priced.

So... we discussed the idea of tiling pi into the back splash. We could use 2" squares of glass tile, and the uniqueness of the design would probably allieviate the issue if it becoming dated.

We would need a ton of individual tiles - we had room for about 160 digits of pi, with columns 10 tiles high - 1600 tiles is a LOT to mess around with. We'll do pretty much anything it takes to see a fun idea through to fruition though, so we ordered samples of 2" glass tiles. Like many of our weird ideas, it went from possibility to decision in NO time.

Hrm... I think that the pi tile backsplash is going to happen. When we eventually sell this house, we are going to need to find NERD buyers! - Facebook, January 8, 2012

To make sure that we were being thorough in our research and exploring all options, we took a field trip to a local tile shop, and immediately fell in love with a green colored granite tile. This ended up being a bit of a complication - for budget reasons, we had decided to go with laminate counters. We'd be having a fair amount of counter space, so anything else would be totally cost prohibitive. Problem: A granite backsplash would look pretty ridiculous with a laminate counter.

I later learned that Porter had ulterior motives in setting up this field trip. Budget aside, he was against the idea of laminate, figuring that we'd regret and eventually want to replace it. He was sure that if I could see good quality granite tiles in person - especially done up as a counter top - that I'd like them and want to go that route instead of laminate.

He was right.

My problem with the idea of tiles was that the only tiled counter I'd ever seen was the horrible one that came with the house. It was made with those 4" square bathroom tiles, with a fairly thick grout line in between the tiles. I hated it, and that's what I had in mind when he mentioned tiles.

At the tile showroom though, I saw that tiles of 12" squares of granite actually looked really good, and I was sold. We took some samples home to run the numbers and sleep on it.

The math actually put the granite tile counter top and back splash as being right in line with what we'd budgeted for glass tile back splash and laminate counter tops, so we figured out our material needs and placed the order the next day.

Hubby is calculating the sum of the 1st 161 digits of pi, so we can place our tile order. Holy crap, we're going to do this! - Twitter, January 10, 2012

Now that we had a kitchen project that we were super excited about, we were inspired to push through with the cabinet building. Beyond that, we decided to aim for having it all done in time to host a Pi Day party - an annual event for us - even though we'd previously assumed that we'd have to forgo it for that year. We figured that having that goal date in mind would be a great excuse to get it DONE - "Eyes on the prize" and all. So, he took a week off work to get a big chunk of work done.

On January 14th, Porter pulled out the cabinet making books for one last go through before starting construction. We were SO excited for him to start building the next day. It would be an interesting set of circumstances to deal with - his first time building cabinetry, him having an exhausted and frustrated wife nagging him to get it done, AND only having a workspace of 8' x 12'. The sheets of plywood he was handling were 4' x 8', for reference!

90

Starting out on January 15th, we had an ambitious time line: The very first day of construction, he made the base cabinet for the sink area, as well as the single cupboard to go above it. It was amazing to have that first glimpse of our new built- in cabinetry, even if it was basically just the skeleton of the final product. We placed some tiles on the counter top and set the sink where it was supposed to be, just so we could admire our preview of what was to come. Damn, we really chose wisely in going with the granite tiles, this was going to be gorgeous.

The next day he built the counter top base - Wood, mortar, cement board, screwed all of that down into place - and we got to tiling the counter. I measured and marked all of the tiles to be cut, he cut them and buttered on the mortar, and I set the tiles - that part actually went pretty quickly. With that counter set, he went on to build 3 of the upper cabinets for our long bank of cupboards.

By the end of the day on January 18th, he had the entire long bank of cabinetry built - both uppers and base. We set the tiles for that counter top that night, and it looked amazing. It's one thing to see a box of tiles, but it really is something else to see them set into a long counter - especially when you've been without a functional counter for so long!

Our main bank of cabinets, before the counter tiles were set.

With the two straightforward cabinet areas built, it was time to turn our attention to the third - and most complicated - section. This was a weird area of the kitchen - the oven would be set into the corner, with moderate sized counter top angling out from one side of it, and a small triangle counter top on the other side. Above all of this was more upper cabinetry, including a big microwave suspended over the stove top.

With the upper cabinetry in place - and the microwave set in - we had achieved a huge step forward. We'd been using a small, beat up microwave since the tornado. The turntable in it didn't work, and it would burn everything. Finally getting to use our shiny new microwave felt almost... luxurious. I can't pinpoint exactly where we started to emerge from our borderline feral state, but I would say that the new microwave was part of it.

As he continued to build the cabinetry, I concerned myself with preparing the tiles to set the back splash.

The tiles came pre set onto mesh, in grids of 6 tiles x 6 tiles - and I needed them separated in order to build the digit columns. I separated them first into strips of six, and then cut them down from there.

I had taken a strip of tiles and used it to mark off the entire length - all 3 - of where the back splash would be, making small marks where each grout line would be. The spaces between the marks indicated a tile, and I numbered them in order, from where the design would start, all the way around to the end. Including the initial "3", we would be laying 159 digits of pi.

I divided the work surfaces into sections, and made a chart of which digits were going where - For instance, the wall to the left of our stove would be 1-27 digits of pi, the center back wall would be digits 28-47, and so on. I transferred the digit positions – as well as the actual digits that would be represented as columns – into a table, along with any notes I felt I needed about the locations. ("The end digit of this wall may need to be trimmed", etc)

I created another document where I not only listed the digits that would be on each wall, in order – I counted the number of times each digit showed up in that wall area, and created a chart.

For our purposes, our main design was 9 blocks tall. 1 green tile = "1?, two tiles = "2?, and so on. No greens = "0?. Once I inputted the needs for green tiles, I figured out how many beige tiles I would need to complement. If I had five "Ones" in green, I would need five "Eights" in beige, etc.

Using the charts, I cut and prepared strips of tiles, trimming the extra mesh from either side of the them. This would prevent mesh overhang from forcing the grout lines to be thicker than we wanted.

Once the final counter was placed, we started setting the back splash. We started at the sink - the first area built, but the second of three large sections of pi - I was so excited. I'm sure that I drove my twitter followers completely batty with the constant tweeting about the pi back splash, and the many progress photos that I was posting. This was going to be the coolest, nerdiest kitchen EVER, and I just couldn't contain my excitement.

It was also the first time that I had a kitchen that was all my own - my whole life, I've lived in places where the kitchen wasn't mine (growing up), or was a rental apartment, or even just the home that my husband owned, that I moved in to. Not once were any custom built and designed to be *mine*. This felt so incredibly special to me, and I found it even more amazing that my husband was building it for me.

You know, when you tile pi into our kitchen, it really does function as a springboard for all KINDS of puns and jokes. Who knew that a back splash could be an endless source of entertainment? For my part, we weren't even finished setting the back splash when I snarked that our kitchen would be "City of Minneapolis" themed - when we were in there, we would be "surrounded by irrationality"! Not a comment on the residents of Minneapolis, just the monumental heap of bullshit we had to deal with from the City of Minneapolis - the municipal entity.

We made sure to take frequent professional photos as were setting the back splash, figuring that I would get a pretty cool blog entry out of this. Sure, my blog may be more of a food blog... but this was kitchen related. Also, a tutorial is essentially a recipe, right? Good enough. I needed to share this with the world... even if it could end up being the most useless tutorial ever. I wasn't sure if it would ever be viewed by someone that would want to do a similar thing - we tend to lack the filter that most people do!

On January 27th, we officially had a fully functional sink area AND our dishwasher installed for the first time since the tornado. One step closer to the end of plastic cutlery & paper plates!

February 1st was the day that the final section of back splash (well, the first one in terms of design sequence!) was grouted - the area surrounding what would eventually be the stove. I was SO completely out of my mind with excitement, that Porter actually banished me from my own kitchen. As soon as the back splash was grouted, my stove would be going in - FINALLY! Beyond that, this was the finishing-up of the very start of the sequence - it was very cool to see that 31415 emerge as a finished product!

The stove went in, and we celebrated. I could COOK again, and would never again need to see the weird, unprotected sides of what was supposed to be a set-in stove. It had just looked so weird and wrong sitting out there in the middle of the kitchen - now it looked elegant and proper!

New cabinetry, and the first hundred or so digits of pi!

I posted a tutorial "How to Custom Design and Install a Nerdy Granite Tile Backsplash" to my blog on February 3rd... and the geek world went nuts over it.

Think Geek - or, as I like to think of them: "The Bastion of Awesome" - retweeted the link to my blog, posted it on their Facebook page, and linked to it from their own blog. From their post, Make Magazine blogged about it... and then PC World magazine... then a bunch of bloggers and Pinterest users.. Before we knew it, ten thousand people had visited that blog entry in the first month! We were completely flabbergasted by the response.

On ThinkGeek's Facebook page, the positive comments were piling up - along with hundreds of "likes" and "shares". People were sharing it to their own walls, declaring desire to do their own kitchen the same way, or just expressing admiration for ours. It was so amazing to see that we were NOT alone in finding our kitchen idea to be completely awesome. We'd been prepared for virtual eye rolls, not for our kitchen tutorial to go viral!

Our back splash managed to get so famous in the geek community, that one friend told us that she was finding it weird to see her family members - that we'd never met, heard of, or had any contact with - posting photos of our kitchen!

We had been completely happy with our tiling job and the design, ourselves... we're both very much the type to engage in what we're interested in. If someone doesn't like it, too bad. In the case of the back splash, same thing... but it really did feel awesome to have that kind of reaction, anyway!

Over the following weeks, Porter continued to work on kitchen construction. Now that the big, impressive work was done, he had to build shelves - something that is apparently far more involved and nit-picky than I would have imagined. He did a gorgeous job on them, taking the time to apply a nicely finished front edge panel to each, apply 3 coats of stain to all of the shelves and interiors - it was long, drawn out, and fussy work.

By the time Pi Day rolled around, our kitchen was pretty much functional - all of the shelves were in, all of the appliances installed and working, etc. The lower cabinets were yet to get the drawers, and obviously the exterior walnut facings and doors were missing. We finally had shelves, though! Being able to move all of the groceries in from the living room and have a functional kitchen was amazing.

I cooked up a huge, diverse menu for our "St Pi-trick's Day" party - everything was either round or spherical and at least vaguely Irish themed. It felt great to be able to go all out for the occasion, when we'd thought - just a few short months before - that the party would have to be cancelled. Not only was the menu better than previous years, but the back splash acted as a stunning accessory to the event!

Porter picked away at building the drawers throughout April. As this book goes to print, we are still missing the pull-out drawers in 4 lower cabinets, 2 toe-kick drawers, and all of the walnut work. Eventually we will get our walnut lumber back from the mill, and the long, fussy process of finishing the kitchen will begin.

Bathroom

While it sucked to find out that the bathroom was also damaged in the tornado - when we hadn't realized that up front - it all turned out well. For the most part, the items of our house that had been damaged in the tornado were all stuff that we either disliked but had no budget to do anything about (deck and porch), or the only two rooms that we hadn't gotten around to redoing before we moved in. The kitchen and bathroom already needed to be redone, we already knew we'd have to, so ... not as big a deal. The scope had increased on the kitchen, and the projects suddenly became urgent - rather than "some day" - but that's about it.

About a month after the tornado, we were finally able to focus some attention on the decisions that needed to be made in the bathroom, in preparation for actually doing the work. In an effort to be as cost-conscious as possible, we decided that we would be doing all of the labor on the bathroom remodel by ourselves.

What we were starting out with was so old and dilapidated, we pretty much had to gut the place. The shower was ok - shiny 4" pale blue tiles - but was trimmed with weird retro styled small rectangular tiles in a darker blue.. The shower had a fairly low ceiling, as overhead cabinetry had been built in, above. A useless decorative header connected the cabinetry to the ugly rusted brass colored mirror shower door below. Getting in to the shower was annoying, as the door would only open from one side - which meant having to wedge between the vanity and the edge of the door.

I hated that thing,

The walls we covered with a weird textured wall paper that was peeling off at the seams. The floor was covered in tiny 1" hexagonal tiles, and all of the fixtures were very old and brass colored. The vanity was old styled and in rough shape, and didn't match the built in medicine cabinet or a secondary medicine cabinet... which didn't match each other, either.

Yep, it needed some help.

I'm surprised that things didn't end up coming to blows over the major design decisions - specifically, the tiles. We had very different ideas of what we should go with for the overall feel of the bathroom, and the tiles were the most logical first decision. I wanted fairly neutral and elegant, my husband wanted blue.

To me, the original bathroom had a fair amount of blue in it, and I really hated that bathroom. I wanted it to be completely different. Porter was very "anti-earthtones", and a bit pissy about the fact that we'd gone with rich neutrals in the bedroom. He'd be perfectly happy if every room in our house was blue, with all blue accenting and everything.

Beyond color, there were the issues of texture, accenting, shape, size, tile material... Wow. So many options to choose from, it was insane. Beyond the tiles colors, there were other considerations to decide on: Did we want to mix and match, or have the tiles all one style? If all one style, we'd need to find a style that came in multiple sizes, rather than only in 4". Did we want trim?

Eventually, we settled on stone-textured "coliseum" style tiles, in a medium olive green color. The walls would be a paler tint of the same color. Further, the cabinetry would be a darker wood, and all of the fixtures would be oil rubbed bronze.

It's amazing how easy that all sounds on paper, this long after the fact. At the time, it was a whole bunch of nit-picky small decisions, on top of all of the other decisions we had to make about every other aspect of the house. Honestly, it's kind of hard to focus on whether or not the trim on the cabinetry set is something that we'll be able to find matching/complimentary baseboard trim for, when there's still a tree sticking out of your bedroom wall.

We knew that the bathtub would need to be resurfaced, and the toilet replaced. This is a very old house - built in 1928 - and the sink, toilet, and tub didn't look much younger. All were in very scary shape. We decided that the new toilet and sink should be in a cream or bone color, to compliment the tiles well - white would look weird.. As the tub resurfacing company offered that color choice, we were all set to go.

Because our bathroom is old and tiny, we were very limited in our choice of toilets to begin - we needed one that was very short from front to back. Additionally, my husband wanted an elongated bowl, and I wanted a taller pedestal. 4 requirements. That's it... you wouldn't think it would be difficult to find something to fit four very basic requirements!

Well, we could find toilets that fit three of the four, at best... but the "perfect" one eluded us. Seriously, I'd never even known there were so many options to consider with toilets. Visits to several different home renovation stores were absolutely fruitless. Seriously, it's cheaper and easier to buy a WEDDING GOWN, than a shorter-length toilet. Less variables, too!

Finally, a sales rep at Home Depot let us know that they had a catalog of special order toilets, and that it was very likely that we'd find what we needed there. Well, that was ... interesting. I don't know if it's common knowledge or not, but did you know that some toilets go for $4000+? A bowl on a pedestal, for you to shit in. FOUR THOUSAND DOLLARS. I can't even imagine.

We got off easier than that, but still paid far more than I ever expected to for a *toilet* - $400. It was the absolute cheapest option that met all four of our entirely reasonable requirements, and would have been a LOT cheaper, if we could have gone for white. I really think that Home Depot needs to change the color options sign from "Additional charges may apply" to "YOU GOT A PURTY MOUTH!"

Luckily, our tiles were on clearance, so we managed to save a ton of money there. It all evened out in the end, but... still!

After replacing the insulation and cement board walls in the shower, we got to tiling. Porter would "butter" the wall with adhesive and cut the tiles that needed it, and I placed the tiles. It went a lot more quickly than I expected, and looked amazing!

Once the shower was tiled, we may have gotten slightly off track in terms of our design... but it resulted in a bathroom far more awesome than we'd originally planned!

As we prepared to start tiling the non-shower bathroom walls, I joked that we should tile Fibonacci sequence into the wall. No sooner had the words left my lips, than I decided it wasn't a joke, it was a NEED. An urgent, desperate, must-do need.

You see, I was a huge fan of nerdy PBS children's programming when I was a kid. Owl TV, 3-2-1 Contact, Newton's Apple, Reading Rainbow... I couldn't get enough. Square One TV was my favorite... and anyone who was also a fan knows EXACTLY where I'm going with this.

Square One was a math-themed variety show for kids... and it was great! Bastardized music videos for popular songs, re-worked to sing about different mathematical concepts (Think The Beach Boys's "Good Vibrations", reworked as "Tessellations"!), skits, etc. One regular segment was "Mathnet" - a spoof of Dragnet. Detectives Monday and Frankly would use math to solve mysteries... I loved it.

In one of the more memorable episodes, "The Case of the Willing Parrot", the protagonists notice Fibonacci sequence represented by different colored bricks in a wall, leading to the solution of that week's mystery. I'll admit it - I may have been only 9 when it came out, but I'm STILL game to drop a well placed "1, 1, 2, 3, 5... eureka!" when the situation calls for it! When setting up to tile our bathroom wall... well, the situation called for it.

Porter just gave me a weird look, and I was horrified to learn that he not only had no idea what I was talking about, but had never actually seen the show! We dropped everything to see if youtube happened to have that episode.

After watching, he still wasn't convinced that we had - HAD! - to do this, so I decided to leverage some peer pressure. I know our friends, I know my Twitter followers - I couldn't see ANYONE suggesting that this was anything short of a brilliant idea. I was right, of course - everyone was all over the idea! Some of the comments:

Chris B: <-- loves him some Fibonacci sequence and some phi.

Candi L: No one likes a boring bathroom with no math in it.

Karen C: Well.. that's a better plan than trying to tile it in the Golden Ratio pattern. Less cutting.

Kimberly K: I have trouble believing Porter was NOT on board with this idea from the start.

I could see that the idea was beginning to look attractive to him, when he mentioned liking the idea of tiling the golden ratio into the floor. I'll admit, I got a little manipulative at that point - I told him that if we could tile Fibonacci into the main wall, I'd be up for tiling pi across the two walls behind and beside the toilet.

Sold! I knew that my husband - who is obsessed with pi, celebrating pi day every year - would not be able to resist the offer.

The idea immediately went from "if" to "how". We would need a second color of tiles to create the pattern, and would also need to employ the same remaindering technique as used in the Mathnet episode. Unfortunately, my idea of building a secret compartment behing an out-of-sequence tile was shot down :(

Sometimes I feel guilty knowing that some people follow for food/wedding/cake, & get a bunch of tweets about stuff like #FibonacciBathroom - Twitter, Sun Jul 10 17:36:51 UTC 2011

So we headed back to Menards and picked up more of the same style of tiles, only in a rich ivory color... and the Fibonacci bathroom wall came into existence.

From there, we tiled pi into the other two walls, as agreed upon. We had no sink, and the bathroom was still the size of a closet... but all of a sudden it was the absolute coolest bathroom I've ever seen. I love being married to a nerdy enabler!

Our friend Holly had a fun comment: "Your house is gonna get beat up by the other houses for being such a nerd!"

Fibonacci Bathroom Wall. 1,1,2,3,5... Eureka!

Our friend Peter came over to level our yard, took one look at our Fibonacci sequence wall, and declared "You should have tiled e into your shower ceiling!". Damn. Our only regret about the whole thing is that the nerd walls were such a last minute idea - we COULD have done that on top of the Fibonacci and Pi walls... and a golden ratio spiral floor!

From there, the bathroom renovations were pretty straightforward. We hired Dakota Painting and Drywall to refinish the ceiling, exchanging the glittery popcorn finish, for flat white "knockdown" texture.

The bathtub looked amazing after being refinished, even if we probably killed a few billion brain cells from the fumes involved.

The tiles were grouted, caulking applied where needed. The toilet, vanity, and sink went in without a hitch. Towel racks were installed, along with a glass shelf in the shower.

101

Finding a shower curtain that went well with everything was a bit of a challenge, but we finally found something suitable in the 5th store we looked in - Ivory, with an antique gold colored embroidered leaf trim.

On August 8th - about two and a half months after the tornado - we were finally able to use the shower again!

The only thing that presented a challenge was the built in medicine cabinet behind the sink. The inset cabinet itself went smoothly, but we ran into a problem with the door. The framed mirror to match the vanity and second medicine cabinet was far too big - there was no way that it would work as a door. Even the idea of removing the mirror, using the frame on the wall around the cabinet, and just having the mirror as the door was not going to work - STILL too big.

So, we had to buy a smaller mirror, completely dismantle the frame, trim all the sides down to appropriate lengths, and reassemble it. The frame would be fixed to the cabinet box, and the door would need to be custom made - Trim the mirror, affix it to a thin sheet of maple wood, trim with piece of rounded wood trim, and stain it all to match the wood used throughout the rest of the set. Easy, right?

Well, it was fussy work to do a bit at a time, but turned out beautifully. On September 11, we finally had a fully functional, gorgeous new bathroom!

Brushing my teeth in the washroom for the first time since the tornado was a great experience. SO much better than leaning over the Jacuzzi in the bedroom!

From my husband's point of view, he was thrilled to have the mirror back, having been forced to shave "blind" in the shower for months on end. Using a mirror felt like such a luxury to him, having taken something as basic as a mirror for granted prior to the tornado.

Backyard

Unlike the fairly basic decisions that need to be made with the roof (Pick the shingle color) and the upstairs (Just make it look like it did before), the back yard involved a lot of planning... and it was all up to us.

The previous deck had taken up most of the back yard, but didn't actually have a lot of useable space. Because of the porch and the "horse barn" enclosure over the stairway, we'd have to wedge between the two to get to either side of the deck - both of which were long and skinny. Neither one really fit even an oblong table and chairs set, and it was all very awkward.

I didn't love the "horse barn", thinking that it was just begging for someone to get down in there and try to break in - completely hidden from any possible witnesses. Also, it was ugly and made the back yard feel even smaller than it actually is.

After much negotiation, we decided not to rebuild the porch, in favor of more outdoor space. We would have a fairly narrow cedar deck built along the whole length of the back of our house, using the same spindles we had chosen for the upstairs mini deck. We would build patio on both sides of the stairway, and the deck would have two small staircases, one for each patio.

It was a bit of an argument to get to that decision. I hated the hugeness of the old deck, and how tiny it made the backyard feel. I was in favor of more patio space than deck, as the lower surface would make the backyard feel much bigger. Porter, however, was in favor of as much deck as we could possibly build in there. He liked that deck railing felt enclosed, like a bit of a barrier to the rest of the world.

After pouring over patio displays, we finally decided on a compromise - we would build a bit of a smaller deck, in favor of a lot of patio... but we would build a decorative wall around both sections of patio. We both loved this idea - it suited both of our needs, plus it looked a bit "Stonehenge", which was pretty awesome.

Together with Peter, we plotted it all out in the yard and figured out our needs for patio pavers and the large bricks.

Then we spent a fortune.

Just dropped $5k at Menards. $2.5k at Lowes yesterday. The costs of even DIY tornado repair are BREATHTAKING. #NoMi #ThankFSMForInsurance - Twitter, Sun Jun 26 23:10:20 UTC 2011

To be fair, that covered pretty much everything for our bathroom, the materials to build the patio and deck, replacement patio furniture, AND the bulk of the lumber to rebuild the kitchen cabinetry. (Our walnut would be used for the faces and doors, but the interiors would be maple). Tons of stuff to buy... and these purchases didn't even represent the bulk of what we had to buy from Menards post-tornado!

On July 16th Peter brought a dump truck and a loader and set about taking the piles of dirt and clay out, filling in the hole left by the downed walnut tree, and leveling the yard, to prepare for us to lay the patio.

As he started to haul out the clay that had been piled up under the old deck, it was apparent that the previous owner had used it as an opportunity to bury random junk, as well. In one particularly stressful instance, he pulled out a rolled up rug. Given all of the stories we'd heard about the previous owner - combined with the neighborhood - we were honestly expecting to find a body in there. Lucky for us, there were no remains in any of the crap unearthed that day!

Over the course of the next week, Peter and Porter worked together in sweltering heat to get the yard ready to lay the patio, spreading out layers of gravel and sand, meticulously going over everything with a giant level.

By the following Saturday, the yard was cleared, leveled, and ready to go. Good thing, as we were expecting a HUGE delivery from Menards that morning - including the 11 pallets of bricks that we'd need for our new patio!

Together with some friends, we laid the bulk of the patio surface that day, including the base of what would become our "Stonehenge" border. I had no idea that laying a patio was so much work - I was honestly sort of considering it to be "grown up Legos" going into it. I'm pretty sure that we all ended up beat up, sunburnt, and dehydrated. Those of us who were wearing work gloves wore the fingertips out of them - I went through 3 pairs, personally!

Just tripped backwards over a tallish stack of bricks, scraped up elbows and backs of legs, hurt hip in the process. Add that to sunburn, heatsickness (literally!), dehydration, pulled muscles, and wearing my fingertips raw... yeah, I'm sick of doing brick work. I'm so tired. :(- Facebook, July 24, 2011 at 4:15pm

As beat up as we were after that, we were so happy to see the progress being made - it looked nothing like when we bought the house. Every bit of progress got us one step further away from the "Haiti" look! We looked forward to a future of being able to hang out back there, rather than labor for long hours on it.

By the end of the weekend, we had laid not only the patio surface itself, but several of the corner towers, and two of the "Stonehenge" walls. It looked great!

The brick work was put on hold for a week, while I dealt with the deck design and permit.

I thought it would basically be me saying "we're making this deck, it'll be cedar, and here are the measurements", but it ended up so much more detailed than that. First we got a printout of the design from Menards, then I had to figure out the dimensions of our yard, where everything was, relative to each other and the house, and draw out detailed diagrams of everything.

The city REALLY doesn't make it easy to get a permit to build a deck. It's like only engineers/people who can afford engineers can have one!- Twitter, Wed Jul 27 22:42:48 UTC 2011

On the morning of July 29th I finished up with tiling the bathroom, then headed out to apply for the permit. Ah, the glamorous post-tornado life.

The plans made it through zoning review, but needed a little bit of adjusting when it came to have it reviewed by the building section. Because of the staircase to the basement, we had to move one post over, creating a longer span of beam between two of the posts. It was because the requirements for how deep a post footing needed to be also applied horizontally out from the retaining wall as well. Ah well, it got approved with the modifications they added for us on the spot.

$323 for papers that say we're allowed to build our dinky little deck and replace a toilet and sink. What a racket. #AtLeastWeGotApproved - Twitter, Fri Jul 29 18:31:12 UTC 2011

With the base of the patio and the deck permit taken care of, I decided to building the last tower and rest of the border by myself. While Porter was at work, and during a heat wave... because I'm just stupid like that sometimes.

"Dear Mother Nature: WHO IS THE BADASS NOW?!!?!

Holy shit, those bricks are HEAVY! I'm gonna have nasty roid-ed out looking traps muscles when this is all finished :(Would be nice if the new muscles came in somewhere useful / nice, like biceps, triceps, or delts.

FWIW, I had to move 5835 lbs (I did the math!) of 40 and 55 lb patio bricks to build a bunch of patio wall today, as part of our massive 2+-months-now tornado repairs. By hand. By myself. I can barely move. If my arms would fall off, like they feel like they're going to, I'd welcome it. I hurt all over, and painkillers aren't working on me.. Damn it, Jim - I'm a chef/author, not a handyman." - Facebook, August 4, 2011

By the end of the day, all of the tower and wall building was done, and I was very proud of myself. Dehydrated and sore, but proud! Almost all of the patio building was done at this point - just needed to cut some small bricks to fill in gaps around the edges of the patio surface.

We planned a "Backyard Blitz" for the weekend to get a bunch of work done - the remaining chunk of deck removed, and start building the deck. I was actually hoping that we'd be able to finish the bulk of deck building, but knew it was only the slightest of possibilities. I set up a Facebook invite, our friend Todd bastardized the lyrics to "Ballroom Blitz" on our behalf, and things were a go - the weekend would see the start of the deck building!

The next step was to get the footings dug for the deck. Before anything could be built, the inspector would need to approve the depth and diameter of the footing holes. We hired someone to dig them to the specifications on the permit, and they finished up right before the inspector arrived.

The inspector arrived, and all of our plans for the weekend seemed to be shot to hell in just an instant.

106

The inspector wanted the footings to be MUCH wider than specified on the plans... and wouldn't be able to come back before the weekend to approve the holes after being widened. I was so upset. The weather was supposed to be perfect for the weekend, and we had all of our help lined up - the idea that we'd have to postpone it was heartbreaking. I was so sick of carefully jumping off the exposed beam from our old deck - it was dangerous, and I was sick of destruction. The idea that it would be postponed because we did exactly what the permits office told us to? Ridiculous.

Fighting back tears, I explained the situation and asked if there was any way that we could dig the holes and email a photo in for approval. I explained that my husband is a photographer, and that we could definitely get a clear photo of a measuring tape across the bottom of the footing holes.

He agreed!

The guy we'd hired hauled ass to dig the holes wider, my husband came home from work early to photograph them, and they both go to work on mixing and pouring the concrete into them. It ended up taking exponentially more concrete than we'd planned for, so a couple of trips were made to the hardware store.

"The footings are done! WOOOO!!! We're getting our deck replaced this weekend! The last obstacle is gone! I cannot WAIT to not have to be helped down off the rotten beam sticking out of what remains of our dangerous smashed up deck!" - Facebook, August 11 2011

August 13th, the "blitz" began. Friends that we hadn't seen in FAR too long showed up, introductions were made, and a LONG day began. It ended up taking most of the day to just prepare the area for building the deck... including the removal of the last bit of old deck.

Peter brought his "MultiTrac" machinery, which we had dubbed "The Grabboid". He drove it right down the stairs, grabbed the deck, and -with help from a few of our friends - ripped it off and hauled it our of our yard for disposal.

In taking out that last bit of deck, we finally got a clear idea of just how structurally unsound it was - it was basically being held together by carpet. You know, because this section just balancing across an 10' drop by resting a couple beams across retaining wall bricks wasn't scary enough! It's a wonder no one seriously hurt themselves on that!

The bulk of the deck was built over the next week, with the railings being built by Steve and Jeff from Iron River. They'd done such a great job on the upper deck, and it was super fussy work - it just made more sense for them to do it.

When all was said and done, we had a gorgeous and incredibly functional back yard.

After the new roof and deck removal, before yard leveling

After yard was cleared and leveled

Beginning of the patio

Start of the walls and towers

Remains of the former deck, as we'd been walking on since the tornado

Before

After

111

Exterior

With all of the time and attention that the major repairs were taking, the exterior cosmetics were pretty much back-burnered until late summer.

When "Prior Fat Girl" Jen tweeted about getting new windows on August 30th, I kind of freaked out. It was such an innocuous tweet, just a happy update on her own progress - Not only did we not have any contractors scheduled to work on ANYTHING that day, I didn't even know when our windows would be going in!

Jen explained that her fiance had a huge network of construction companies that he worked with, so they were able to speed up the process. Then she unknowingly twisted the knife a little, mentioning that they were still a "couple" weeks away from being done with their repairs.

Oh, I was upset. I couldn't believe that some people could be finishing up, when we were many months - probably a year, realistically - from finishing, ourselves. Rather than mope about it, I decided to take it as her lighting a fire under my ass, and I got to work on getting the ball rolling on our exterior work.

It took two weeks of researching the options and getting a couple of quotes, but I finally settled on a company that seemed to have a good grasp on what needed to be done, and didn't sound like they were going to fleece us. Though we were planning to get the windows replaced first, we decided that it would be a smarter idea to just get the stucco repairs made. It'd be cheaper, anyway - they didn't have to put a bunch of labor into blocking the windows, as they'd be replaced anyway. Additionally, the fact that we were planning to paint the stucco meant that they didn't need to tint their material - again, cutting down on the labor. They were really great about talking us through reasonable ways to cut back on expense, and the areas that we could handle by ourselves (caulking really thin cracks ourselves, etc).

On September 13 - 115 days after the tornado - the holes where the trees shot through the wall were finally repaired, along with some other miscellaneous stucco damage from the tornado.

In addition to the big tree holes, there were fairly large sections of bare wall, where the little beams that supported our former roof were pulled out. The new style of roof did not require them, so they were left bare, ready to be covered over. The debris had left some damage in other areas, and something had shot through the back wall of our garage - a fact that we were not aware of, until the estimate. Yay for finding more damage!

I had NO idea that fixing stucco was such a noisy job! I was going insane inside, trying to work - it sounded like the house was going to fall down around me. Just awful. In the end, though... they did a great job, at a great price. No more holes in our walls! Woo!

From there, Porter repaired the remaining small damage, then used an industrial airbrush to apply exterior primer to the areas that needed - including the brickwork around the base of the house. If we were going to go to all of this effort to repair and replace, we were going to take the opportunity to correct some ... interesting... design decisions that the previous owner had made.

Well, that and we wanted to cover up the skid marks that the tornado had left across one side of our house. Skid marks. Seriously.

So, bit by bit, we painted the house.

The day that we picked out our shingle color, we'd decided that we should do the whole house blue. The old white stucco would be repainted a pale grey-blue, The windows would be trimmed with a medium-dark grey-blue, and the bricks would be painted with a medium blue, then sponged over with a dark grey. Yep, we were feeling ambitious.

Once the stucco was painted, we did the bricks - bit by bit, as it took FOREVER to get even coverage, over all of that texture. Towards the end, when it started to look like we'd run out of time, Tara helped out with airbrushing the brickwork. For my part, I sponged the dark grey paint over the bricks, leaving the mortar lines untouched. This gave a lot more depth to the paint job, looking so much better than just having it all as one solid blue. I only got as far as completing the front of the house, deciding to paint the other three walls in the coming spring.

Beyond the painting, we had decided to keep a blue color scheme throughout the gardening, also. The two flower beds against the front of our house used to be edged with chunks of flat stone, maybe it was some sort of slate... but that had all gotten destroyed when the arborvitae trees up front were knocked over. We decided to rebuild the beds with grey retaining wall blocks, then plant some blue junipers in there. We also decided to create to long flower beds to flank the front sidewalk and meet up with the juniper beds, which would contain all sorts of blue flowers.

We also decided to get an mp3-tone doorbell, and set it to play Eiffel 65's "Blue" whenever someone rings the bell. Awesome!

I mentioned that blue is Porter's favorite color, right? We tend to get a bit crazy about things around here... :)

The windows... were a bit of drama.

We'd intended to replace the windows before we moved in, and bought the bulk of them. Times got away from us in the course of the initial fix up, though, and the windows were banished to the basement until we found some time to deal with them. We thought we had bought them all except 3 big ones, but found out that we were missing two others upon counting and recounting. Then came the task of figuring out which were missing - the windows were odd sizes, and a few of the sizes were pretty close to each other.

Then it turned out that we were missing four more, and that those sizes needed to be special ordered with the big picture windows. To this day, I have no idea how we managed to keep miscounting the windows!

September 16 was when the window replacement started - what a difference it made! Not only were windows busted up by the tornado, they were in rough shape before it hit - very old windows, probably original to the house. One had a vine growing in through it, between the two panes... not sure how that happened. The new windows looked great, and really ended up making the house look like new construction, in combination with the new roof and paint job.

114

On September 27, I set about painting our front door. It was a weird purple-red color, which definitely did not match the new blue exterior. I chose to use the same medium blue paint that we had used for the base color on the bricks.

Our door is a heavy old door, the kind with 8 square panels set into the design - four rows of two each. I have NO idea how I missed realizing that it would look like a TARDIS before starting, but I sure noticed when I finished up the first coat of paint. I stepped back to see if I could see any missed spots, and.. there it was. We had a TARDIS door. I had to post a photo to Facebook:

You know what happens when you paint our front door blue? Not only does it cease to look "unoccupied foreclosure"... it, um... looks like something else. I have NO idea how we didn't catch this before we started painting, LOL! Strongly considering getting the sign to go with it... - Facebook, September 27, 2011

My friends lost it. Some of my favorite comments:

Wendy C:I would! :)

Amy K: OH MY GOD YES. And get a photo of Matt Smith, and put it on the door so it looks like he looking out the window at you!

Kate S: OMG YES. THIS. Post the notice on it. Bonus points if you install a light at the top on the exterior. Put the sign on the interior so people feel like they are entering the TARDIS when they leave your house. You are going to have the geekiest house ever. EVER. And I love it!

Todd M: I'd skip the sign that says people can step inside to call the police, though. You might get some unwelcome visitors.

AmandaJean B: Love it! So if I come to your house will I be able to time travel :-) ?

Jeanne K: and your house will so much bigger on the inside... tee hee

Wendy C: Definitely a blue lightbulb if you have a light over the door, and...hmmm. Maybe you can make a sign that says something a little different?

As luck would have it, the exterior light that we'd picked - centered above the door - was cylindrical and would totally suggest the TARDIS light style, if not for it being a white light. Ah well.

We did talk of possibly making three laminated signs to the door, each to fit a square: One white with blue bars, one white with David Tennant peering out from behind the blue bars, and the third being the public phone sign. Maybe a long one for across the top.... hmm...

The windows were finally trimmed on October 13th, and that was the end of the major tornado repairs/renovations to the exterior of our house. It ended up looking extremely cute, but it was a TON of work. I'm not sure we would have taken on all of that expense and labor, if not for the tornado.

On December 26th - with the temperature soaring to 50 degrees outside - Porter put aside clearing the basement out. with the weather that warm, it was a perfect time to finally install the replacement storm door in the front. Insane weather... but we were glad to have the exterior finally finished!

The Worst of People

While we were dealing with cleaning up, rebuilding, and healing from the tornado... we were also learning about how such a disaster can bring out the worst in some people.

Vultures

As I mentioned in an earlier chapter, vultures were a huge concern ... all the way from day one.

The door to door salesmen started up within hours of the tornado... on a Sunday afternoon. I'll never understand what kind of a mind would be so quick to jump on such a disaster, so fast, as to mobilize their SALESMEN on a SUNDAY, to get all suited up and hit the ground within hours.

That first day, there were times where there may have only been 5-10 minutes between salesmen walking up. The tornado wrecked a huge swath of the city... knowing the volume of salespeople who knocked at out door that first day - and daily, in the weeks that followed - I can only imagine how many of them were swarming the area. Absolutely disgusting.

Aside from the issue of the door to door contracting salesmen, there was the issue of the salvage companies. These were the companies offering piddly amounts of money for cars that were damaged in the tornado - some of which only needed, say, a new windshield.

For the most part, these companies were literally driving up and down the street, scouring for victims, looking to take advantage of desperation and shock. They'd be driving oversized pickup trucks, just handing flyers out to anyone in the street.

I don't know why, but the way they did this rubbed me even worse than the door to door salesmen. At least THEY put in some sort of effort, walking door to door. At least they weren't in the roads, which - where even passable - were extremely narrow.

117

As I see it, the salespeople and scavenging companies had no business being on our roads. The roads should have been reserved for people who had actual business being there - the residents, volunteers, HIRED contractors, police, and city/utility workers... NOT people looking to profit from it. Aside from the annoyance and predatory nature of their actions, there just plain wasn't any room for them in the area. The entitlement mentality of these companies blew my mind.

The interesting thing, to me, is that the vast majority of the sales vultures managed to show up the day of, and the day after the tornado. This was when we supposedly had police check points in place, when many residents were reporting having problems getting friends and family through to help out. Why should the salespeople have been allowed through, especially in such droves?

With so many people hurting - and, let's face it, many were in shock - no one needed to be exposed to that. This was predatory sales in the extreme.

I honestly think that they were specifically trying to get people while they were discombobulated from the whole deal, and not really in a position to make educated decisions about what to do.

Had someone driven by and offered me money for my car just a few hours earlier than the first one did, I may have gone for it. I may have been so upset by the whole ordeal, in such despair at the sight of my car under a tree, that I may have taken this ridiculously insulting sum, figuring that the car was a write off anyway. They may have caught me before we had a chance to cut it out from under that tree, and realize that it was fixable. That we COULD work with this, even though it wasn't insured.

They may have gotten to me, say, moments after my meltdown. They may have gotten to me when I was wandering the streets, handing out those bottled drinks - completely convinced that saving those drinks was a HUGE IMPORTANT PRIORITY - completely in a daze and NOT thinking straight. Who knows what I may have agreed to at that point?

I know that I was far from the only one who was NOT in a position to be making such big decisions. I'm sure that these companies were well aware of that fact.

118

Additionally, we live in an economically disadvantaged neighborhood. My husband and I have a decent income, and we're very resourceful - not everyone in the area can say the same. These vultures were well aware of that. We were FAR from the only people whose car insurance didn't cover the tornado damage.

Given a night to sleep on it, time to cut it out from under the tree, and my husband's knowledge of car repairs, we knew we could save it. We called around to salvage yards to find replacement doors, and handled it.

For many others, with just a couple of weeks for help to get set up, they would have found out that various charities, government agencies, etc... would have been able to help get their cars fixed. Hell, with time to think, they could have gone online and found companies that would have paid more than $100 for their cars.

These vulture companies got in there and swept the area, offering far less than many other companies, taking advantage of the pain and confusion for their own benefit.

... and people wonder why I say that "I hate people"!

Another issue that I had with the salvage and contracting companies was the ridiculous amount of litter they generated.

The contracting companies adopted a habit of just leaving their literature EVERYWHERE. Stuck in my door. Left on my sidewalk, dumped in the yard. Walking down the street, you'd see masses of tornado debris... and then brightly colored sheets of cheaply photocopied ads just blowing in the wind.

You know, because we didn't have enough shit to clean up.

At one point, I was cleaning up the back of my car, when some canvassers for a salvage company put one of their "We'll pay you $$ for your car!" flyers in what was left of my windshield.

I stopped what I was doing, told them off, and ripped it up right in front of them

119

One of the two guys swore at me, the other gave me the finger, and then they walked to my neighbor's car and papered it as well.

I figured I was doing my neighbors a favor when I followed, plucked the flyer from their window, and ripped IT up also. It may have only been 2 days since the tornado, but I was just DONE with this crap.

Well, they made the mistake of threatening me at that point. Yeah. Yelling at me, on any day, is just not a smart idea. Tornado or not, I have a temper and a set of lungs on me, if you get in my face, I will not be backing down.

I mean, hell... I once punched out a friend of mine, in a bar, on his 30th birthday. (He deserved it, and admitted as much, later!) . Strangers behaving badly towards me, just days after my house is destroyed? When I've been one a two day streak of adrenaline and overstimulation?

Oh hell no.

So, I yelled back. I swore back. I'm sure I looked like a crazy person, and I'm sure they realized that I was about two seconds away from laying them out.

They backed off, and said that they were going to call the cops on me. Yeah? Bring it.

As luck would have it, there was a police cruiser heading our way. I flashed them a grin and declared that I would save them the effort, and flounced off towards the police car.

Now, if you knew me, you would know that I never "flounce". That is how completely broken I was at this point. I literally flounced. I may even have skipped.

So I discussed the situation with the driver, who took off after the two vultures.

A few minutes later, they walked past my house, empty handed. The officer had confiscated their flyers!

One of them spit on my car, while the other - on a phone - read my address off to whoever they were talking to. I think it was supposed to intimidate me, as he did it in an overly loud voice, while looking at me.

I went over to the neighbor on the other side, that they had papered before reaching my house the first time. I took the flyer they'd left, and called the company they represented, to let them know what had happened - from the initial altercation, though to the employee spitting on my car, and the perceived intimidation move. I let them know that I had their company information on record, and that - should anything happen - I would be holding them accountable.

Nothing happened. Never heard a thing from them since, never received another flyer from that company. Good riddance.

Marie: 1 Vulture: 0. Don't yell at a homeowner and make obscene gestures while papering the neighbourhood. Apparently the cops don't like it:) - Twitter, Tue May 24 16:01:23 UTC 2011

The day after that incident, I had a brilliant idea to deal with vultures.

Just had the BEST idea for dealing with vultures: water balloons. Gonna go pick up supplies... heh heh heh - Twitter, Wed May 25 22:09:27 UTC 2011

As I went to the dollar store nearby to pick up balloons, my twitter lit up with messages of support and approval.

RT @AmJayBakes: Now I want to meet @celebr8ngenr8n in real life, so I can play bomb the vultures with her! #reallifeangrybirds #GoNinjaGo - Twitter, Wed May 25 22:34:01 UTC 2011

Seriously. Anyone who's going to use the hashtag "Go Ninja Go" is alright in my books!

Also considering spray painting red Vs on signs put out the night of the tornado - V for Vulture, of course. About as not-human as Visitors! - Twitter, Wed May 25 22:51:13 UTC 2011

I really wanted to be able to fit the hashtag #Mousie on that last tweet. - Twitter, Wed May 25 22:51:59 UTC 2011

I never did get around to buying red spray paint and following through on that idea - which I kind of regret, even now. I know that my husband and I - not to mention the vast majority of our friends and volunteers - would have gotten a serious giggle out of it, but it may have been a really obscure reference for non-geeks. I have no idea how popular the original "V" was, but it WAS over 20 years ago...

Oh well. I can giggle at the idea!

The unfortunate thing about my water balloon idea is that it sort of backfired on me.

You see, as soon as I bought and filled the balloons, I went from being annoyed at the idea of vultures approaching, to welcoming it. I looked forward to it, and was completely convinced that this would be a ridiculously therapeutic approach to our problem.

I put the basket near the door, and waited.

... and waited.

You see, Murphy's Law has always had a bit of a stranglehold on my life, and this was no different. From the time those balloons were filled, I was not approached by another vulture.

Not that they didn't come to our door, they just seemed to have impeccable timing. I could be home all day, save for a few short trips for supplies - but THOSE were the times that they would show up, after I "armed" myself.

Boo. I didn't have the opportunity to lob so much as ONE water balloon! What a waste of a good idea!

The city had sent an email to residents of the area, instructing them to ask to see a City of Minneapolis "peddler's license" from anyone who showed up at the door, and call the police on those who could not produce one. This seemed to slow the flow of vultures a little bit, but those that remained were persistent and aggressive.

They would knock on the door, and nag whichever friend answered the door about talking to "the man of the house" - who was, of course - very busy. The friends would ask to see the peddler's license, the vultures would refuse to show it to anyone but my husband, and then he would come out and yell at them. Lather, rinse, repeat. I have no idea why they thought that they were entitled to anything, or in any position to demand to see ANYONE.

At one point, while I was filling the water balloons, the ONLY vulture to come the rest of that day showed up, and caused some drama. As my friend Shawn recalls:

"Jen got up in his face and asked what he was doing there. He kept asking to see the homeowner and she got closer and closer during her... very insistent questioning. When Porter finally showed up, he demanded to see the guy's peddler's license. (Apparently, the city told Marie and Porter that if someone dropped by who didn't have a license, they should call 911. I'm not kidding.)

The vulture showed them a Brooklyn Park license and said they had one for Minneapolis as well. Jen took a picture of him and the license with her cell phone, then they shooed him away in an extremely rude and appropriate manner. (Hey, I hadn't been dealing with that shit for the last three days and I thought he was a nuisance.) As he started walking down the street (without stopping at anyone else's house), he turned and said, "Take another picture." Jen followed him and asked him to stop so she could.

He finally got to the bottom of the hill, the end of their block, and met two other vultures there. Jen got some pictures, then started walking back to the house. I thought the whole incident was kinda funny, but couldn't see what was going on at that point because of the large piles of branches and stuff on the side of the road. When I stepped out between some of the cars, I saw three people at the bottom of the hill starting to walk up. When I headed down toward Jen, they turned around and walked away.

Both of us agreed that was one of those instances where we almost wished I hadn't walked out into the street when I did. She knew they were behind her... she's 5'4? and on the heavy side... what would three guys do to her? Or what if I'd poked my head out a minute later when they were halfway up the hill and couldn't casually turn around and pretend they weren't following her? We're probably better off not knowing, but still..."

Oh, the fun we could have had if this had happened just a few minutes later, when I had my basket of filled water balloons....

I've lost track of how many contractor salesmen I've yelled at and/ or threatened with violence since the tornado #YouWouldntLikeMeWhenImTornadoed - Twitter, Wed Jun 01 19:05:42 UTC 2011

I'm still struck by the way that so many people tried to take advantage of the situation, and prey on the tornado victims. Even things like... satellite TV companies.

While the company we were with - DirecTV - was VERY good to us when we called in about the tornado, the people on DISH in our area weren't as lucky. There were a lot of reports of people being charged hundreds of dollars for the damaged / missing equipment!

After reading how @dishnetwork is charging #NoMi victims $100, even more thankful we changed to @directv. NO charge to replace/reinstall! - Twitter, Fri May 27 22:54:40 UTC 2011

#NoMi @DIRECTV suspended our account AND refunded the few days of non-usage between tornado & time we called! <3! - Twitter, Fri May 27 22:56:49 UTC 2011

Ugh... and I read that Joplin had to go through the same thing, with many other TV companies. I think it all got sorted out in the end, but it should never have been something that people had to deal with in the first place.

Trolls

Much like how I still can't wrap my head around the way the vulture companies think, internet trolls were another ... disappointment. I think that's the word I'm looking for here. I was disappointed in humanity. Well, or what passed for "humanity"... "human" isn't exactly the first word I'd come up with for some of these people.

Now, I know better than to so much as glance at comments on many news articles - anything regarding religion, women, politics, health, etc. The internet gives courage to the most insane of the spineless, and their vitriol is something that I'd just as soon avoid.

The thing is, we needed to follow online news in the weeks following the tornado. With the city being incommunicative to residents - it was one of the very few ways that we were actually able to receive certain information.

The comments sections on any newspaper or tv news station's articles about the tornado? Wow. Just... wow. I really don't understand how people can be so hateful and devoid of even base levels of compassion.

To start, there were many people who expressed over the top outrage at so much as one government dollar going towards tornado victims. Not annoyance, and not regular anger.. I am talking seething rage.

6 years living in America, and that's one thing I've never gotten used to. The culture, as it pertains to insurance, healthcare, government ANYTHING... completely different. I've never gotten used to the idea of masses of people teeming with anger at the idea that any of their money may go to help someone else. It's never made a lot of sense to me, and it seems ... I don't know. Hateful.

The thing is, whenever anger boils over at the topic, it's always related to benefitting *people*, on a personal or basic level. Not wanting any tax money to go towards someone else's healthcare. Not wanting to put money into helping a tornado victim, or single mothers, birth control, or... whatever.

You don't really hear people complaining about, say, tax money going towards a road that they don't personally drive on. It seems like it's well and good to contribute to and benefit from a pool of tax money when it's applied to something like roads... but find it a completely different issue if that pool of money is applied to people.

I'm used to not stressing out and trying to micro manage where my tax dollars are spent. Back home, sure... some of my tax money would be in a pool that paid for, say, treating a smoker... though I'm not a smoker. That same system would cover any injuries that I received from figure skating, though - a risky activity that I chose to do. I'm sure everyone has had something covered, that someone else would disagree with. So what?

I could rant for hours on the subject, but let's just sum it up as... the fact that so many people work so hard to make sure that other people don't get something - help, benefits, rights, whatever - it's new to me. Culturally, I'm used to the idea that a country is only as strong as its weakest link... and people caring about each other.

By contrast, I read many, many comments to the effect of:

- The people in North Minneapolis should just rot.

- God hates the people in North Minneapolis, and/or that the area deserved it somehow.

- That the city should "level"/ bulldoze this area of the city, entirely... to the extent that "Wipe it right off the map" was used by one person. Awesome.

- Anger that the government was even calling a session to declare the area a disaster zone. Apparently, North Minneapolis was inconveniencing / wasting the time of the government.

- Loads of entitled, classist bullshit.

... each of these themes was represented many, many times, across many different news outlets.

Of course, the fact that the media was aiming for sensationalism for the most part... really didn't help anything. There was a huge focus on the negative, while completely ignoring positive stories to come out of the area.

For instance, so far as I can recall, there was only one instance of looting, at a liquor store. Listening to the news, however, one would be convinced that the area was under siege, that everyone should sit at home with guns, and just wait to fend off these apparent droves of looters.

Not once did I hear a story about, say, the neighborhood cookouts being organized. There was very little - if any - coverage about how neighbors were coming together, how people were helping each other out. The majority of positive stories to really come out of the area tended to be whenever the city was patting itself on the back for something.

Aside from the comments that were obviously area/race/class specific, there was a repeating theme of how much worse things are, elsewhere. Comments that we should consider ourselves lucky, about how Joplin "got it so much worse", that North Minneapolis was whining for nothing, should consider ourselves lucky, that we need to "suck it up", etc. To quote one troll:

"Fucking 1st world problems! Grow a back bone, people! Get your narcissistic heads out of your asses. There are women who walk 5 miles, each way, to get water they will probably catch Cholera from who will get raped twice during the trip. And they have to get up tomorrow to do it again because there isn't any choice"

I don't get why anyone needs to diminish anyone else's difficulties, by comparing them to something else. There will ALWAYS be something worse than whatever anyone is going through, but that in no way lessens the pain that the affected person feels, or the work that they have in front of them.

It was a disturbingly common sentiment, too... not just towards our particular tornado, but being lobbed in various directions, over various incidents.

Comments about how one tornado area shouldn't complain, because another one got it worse.

Comments from people on the west coast, stating that people affected by the earthquakes on the west coast were somehow wimps, because the west coast had so many more of them.

"We had it worse!" or "Suck it up!", or "You should be happy you only had ___ happen" are really awful statements. I don't know if people consider how harsh and unnecessary such statements are. Natural disasters aren't a contest.

Racism

In addition to the classism and generic trollish bullshit on the media coverage, racism reared its ugly head MANY times over the tornado. I won't even dignify the racist commentary by quoting it here.

I realize that this is a delicate subject, but let me be clear with regards to three issues:

1. North Minneapolis is a very diverse neighborhood, with many people of pretty much every nationality, culture, color, and religion represented. That's a big part of what attracted me to it!

2. The racism came from both sides of the divide, and both were equally responsible not only for the strife that occurred over the tornado in specific, but for the race wars in general.

3. Defining a person's worth by the amount of melanin they have is one of the most absolutely retarded ways to judge a person, no matter the skin color of the judging OR the judged.

Now, I understand the reasoning behind racism, even if I don't agree with it in the slightest. Some people are raised to be afraid/distrustful/etc of people different than them. This applies whether talking about gender, color, religion, sexual orientation, etc.

A lot of the hatred being lobbed at North Minneapolis appeared to be rooted in the ideas that the entirety of the area consisted of black people, and that - in the commenter's minds - black people were somehow less than human. Gross, narrow minded bigots, expressing their own personal hatred.

In addition to the "everyday, run of the mill racists" were the race-baiters. The thing I really don't understand is why some people seek to perpetuate the divide. I don't mean just in the "this is how I was raised to believe, and I refuse to seek to change my ways", I mean in the sense that some people seem hell bent on creating racial strife, in making both sides hate each other. It's like they're not happy unless they're causing inter-racial drama of some sort.

There are two main people that come to mind as I try to describe this phenomenon, but they weren't alone - they just had the most "reach" with which to use the tornado to further their agendas.

The first is a semi-local guy. To the best of my knowledge, he lives somewhere in Minneapolis or its suburbs - but NOT in North Minneapolis.

From early on in the aftermath, he was hell bent on making the tornado a race issue. Everything was Black this, or White that... not "people". No acknowledgment that everyone going through this was human, and shared that in common. Pretty much everything he said had this apparent goal to draw lines, to divide sides, and to undo all of the good will that was being created by neighbors - of all colors - getting together, WORKING together, on rebuilding from the tragedy.

You see, tornadoes know no colors, and don't seek out victims based on race.

One day, I posted an article on the tornado resource page about - if I recall correctly - FEMA approving Minneapolis for sidewalk/road repair funds.

In response, I was treated to long, rambling, and fairly incoherent rants about how people in North Minneapolis were worse off for it, that this was all about white privilege, that everything since the tornado was all about white privilege, *"DFL political plantation"*, and more.

Ugh . What does one even say to that? Using the tornado to cause derision and hate between people - clouding the ACTUAL issues - is exploitative at best. Why couldn't he roll up his sleeves and actually HELP, rather than cause more bullshit?

When he sent me a link to a rant where he referred to himself as "Minneapolis Black Jesus", my head just about exploded. Well, I it was himself that he was referring to... I couldn't really wrap my head around most of it.

To me, if a person is going to invest himself so heavily in an event that didn't even affect him directly, the efforts would be better off used to bring people TOGETHER, rather than to divide.

Eventually, he told me:

"Hey Marie, I'm not going to argue with you. "Anyone that makes cakes is cool with me." All I'm asking is that you make a couple of phone calls to find out for yourself something stinks."

I replied, and the thread ended:

" I know something stinks. I've made calls. I've made a TON of calls. Do you have any idea how many calls are involved when ones house goes through over $120k in damage? A LOT.

This whole time, the city has worked actively against ALL OF US in the city. The lack of melanin in my skin has not only NOT prevented my house from getting hit by the tornado, it hasn't prevented me from dealing with idiocy (at best) from the city. There are enough issues with scammers (including some of those who received tornado donations!), the city, insurance companies, contractors, etc... it would be really, really nice if people on the sidelines weren't just throwing shit on the pile. Yes, I see attempts to create a race issue out of it to be just that.

The one good thing to come of this has been seeing neighbors come together - of ALL colors. Getting to know each other. HELPING each other. Please don't mess that up."

By the time I'd blown up at him over this particular attempt to flame a race war, I'd already had it. I'd had it with this crap, I'd had it with the racists online, and I'd just had it in general.

Shortly before this incident, I'd read a blog post from Debbie Hines - a woman in Washington, DC, blogging for the Huffington Post... NOT a local.

Her blog post was entitled "FEMA Denies Aid to Black Tornado Victims in Minneapolis", and opened with several statements about how FEMA *"once again refused to provide aid to black disaster victims."* and *"is now refusing to provide individual aid to help black families living in the north side of Minneapolis."*

Like the rest of us were somehow approved... or worse yet, just didn't matter. I had to reply.

" My husband and I are both white, were hit by the north Minneapolis tornado, and suffered $120k in damage. We're covered for $75k.

Several sets of neighbors on one side of me are white, and many neighbors on the other side are Asian.

NONE of us have been approved for FEMA relief, nor are we going to. This is not a "black" area, nor is it white, Asian, or Martian. This is our neighborhood, it's VERY mixed, and you don't do a service to anyone by trying to claim that "black tornado victims" got denied aid. We ALL did. ALL.

Don't try to capitalize on our -ALL OF OUR - losses by coming up with ridiculous, sensationalistic headlines. It's disgusting. Why are people like you - and by "people like you", I mean sensationalistic pot-stirrers - SO up for trying to create even more of a race issue than there already is? Why do you aim for segregation? Do you hate people so much, that you need to try to cause further rifts?"

How quick would everyone freak out if "black" was swapped out for "Asian" or "White" or whatever, in any of this nonsense? If some blogger on the other side of the country loudly declared that "FEMA denied aid to white people!"?

I don't care WHAT side of the melanin spectrum it's coming from, segregation and discrimination like that is sick, and doesn't do ANYTHING to heal any of the issues - physical or emotional - going on in North Minneapolis... or the world. People from all sides need to respect each other and CELEBRATE differences. Not hate or "tolerate".

I mean, come on - it's 2012! People should be evolved enough to find a much better reason to hate people, than the color of their skin. Personally, I'm just anti-stupid, and anti-bigot. Stupidity and bigotry are genderless, have no race, and know no sexual orientation.

Speaking of bullshit discrimination, morons, and the fact that it's 2012...

About a month after the tornado, I made one of about a thousand trips to Menards. Unlike the vast majority of the other trips I'd made over the months that followed the tornado, I made this trip alone.

131

It was fairly early in the morning. My husband was at work, and I was preparing to demolish the bathroom by myself. I'll let my tweets from that day tell the story...

Man, shopping at Menards is a VASTLY different experience without my husband in tow. :/ Not cool. - Twitter, Wed Jun 29 14:09:35 UTC 2011

At no point, when buying TONS of stuff, has anyone ever made cutesy, condescending comment to US like "SOMEONE has a big project".Today? 4x! - Twitter, Wed Jun 29 14:10:35 UTC 2011

Like NO ONE ever comments on our purchases, ever. I had FAR less items today than we have had any other trip, too. - Twitter, Wed Jun 29 14:13:30 UTC 2011

You see, I'm not talking about employees trying to be helpful. Random guys would walk by, look at my cart, and make a comment - usually condescending. I had a shopping list and was on a mission. I was tired and disheveled and I'm pretty sure that NOTHING about my face or posture gave any signal that I was looking for any sort of interaction - especially from random sexist guys that morning.

I mean, can you imagine reversing the situation? That would be like me approaching a random dude in a grocery store and condescendingly commenting about how cute it was that he was going to try to cook.

2012. Blows my mind.

The Tourists

Let's move on to another brand of loathsome... the "tourists" that swarmed the area in the days following the tornado.

To start off, let me reiterate - the roads were narrow, barely passable, and really should have been reserved for people who had legitimate business in the area. This was a fact that should have been blazingly clear to anyone who entered the affected areas.

Yet, for some reason... many people seemed to think that it would be a fun idea to tour the wreckage and gawk at the damage. Yep. Not only did we become disaster victims that day, we also became cheap entertainment.

The tourists were easy to spot. They were usually driving really nice SUVs, filled with entire families. The people were usually well dressed, the women sporting coiffed hair... a stark contrast to the dirty, sweaty, and bedraggled residents and the volunteers who were there to help.

They would drive slowly up the streets - with little to no regard for the legitimate traffic that they may be holding up - noses pressed to the windows, delighting in the spectacle they were viewing. Really, the expressions on their faces were no different than those of young children watching a parade. The way they would look excited as their gazes would come to rest on a particularly bad area of damage... very similar to how one would react to an especially ornate, exciting float.

I couldn't believe what a disconnect they had, from this reality that those of us in the area were actually living with. It was like those of us affected had suddenly become characters at a surreal Disneyland, our struggle and pain now a twisted form of entertainment for these people. I can't imagine getting off on something like that, and encouraging kids to do the same. To gawk, like we were animals on display.

Loads of gawking tourists in #NoMi. Makes us feel like characters @Disneyland. Need signs. "Have your photo taken w/ tornado victim-$5!" ;) - Twitter, Mon May 30 03:18:38 UTC 2011

A neighbor and I ended up really sarcastically waving at one car - they WAVED BACK.

I joked to the neighbor that we could make a fortune by putting out a sign "tour a tornado house - $10" or maybe do up one of those displays you stick your head through for photos... the picture on the front could be a tornado, or someone dressed in grubbies with a smashed house in the background.

The douchebaggery didn't stop at gawking, either. Some of the tourists decided to treat the area like their own personal garbage can! It was as though the fact that there was debris on the ground was an invitation for them to throw their pop cans and lunch wrappers out the window!

133

As one local friend, Lisa, described it:

"One thing that really pissed me off were the gawkers! One chick had the audacity to throw some trash out her car window while driving 5 mph down our block. I snapped! We were out cleaning up debris and I yelled WTF? Doesn't it look like we have enough to clean up?! The driver actually made her get out and pick it up. Awesome :)"

I was so sick of having to deal with someone else's garbage, while we'd been working our asses off to clean our house/yard and get some NORMALCY.

On another occasion, some douchebag hipster - who lived in another area of the city entirely - put the following as his facebook status, raising the ire of many of us in the tornado zone:

"Hey! Join me for a Surley at the Finish Line!!!!on Sept. 10th. Running the beautiful trails of Wirth Park and through the Tornado Zone! Mpls wilderness in the city..."

Yep. I hate people!

Contractor Drama

We started calling roofing companies the day after the tornado, desperate to get the roof repaired and save the house. There was a lot of rain over the early part of the summer, and the threat of further water damage or mold was just killing us.

Looking back over the whole ordeal, I'm still flabbergasted by the degree of difficulty we went though in trying to hire a roofer.

Most were not answering their phones. It was incredibly difficult to even get someone to return a phone call. I'd estimate that maybe 1/6 of our messages ended up returned.

When we could actually get a hold of a human, they were extremely quick to come up with an excuse as to why they were not willing to come out to even look at the roof.

If the excuses had been along the lines of them being over booked because of all the tornado jobs, that would have been one thing... but this was something else.

Many claimed they'd get back to us with availability, and never did.

One claimed that because our roof was in North Minneapolis, it would be full of lead, and that they were not certified for that. Sight unseen, mind you. Who ever heard of needing to be lead certified to work on a roof, anyway? If this is actually a thing - and a common enough thing to have to turn down business, sight unseen... wouldn't a *roofing* company obtain whatever certification they needed, to do roof repairs?

My favorite - and by "favorite", I mean "The one that disappointed me the most" was from a company that advertised themselves as being a couple of school teachers, who were also running a construction company together. The recommendation came from a friend, and we were thrilled at the idea of being able to give our business to school teachers.

That is, we would have been, if they had been interested in said business. Their excuse had been that the homes in our area had incredibly steep roofs, and that they weren't set up to deal with that. No matter how many times I assured the person that no, our roof wasn't steep at all... no dice. Not even interested in coming out to take a look. It was incredibly frustrating to us.

With people - including the vultures themselves - so quick to refer to the down economy as an excuse for the predatory marketing actions, I'm still just really surprised that it was so unbelievably difficult to even get someone to come over for a quote.

I still suspect that it was either classism and/or racism at play. We hadn't had such difficulties when we lived in the suburbs, even after a major hailstorm had caused widespread damage in the area. Phone calls returned quickly, appointments made right away, and businesses seemed eager to compete for available jobs.

Almost a week and a half after the tornado - and dozens of calls later - we were no closer to having our roof repaired.

Sick of hearing construction on other roofs. I don't know why it's so hard to find someone that follows through on communication/promises! - Twitter, Fri Jun 03 18:27:02 UTC 2011

Then we went through one of the most demoralizing experiences of the tornado recovery. The report that I filed with Angie's List and the Better Business Bureau details it well:

"On the afternoon of Tuesday May 31, 2011 we were approached at our home by Andy of Pro 1 Construction. He was canvassing the neighborhood after the tornado, and our roof had extensive damage.

We'd been waiting a week and a half for the roofer we'd been recommended to, to actually give us a date for a consult/work to start/etc, and we were tired of waiting. Against my better judgment, I listened to what Andy had to say. I had sworn that I wouldn't hire any of the "vultures" who came door to door, but he seemed nice, honest, and well... he was the first one not wearing a suit. He seemed nice and helpful, and didn't come off as a smarmy salesperson.

Andy went right up on our roof, looked over all of the damage, and gave us a rough estimate of what it would cost. He seemed very thorough, and even talked to my husband on the phone, right there, about some of the concerns my husband and I brought up (insulation, our choice of shingles, etc). It all sounded good, but I'm not one to sign a contract for something like that on the spot, so I told Andy that we would think it over and call him if we would want to go ahead and make an appointment to sign contracts the next morning. He told me that we could call "anytime", and that he's even taken calls up til midnight.

Well, by 9 or 10 pm that night, we'd decided to sign with them. He DID take the call, and arranged to meet up with us at their office the following morning. We found it a little strange that Andy wasn't able to meet IN the office - his parents/owners weren't in yet, and he didn't have a key to get in. We went over everything, it looked good, and we signed anyway... leaving a $2000 deposit. Andy told us that he'd be able to get the order for the shingles in that afternoon. The materials would be dropped at our house on Friday, work starting on Saturday... likely taking 2 days. He would call that afternoon to confirm that there was not a problem getting the shingles we wanted.

136

We didn't hear from him that day, so got a hold of him the next day. He said he'd have an answer by the afternoon (Thursday, at this point), but we didn't hear back. We called around 6pm, and again around 8... nothing. Apparently "call anytime" only counts before they have our deposit money. He did not return our call that night.

Friday morning, I called the office and got a hold of his father, the owner. He claimed that Andy had "over promised", but made no attempt to even try to live up to the promises that were made in order for us to sign. He was very short with me on a few occasions, but I tried to ignore it - I just wanted our roof installed.

According to him, the shingles hadn't been ordered, were going to be a "special order", but that he'd start making calls to see if anyone had them in stock- this is now 2 DAYS after we were told the shingles would be ordered that same day. Friday - the day we were supposed to have them dropped at our house, for work to begin.

The owner wanted to come by to see the place himself - which seemed a little weird to me, as our contract had detailed measurements, all of the specifics, etc. He asked if I'd be around in a couple hours, I told him that I would have to be going to a meeting at some point, so to call when he was on his way.

He called to say he'd be here at 12:03. At 12:02 he called to say it would now be 12:15. He showed up at 12:25. Almost immediately, he began making disparaging remarks about the area, repeatedly stating that "most of the people who live here are scammers, are bankrupt / trying to screw the system / on welfare, wouldn't pay him, etc. He followed it up with "I'm not saying this about YOU, specifically...", but it struck me as weird. I tried to ignore it, as I just really wanted the roof replaced as contracted.

When he walked around the house, he started coming up with all sorts of things that Andy "didn't see" (Yes, Andy saw and made mention of all of it), and started trying to add stuff to the whole thing. That we needed new supports for the overhang. That Andy "hadn't factored in" something else. I didn't even care at this point, I just wanted the roof on, and SOON.

I asked when he can start, he said that he can pull a permit and have his guys there tomorrow. Two minutes later, he says something about not starting till Monday. (This wasn't the first inconsistency of his). I asked him about this, and pointed out what he'd said just a few minutes before. He tried to backpedal, claimed I'd "put words in his mouth", when all I did was directly quote his response to my asking for the bottom line time line. He finally agreed that he HAD said that, but that it was contingent upon him getting "all the way to St Paul" for a permit within the next 3 hours, and that MAYBE he could, but they wouldn't start till Monday or Tuesday now. I pointed out that the city had set up a special permits office in N. Minneapolis to deal with the tornado damage, and he brushed it off with "I don't have my checkbook on me", saying he'd have to go back to Maple Grove and then back to St Paul. He had NO desire to go to the North Minneapolis office, I have no idea why - well, aside from maybe the condescending attitude he had towards "those people" in the area.

He kept getting even more rude - he'd been condescending this entire time. Raised his voice, asked if I "Know how business works" (I do, I've been a business owner for over 15 years), and "Do you even know what 'condescending' means?". Oh, the irony on that last one. I told him that I am an educated, intelligent woman, and did not need him to be talking down to me. He fired back at me, asking if I was saying that he was UNeducated (?!), and got very belligerent. He started trying to back out of the contract, by saying that if I was going to question what he says, than he "obviously couldn't make (me) happy", while I explained that yes, he could, ALL we want is for him to do the work that we contracted them for, and to give us an answer as to a start date.

At one point, he said - of my question about a start date - "That's a very easy question to answer, but I'm not going to, because nothing I can say will make you happy". He just refused to give us any sort of idea, even though a time line was easy to promise BEFORE they had our money.

I don't beg, and I don't cry easily, but he had me doing both, right there in my front yard. It was almost 2 whole weeks after the tornado, and I did NOT want to be sent back to square one. All I wanted was for him to honor the contract that we'd rushed to sign, and paid a hefty deposit on.

He gave me my contract and deposit back, and walked out. I'm glad I don't have to chase down our money, but I was very upset that they wasted 3 days of our time.

That was 3 days we could have spent with someone who actually intended to do our roof. It was 3 days of relief at FINALLY knowing we had someone to do the work, and about excitedly looking forward to being able to move back in. 3 days, ripped away from us, and THAT can't be returned.

Looking back over the entire deal, it seems to me that he wasn't happy with the quote we were given on our contract, and wanted it higher. When I questioned some of the things he was saying - in terms of the logistics of the repairs, etc - he got mad. If he's going to try to add stuff on, of COURSE I'm going to ask about the options, what he means by certain things, etc. I think he wanted someone who'd just blindly let him rack up the bill, and when he realized that I wasn't like that, he just wanted out. For all I know, Andy under quoted on the contract (I'm not a roofer!), but if that was the case, he should have lived up to it.

If you're going to give someone the power to make promises and sign contracts on behalf of the company, you're going to have to be prepared to live up to those contracts and promises, not just berate your client repeatedly and try to say that they wouldn't "be happy". Like I explained to him many times - while BEGGING - all we wanted was our roof replacement, and an answer as to when. That's not unreasonable. We're not hard to deal with... and we certainly didn't deserve what they did to us. I felt personally violated, that this company - that we paid a big deposit to - came to our property, to our house... and treated me like that."

- I wrote those words just minutes after he left, making sure to cover every detail with explicit accuracy.

I was in tears as I typed out every detail of the disgusting encounter. This had happened just short of two weeks after the tornado, and I was at my breaking point. I'd been SO thrilled to finally be past the hurdle of even having someone quote the job - never mind be on track to having the work done, contract in hand. It was just beyond cruel to have that hope ripped away from me at all. The verbal abuse and condescension I was subjected to was just... icing on the cake.

There was so much about the whole tornado situation that I wasn't used to having to deal with. Tornadoes, for one. Having to DIY it, being "homeless", etc. Most of it completely out of my control, and not a specific attack on me from anyone.

Being talked down to, however, was another matter entirely.

When you have a decent IQ, the opportunity doesn't tend to present itself often to those who would be apt to do so. When you're large - and fairly mouthy - on top of that? People just... don't talk down to me.

For most social situations, I've learned my way around almost anything that the Aspergers had me disadvantaged at. This is because when you're subjected to a situation - or even just a facial expression - repeatedly, it becomes a matter of ... well, patterns. I can learn from patterns.

When something happens that's outside my realm of "figured out", it throws me off - even at the best of times. When it happens after almost 2 weeks with big gaping holes in my smashed up roof... then it gets ugly.

As the owner of the company turned to walk away, smug sneer on his face, I calmed down enough to tell him that I would make him regret the way he treated me. He laughed at me.

All these months later, I don't have adequate words to describe the mixture of hopelessness, disappointment, and rage that I was feeling, as he walked away.

I thought back to our first meeting with this company, how their represented had come to the door. I called out to him to ask to see his peddler's license. I mean, if the city wanted us to call the police on people who would not produce one, who am I to disobey those orders?

He refused to produce one, so I called the police as he drove off.

The officer that arrived had not heard of the city's email, had no idea what to do about it, and ... that was that. I have no idea why the city would send such emails, then neglect to tell the police to expect such calls... but I later found out that I was not the only person to run into that.

I went inside and wrote down the details of the whole sick encounter, with the intent to submit it to the Better Business Bureau..

I don't cry easily, and I don't beg. This company had me doing both, in my own front yard. I can't even describe how upset I am. #NoMi - Twitter, Fri Jun 03 18:51:11 UTC 2011

As I thought about his comments about "welfare scammers" - another instance of the racism/ classism that people in the tornado zone had to deal with - I ranted about the ordeal on Twitter. Along with the comments being made to commiserate / cheer me up, there was a great suggestion: Post the review on Angie's List.

I'd never even looked at Angie's List, much less posted to it. I did know, however, that they were very proud of their A+ rating on Angie's List - they had it proclaimed loudly across all of their full color, glossy business materials.

After looking at Angie's List, I found a coupon code online and bought a membership - spite shopping is the best shopping, especially when done with a discount code.

When I looked up their profile, I noticed something that made me almost fall out of my chair, I was howling with laugher THAT hard.

Their big A+ rating that they were so proud of? Yeah... it was based off one review. ONE.

I can't imagine what thinking went into being THAT proud of the review. One review says absolutely nothing about a business. Also, slapping that logo and statement across everything they put out there? Not smart, as it only takes ONE screw up on their part to elicit a review that will obliterate it.

Then again, if they had good business sense, they wouldn't belittle and abuse a client on their own front lawn, making them BEG for the company to just honor their own contract.

I'm taking some solace in the fact that their Angie's List "A+" that they advertise on their stuff was based on 1 review. WAS. Hehehe. - Twitter, Fri Jun 03 20:06:12 UTC 2011

So, I posted the account on Angie's List, and gave them an F, overall.

I was fair in my rating - N/A for quality of work (as they didn't end up doing any), F on both punctuality and professionalism (for obvious reasons), and C on responsiveness and price. They were quite responsive before we signed, not as responsive afterwards, and their prices were just ok... before the owner tried to raise the quote, anyway.

Because they didn't end up doing work for us, the review wasn't give as much weight as it would have if they had, and only brought their overall rating down to a B. Boo.

The other interesting thing was that the sole review there was about Andy. Aside from not being so quick to reply to our calls after we signed, I didn't have a problem with Andy. Andy was nice, seemed honest, and seemed very willing to do the work. I have no doubt that if the father hadn't gotten involved, the whole thing would have turned out very - VERY - differently.

I actually felt bad for Andy, as his father repeatedly threw him under the bus. That's got to be a horrible environment to work in... and a horrible person to work for.

I was NOT in the mood to deal with the father again, so it was Andy that I called after I posted the review. I very pleasantly let him know that Pro 1's advertising was no longer accurate, as they no longer had an A+ rating on Angie's List.

An interesting thing happened, at some point after that. Although this company loudly advertised their former Angie's List rating on all their advertising, they claimed to be an "unwilling participant", and tried to get Angie's List to remove the review and/or their listing entirely.

From their Angie's List profile:

"This provider has asked to be removed from Angie's List. While we do not honor requests to remove a provider from the List, we do withhold unwilling participants from Category and Keyword requests."

So, they'll no longer show up when someone is searching for, say, a roofer... but if someone looks them up specifically, they'll find them. That honestly kind of made my day to read. I don't think that the business owner realized that it's a bad idea to abuse someone with a vocabulary and an internet connection

The kicker? In stark contrast to the above notice - which was highlighted with a very obvious warning box at the top of the profile - was their business description:

"Pro 1 Construction is proud to say we have an A+ Rating, also we are members of the NRCA as well we are Certified Contractors of GAF-ELK"

Unwilling participant, but proud of their former rating? Awesome. Way to have a spine, there.

Major kudos to Angie's List for not removing the profile, by the way. I'm glad that they have the honor to show both sides of a business's reputation and actions, and not just accept payment to showcase the positive only.

Now that I'm calming down, I find the "Do you even know what condescending MEANS?" comment hilarious. - Twitter, Fri Jun 03 20:14:20 UTC 2011

The converse of that, however, was how the Better Business Bureau dealt with it. While I will have respect for - and patronize - Angie's List for the foreseeable future, I will always look at BBB as a joke and a racket as a result of their actions.

Going into this, I looked at BBB as being pro consumer. It was where you go to check on a business, for better or worse. If a person had a bad experience with a business and complained about it, it would be there on BBB for the world to see - and take heed.

Of course, this was because I didn't know about BBB "Accredited Businesses". Apparently, you can pay a membership to BBB, and they will protect you from negative reviews.

Isn't that akin to mafia behavior? Am I missing something here?

143

Anyway, at some point - a few months after the debacle with Pro 1 Construction, a friend messaged me to let me know that I should complain about them to the BBB. I informed her that I had... and then she informed me that their profile was listed as "A+" standing, with 0 complaints in the last year.

Now, not only did I submit a complaint about this company, I had received a reference number for the complaint. Surely, this had to be some sort of oversight.

Nope. After many calls, a few emails, being told that they "hold complaints until they see a pattern", and even a "Whistle blower" article about the situation in the local newspaper, the complaint was marked "Info only", and - to this day - does not show up against the business profile. The profile still erroneously states that BBB has received NO complaints about this company, even though one can access my complaint directly - IF they have a link to it. It's not available through any other search on the site.

To quote the article ("Not every gripe goes on a BBB record", by James Eli Shiffer - Star Tribune), *"Minnesota BBB spokesman Dan Hendrickson said his organization logs all complaints, but a company's public profile generally lists only those in which the customer is asking for a refund or other action."*

So, take a lesson from this - when the Better Business Bureau claims that they have not received any complaints about a business, it doesn't necessarily reflect the truth. They're not pro consumer, they're pro-"Accredited Member". It's an advertising agency, no more.

The article did go on to say:

"Because of Porter's concern, however, the BBB reopened the complaint and asked the company for a response, which will eventually show up on the company's record, he said."

... which has not happened, even 10 months later.

After the article, the BBB finally did one thing, anyway - they forwarded my complaint to Pro 1 Construction for comment.

Here is the response that they sent to the Better Business Bureau:

"At this point, and after much thought of the harassment incurred by Mrs. Porter, I am CC this response to our council as well and will be seeking a civil action against the Porters, due to the erroneous allegations made by Mrs. Porter, not only to our BBB ratings, but Angies List as well, whom allowed her erroneous allegations to be listed on there web-site. We will be seeking full restitution in this matter, to the fullest extent of MN law, now at this point."

I love it.

Apparently, posting a true and completely accurate account of their actions in two places - and one photo call to notify them that their advertising is no longer accurate - constitutes "harassment".

Additionally... BBB won't even mention that there IS a complaint against them, so I'm not sure why they're (Or would that be "there", using their creative grammar rules?) fussing about that.

Finally, the "At this point, also, now at this point" of the statement reads like a Miss Teen North Carolina 2007 pageant answer, again now, at this point. I honestly kind of wanted to forward their reply back to them, with "Like the, such as, BITCHES!". But, you know... I'm sure that would be seen as harassment.

I kinda hope they actually do sue me - I'm still sore at being abused like that on my own lawn. It was embarrassing and felt awful. I've never been treated so awfully in my life, and it's the first time I've ever experienced what seems to be sexism. While it would be extremely draining to recount the experience in front of a judge, it could be worth it to have him/her point out that truthful statements do not constitute any sort of actionable offense.

I guess we should count our blessings that they at least gave our money back. Many people in the area weren't so lucky, having fallen victim to one of the many scam artist "contractors" that preyed on the area in the months following the tornado. Some people paid deposits, then never heard from the company again. Others had contractors take their money and do either shoddy work, or only partial work before disappearing.

I can't even imagine what kind of a sick mind it takes to pull that shit, especially given the circumstances. That's just... a special kind of depraved.

The Alarm Company

I think I should mention: Tornado aside, ... I don't cry easily, and I don't beg. The douchebag contractor wasn't the only business owner to get me to that point, post-tornado. The alarm company we've been signed up with since we bought the house did, as well.

Some time after the tornado, I wanted a clearer understanding of certain things about that day. I had decided to write this book, and certain memories were a little foggy. For instance, I remember generalities about our first trip through the destruction - approximately where we entered the area, that we had to zig zag, the fact that there were trees blocking most of the roads, approximately where we stopped / ran from, etc - but the rest of it is locked under a haze of blurry confusion.

Around the time that I was ready to see a video of the tornado itself, I decided that I should try and get ahold of the recordings the alarm company would have made of the calls that day. I knew that I was on the phone for the majority of the trip through the tornado zone, and I figured that maybe there would be some clues in my - probably fairly incoherent - screaming. If not specific clues, I figured that hearing myself - at the time it was all going down - could help bring me back, maybe allow some memories to come out of that fog on their own.

To this day, I still consider it to be an extremely reasonable request. I don't see how anyone could possibly have a problem with it, short of, say, maybe someone's psychologist disapproving... given the same/similar situation.

Not under the care of any such professional, myself - I'm left to determine what would be needed and/or healthy for my own emotional recovery from this trauma. To me, being able to put those pieces together would have been incredibly therapeutic and helpful.

So I contacted the company, and asked for the recordings. I figured this was a simple, unoffensive request. I explained what I was looking for and why, and awaited the file.

Shortly thereafter, I received an email with a single file. Upon listening, I learned that this was the recording of only one call, and I knew we'd had two or three that day. This call covered only the first call, where they let us know that our house was on fire - the one call that I already remembered clearly.

I replied to let them know, and to ask for the other clips - the ones where we were actually entering the tornado zone.

A few days later, I received a reply. It stated that the alarm company was charged for every audio clip that they have sent to them, and that I would need to contact the owner of the company for authorization of the rest of them.

... and that is where things got weird.

In talking to the owner, I was completely shot down. He had me explain why I wanted it several times, each time expressing confusion at why I would want it.

Each time I had to reiterate what I knew of the sequence of events, and my desire to know, I got more and more upset. It was still a fairly traumatic thing to walk someone through, and I was very frustrated that someone was putting me through it, repeatedly. I cried. I was shaking. All I wanted was the damn files, so I could fill in my own, personal blank spots from that day. It felt very sadistic of him, and he expressed absolutely no compassion whatsoever.

When he started mentioning his lawyer, I came to understand that he was afraid of a lawsuit.

To this day, I still don't understand it. I don't understand how allowing me access to recordings of myself freaking out at my first views of the disaster have any bearing on their company whatsoever.

Am I supposed to sue because tiny electronic devices we were leasing from them somehow didn't wrap our house in a protective bubble, preventing damage to it?

Am I supposed to see them as somehow negligent, that their operator couldn't magically transport us over the damage, and get us to our house faster than we were able to?

In the months that followed, we saw several accounts that people were able to record of their own personal disasters. People who videotaped it as it happened, etc. I just... wish I had that. The conversation that I had with this alarm company's operator was the closest thing I'll ever have.

It may be twisted, but it IS a sentimental thing for me. I feel like I'm being denied a part of my own history. I want to know. It drives me insane that there IS something out there, from those first moments of our tornado experience... and that I'll likely never have access to them.

The fact that I'm being denied access to them for what appears to be illogical, selfish reasons? Just makes it all that worse. I just hope that the alarm company owner comes up with the compassion to release the files to us, before they're gone forever.

The "Friend" Who Wasn't

While the actions of strangers were hurtful and uncalled for, I was completely blindsided by what happened with one of my friends.

We'd been friends for a few short years. We had many of the same challenges and stories from running our respective businesses, so we bonded quickly over them. She was a sweetheart, and very easy to like.

In the community, she was very well known and liked. She was known to be very generous, and a lot of people took advantage of this - to the point that her business was suffering. She was far too MUCH of a giver.

Both myself and another friend were trying to help her out - mostly with updating her marketing materials, to help her attract new business. For my part, I'd offered to redo her website, free of charge.

Then the tornado happened.

From early on in the recovery, I made it clear to her that - though I may be a little slower with it now - I still wanted to redo her site. It would be a welcome distraction from everything else, after all... and, once I got electricity back a few days later, I'd be able to do so while "babysitting" contractors.

She agreed. She also went way above and beyond what I would expect/ask of anyone, and set up a fundraising special through her business. For a set period of time, a percentage of certain sales would go towards helping us with our tornado recovery expenses. She advertised the fact on her social media profiles... and we were so touched by the gesture.

The announcement got many "likes" on Facebook, and we were shocked to see one comment stating that the person - someone we'd only met once, briefly - would be sending in a check as a straight up donation.

Shortly thereafter, I received a voice mail from her, excitedly telling me that she had a check from me. I had to book a time to come in and do a website consult with her anyway. I left her a voice mail to say as much, and waited to hear back from her. I really, really needed a distraction from dealing with the crap at my house.

She didn't get back to me. I followed up a couple times over the following months, but she didn't reply to her messages or emails, and never answered her phone when I called.

I was hurt, but wanted to give her the benefit of the doubt. She was always such a sweet, good hearted person. I knew she'd come into some very difficult times, financially... VERY difficult - but I couldn't wrap my head around the idea that she may have scammed her own customers, benefitting from my tragedy.

Four and a half months after the tornado, I finally unfriended her, and unfollowed her on Twitter. It had just become too painful to see her cheerful messages, about all the great things she was doing... when she couldn't be bothered to reply to my messages.

When she couldn't be bothered to so much as check in on how I was doing, too. That's just not.. Friendship. Also, I was fairly insulted that she apparently completely dropped the idea of me doing a website for her, without telling me about it directly.

Four and a half months, I figured, was plenty of time - MORE than enough time - for her to come clean about what happened after "I have a check for you!"

To add insult to injury, I was pretty sure that we were talking about less than $50. After talking to the person who sent in the stand alone donation, I learned that she had sent $35. Now, I'm not going to knock any donation - every little bit helped! - but I want to be clear that we're not talking about thousands of dollars here.

Nope. My friendship was apparently valued at somewhere around $35.

It wasn't even as though $35 could have made the difference between eating and starving - I was constantly reading her messages about road trips, vacations, going out dining and drinking. It was just too much.

I was never upset specifically about the money, though. It was the betrayal. How can a friend just drop all communication like that? Turn around and drop me off her radar entirely, even abandoning plans that I'd agreed to, without even telling me?

I was incredibly saddened by it all.

Interestingly, while voice mails, email, text, etc wouldn't catch her attention - unfriending her and unfollowing her sure did.

VERY soon after I unfollowed her on twitter, she called me. I wasn't in the mood to take her call. It took a lot to finally getting to the point of unfriending her, and I just couldn't handle her at the moment. I let it go to voice mail.

Her message sounded both perky and concerned. She said that she'd noticed I'd unfollowed her, and hoped that it wasn't something she said.

I had NO idea how to deal with it. The fact that she was so warm and sweet was starkly contrasted by her (in)actions of the past few months, and also by the fact that she was good friends with a local con artist - one who's scammed several people that we both know.

I do believe in "birds of a feather". To me... if you're willing to be friends with someone who will solicit donations for a cause, then keep them... then pull this on me... well, that's it, really. I think it says a lot about a person's character.

I didn't return her call. Gutless and/or spitey of me, maybe... but I'd been waiting on a return to my messages for around four months. Not only did I not feel up to it, I really didn't feel I owed it to her at that point, either.

She called a mutual friend - one who knew exactly why I was upset.

Apparently, she honestly sounded confused about the whole thing. I believe it, she sounded legitimately surprised on the voice mail she left me. She asked if this other friend had any idea why I broke off from her social media presence.

Our mutual friend remained diplomatic and neutral. She told her that just breaking off like that for no reason didn't sound like me, that I'm an adult, and that if I want to talk to her, I would.

She also pointed out that I'm not one to be passive aggressive, that if I make the decision to walk away... that's it. That when my door is shut... it's shut.

After another voice mail from her - and some discussion with the mutual friend - I decided to finally contact her.

Our discussion was incredibly strained and awkward. I was very hurt that she dropped and ignored communication for months, and I just wanted to be done with it. When someone hurts me, I ... don't want to be around them. I don't really want to hear from them, and I don't want to try and save a friendship that apparently wasn't there to begin with.

Her stance was that she did not sell any of the certain items she'd advertised for the fund raiser, and that she must have misplaced the check she called me about, and then forgot about it. Her reason for not contacting me for several months was that she just got "too busy".

She sounded sincere about everything, but it really came off like she was more upset that I unfollowed her.

151

She offered to mail me a check for twice the amount that the original standalone donation was, I told her that it wasn't about the money, and that she really didn't need to do that. I told her how hurt I was, and that I'd need some time to think about whether or not we could have a friendship after this.

In the end, I decided that I couldn't handle being friends with her. I really do want to think the best of her, and to believe her... but the math doesn't add up for me. How do you go from talking a couple times per week, to nothing? From desperately needing a new website, to just dropping the plans without letting me know?

How do you get so busy that you can't reply to a friend's messages - ESPECIALLY in the wake of such a disaster - but not be too busy to go out partying several times a week, tweeting about each time?

The last message I had sent her - that she had ignored - I asked her what I did, why she had cut off all communication from me. I was so hurt - and I really wanted to know if I'd said or done anything. I honestly would have understood if she'd even come back with... I don't know. That the idea of tornado damage was so upsetting to her, that she couldn't bear to hear from me. How does a person - a friend - just ignore that? I sure as hell couldn't.

How can one claim to "forget" about a check for tornado damages, in the face of messages on several platforms? She followed me on Twitter, where I frequently tweeted about tornado stuff, including the insurance and financial difficulties we were going though. Not one of those messages could have triggered a thought of "Oh, right! Someone sent me a check for her, I bet she could use that... let me mail it now!"? I couldn't even write it off as "maybe she didn't see my tweets", because she specifically mentioned following along, in our awkward conservation.

In the end, she did end up mailing me a check for $70, which we were grateful for, and put to good use.

I do still wish her the best in life, and I would have even if she hadn't sent it in the end.

The Best of People

While the tornado had definitely brought out the worst in some people, it also brought out the best in many others.

The Geek Community

A running theme throughout this entire ordeal has been "We have no idea how we would have managed, if not for the geek community".

A little background, so I can properly frame JUST how blown away we were by the overwhelming love and support we received from this wonderful extended "family":

While Porter's brother in law, niece and nephews to came out and help with the cleanup, and his father put up the cats for 6 weeks, neither one of us are super close to our families. On my side of that, I've been estranged from the vast majority of my family since I was about 12 - aside from my grandmother.

The both of us had lived the typical life of a high IQ kid: Ostracized in school, bullied, not fitting in with anyone, etc. Both felt like we'd been dropped off on the wrong planet. We made small handfuls of friends throughout elementary, junior high, and high school, but sort of "friends at arm's length", if that makes any sense.

While I can't speak for Porter, I feel like the friends that I made while in school were mostly... I don't know... that the friendship happened because they were just gracious enough to include me, more so than any real commonality between us. When it came to outside-of-school-hours get-togethers, I was usually not included. I guess it's just as well, that sort of distance was probably more comfortable than actually learning the social skills that after-school friendships require, at that point in my life.

As adults, we'd both found our way to Mensa - albeit for different reasons. He was looking for a way to meet people and make new friends, I was trying to fail an IQ test. (Long story short: Was trying to prove to the insurance company that I was "going stupid" after my car accident, when medical tests were turning up nothing to explain issues I was having after it: far slower processing, as well as a change in how I talked)

When I, uh... failed to fail... I joined in on local activities, figuring I'd at least get my money's worth out of the deal.

I still remember my first event. It was at a member's apartment, just a casual get together. As I reached to knock on her door, I almost chickened out - the idea of entering this apartment - filled with people that I did NOT know - terrified me.

I did end up summoning enough courage to knock, and I'm glad I did. I was barely in the room when I just... went calm. It's like something in the air said that I was somewhere safe, that these were "my people". Instantly more comfortable with everything... and I began to learn social skills that day - at age 24! Once I learned that I could be comfortable with strangers who were "like me", I quickly learned to be able to be comfortable with random strangers, as well. Learning that there were people like me, who spoke my language... just not feeling so alone any more, it just gave me the backbone to be more social in everyday life.

Porter joined Mensa around the same time, and was also making friends in his local area. One of those friends vouched for me when I visited Minneapolis, and was looking for things to do. He volunteered to pick me up at the airport and show me around, and we were married six and a half months later.

When we heard of a local sci-fi / "fandom" convention - Convergence - our social circles expanded quite a bit. Between Mensa and fellow Convergence nerds and geeks, we no longer felt alone on the planet, having finally met up with "our tribe".

Our social life as adults now... it's wonderful. Nothing I could have ever imagined as a kid. Not only had I never really dared to imagine myself as someone who could BE social, I never could have imagined having such a diverse group of such amazing friends.

The great thing about having nerds and geeks as friends is that things are always interesting. You're always learning things about people in your social circle - such diversity in experiences, interests, and skills.

Anyway.

While we had gotten used to being social and having real friends, we hadn't ever been in any sort of crisis that would provoke any sort of massive geek community response. Hell, we hadn't really been exposed to anyone else being in any sort of situation like that, either.

Almost as soon as we posted that we'd been hit, the local geek community started mobilizing for us. Friends started sharing the news on Facebook and Twitter, asking anyone in the area who was willing and able to aid in the cleanup to contact us.

I've got to say, I'm still worried that I may have not responded to someone during the first few days - my Twitter, Facebook, and voice mail were hit with a deluge of offers, and it was hard to keep everything straight. Before we had even figured out what we needed, there were offers of labor, places to stay - from complete strangers!

At one point, I received a text message from a Twitter acquaintance - from Convergence - that I'd never really met. Although she's even more of a misanthrope than I've ever been, she was offering up her spare room. I was super touched - this was someone who comes off as disliking everyone with a pulse (I can't say I blame her, at times!), going out of her way to reach out to us.

In the local geek community, there seem to be a few "hub" people - the people that absolutely everyone seems to know. While "Six degrees of separation" seem to apply between any two people in general, these are the people that can be reached with only 1-2 degrees, from anyone in the local - or even national/online geek communities.

One of these people - "Uncle Mikey" - tweeted about what we had gone through, asking if anyone he knew could help out.

One of his friends - someone we'd never heard of - contacted me about helping. She was currently between jobs, and wanted to help out. She'd been through a tornado when she was younger - one that destroyed her house - and had an idea of what we were going though. She was very much "A friend of Mikey's is a friend of mine"... and a new friendship was formed.

Tara worked tirelessly to help us out, not only through the immediate clean up efforts, but in the rebuild as well. She showed up the first day of the tornado with a trailer, contractor bags, and tools... more prepared to do this than WE were. She was there almost every day through the cleanup, I have no idea where she got the energy from.

As our immediate, emergency needs - the sprint - were dealt with, and we entered the "marathon" part of recovery, she was still there, helping us grout our bathroom tiles and paint our exterior. I am still amazed at the dedication she showed in helping us out, complete strangers on the day she showed up.

Throughout the cleanup and rebuild, we learned that we had a lot in common. Truly, I have no idea how we hadn't met her sooner! We not only shared certain personality attributes and past experiences, but our social circles actually had a significant overlaps.

On the days where we weren't working - for weather reasons, lack of energy, or just needing a break, we would often just hang out and do non-tornado stuff - visiting the state fair, roaming Asian grocery stores, attending the local Renaissance Festival together. When Porter decorated a cake for the first time ever, it was for her birthday party.

If it weren't for the tornado, who knows when we would have met her, or if it would have been in such a way as to actually get to know her, rather than a brief introduction at an event.

I really want to thank you guys! My tweeps, and the local nerd/geek community. You've made getting through this much easier on our heads! - Twitter, Tue May 24 13:06:18 UTC 2011

"A brief introduction at an event" was exactly how we knew Peter, who would go on to be a COMPLETE rock star throughout the clean up and rebuild.

We vaguely knew Peter through the local geek community and Convergence. We knew him as the DJ who would work the sound at local "Geek Partnership Society" movie nights, and I had him friended on Facebook.

When I announced that we had been hit by the tornado, Peter stepped up and volunteered. Not only was he contributing labor, he had vital expertise and equipment, having previously owned a landscaping business - we'd had NO idea!

Peter was also coming at this from a place of understanding - he knew what it was like to buy a house, then be faced with unexpected, major repairs. After he purchased his house, he discovered mold in the basement, water leeching through cement walls, and all of the fallout from that. He had to pull out the drywall, re-coat concrete and more... while dealing with a mold allergy.

Having been through that sort of situation, he had a good idea of what we were going through in our brand new house. As he put it, he was delighted to help.

In addition to our mess, he was able to use his equipment to help several others. His ex-girlfriend's parents lived a few blocks from us, and their vehicle was stuck between two fallen trees. He was able to use his truck - formerly a plow truck - to move the trees enough out of the way, that traffic could move through that street.

Peter showed up within a day or two of the tornado, and was just amazing. He used his towing dolly to bring my poor, beaten up car to my father in law's house - out of the area, out of the way, and safe. I still remember the relief I felt, watching him drive off with my car, knowing that the car was on the road to recovery.

I LOVE BEING A NERD! I LOVE THE LOCAL GEEK COMMUNITY! You guys are awesome! - Twitter, Tue May 24 16:41:33 UTC 2011

That sentiment was one that I shared with my Twitter followers - probably ad nauseam - across the months that followed.

As Melissa / Chebutykin put it, in response to one of those tweets - "Our geek community rules mightily, doesn't it?"

Yes. Yes, it does.

While heavy equipment hadn't crossed my mind in the day or two following the tornado, we would find ourselves constantly grateful for all of the different ways that Peter was able to utilize his, in the cleanup and rebuild efforts.

He used his truck to pull our HUGE tree stump down the alley, to a point where it could be collected by the tree debris removal crews.

Peter with our Tree Stump

He used his bobcat to pull out all of the random earth and debris that were piled up under the original deck, and his dump truck to haul it to the county waste transfer station. .

We didn't know anything about building a patio, so Peter's knowledge was invaluable there. He calculated what materials - sand and gravel - we'd need for the base, let us know where to order it from, and directed us in what we'd need to do. Using his bobcat, he leveled the yard for us, and hauled the sand and gravel to the new patio areas... spending hours on this, in 100+ degree weather.

Like I said, a total rock star.

Had he been completely able bodied when doing all of this, it still would have been amazing and over-the-top generous and kind, especially as we were only about one step removed from being strangers, at the point the tornado hit... but he wasn't.

Peter had suffered a major bicep injury just a few short months before the tornado. The bicep hadn't ripped completely away from the bone, but it was torn up enough that he could only lift about 5 lbs at the time it happened, and shouldn't have been lifting more than 20 or so lbs at the time of the tornado.

... not that it stopped him from pushing it WAY too far, in his efforts to help us out!

Stubborn, bad ass, and awe-inspiring... even if we do hope it's the last time he ever risks serious injury on our behalf again!

The strain on his already injured bicep wasn't his only fallout from the tornado cleanup - while hauling our tree stump, the transmission on his truck overheated, and he ended up having to replace his torque converter - not cheap.

He's been ridiculously gracious and understanding about us not being able to contribute much (if anything) to the repair - we'll be digging out from the tornado repair costs for the next five years or so.

Beyond the immediate cleanup, Peter was a huge help in designing our deck and landscape design. He was such a source of calm to us throughout the whole thing, so reassuring and ... steady. When he came over on a rainy June day to help us figure out a game plan, I swear it was part therapy session.

That was such a special day to us. The mail had arrived shortly after he showed up, and there was an envelope from Anime Twin Cities in there - a local group that runs an Anime convention in the same hotel as Convergence.

Now, as far as anime goes... I watched Astroboy as a kid. As adults, we were invited to watch a fairly mainstream anime movie with a friend, a couple years before the tornado... and that's about it. I didn't want to be rude and open mail while we were in the middle of our "consultation" with him... but our curiosity was definitely piqued.

Well, I almost fell over when I opened that envelope. It was a check for $1000 towards our tornado repairs, courtesy of their charity arm.

I cried, and could barely get the words out to tell Porter and Peter what it was. I think I ended up just handing the check over, speechless.

BLOWN AWAY by the kindness and generosity of the local geek community. Just received a donation from Anime TC that brought me to tears. / "Thank you" just doesn't even come close. I don't even know what to say. 1st time we've ever needed to accept charity ... I just... / I just don't have the words. We are racking up a HUGE karmic debt, and appreciate you all SO much. Looking forward to paying it forward. / You geeks make it hard for us to be misanthropes. Nothing but MAD love and respect for you. Proud to be part of such an amazing community. - Twitter, Sat Jun 18 22:27:04 UTC 2011

To this day, I'm still amazed at the generosity, especially considering that we had never even attended any of their events.

It was explained to me that as a member of the geek community, we're all family - regardless of what "flavor" of geeks or nerds anyone happens to be. Anime Twin Cities was looking to help out people in this wonderful community, and we were suggested to them.

Their generosity didn't stop there. When they heard of what happened to Peter's truck, in the course of helping us out, they also cut HIM a check, covering 1/3 of the total bill!

I'm still amazed and touched by the generosity... and I still find the timing of it amazing. Peter got to experience their actions twice, both being present when we received a check, and when he received one, himself!

We ended up spending Christmas with Peter and his friends, when he hosted a Doctor Who Christmas Special marathon. Great times!

160

That house party was where we met his girlfriend, Michele, who I just adore. They're both such wonderful people. I was happy to see that this guy... someone we'd only known in passing, but who'd really saved our asses over the tornado - was with someone equally good hearted. Love them!

I'm really not good at the whole stranger-to-friend process, so who knows if we would have ever gotten to know these amazing people, beyond those brief introductions at events. How was I to know that the guy who handled sound at movie nights was such an amazing, selfless person, or that a friend of a friend would not only be so driven in helping us, but end up becoming one of the few "chick friends" I've ever had?

It makes me look at strangers a whole new way... you never know who you'll meet. It's sort of weird to be thankful to a natural disaster for not only meeting these people, but for teaching us anti-social misanthropes a few lessons along the way!

At it turned out, Anime Detour found out about us through a couple of our friends, Dave and Charlotte... and it wouldn't be the last time that they came to our rescue over the tornado.

Two weeks after the tornado - with my car still incapacitated - we found ourselves in a pretty crappy situation.

When we stopped at our house to finally fix the air conditioning, the water pump blew up on our only car, right at the end of the work day. We were stranded at our house, in a heat wave, with no air conditioning - a dangerous situation for me, as I physically can't handle high temperatures.

A comedy of errors ensued .

As Porter worked on fixing the air conditioner - the temperature in the house had soared to over 90 degrees, and it was climbing - I took a cab to the local auto store to get the needed part.

I had to wait in line for over 30 minutes, as the heat wave had driven people out in droves to repair or replace their air conditioners, or replace coolant. It was the only auto parts store in the area, and it was a mess. Right after I left with the part, they closed for the night.

Well, it turned out that they had sold us a broken part.

As we were unable to fix the car at that point, I started looking up car rental places... all of whom had also closed for the night.

Gave up on rental car companies, cabbed to hotel. Homeless AND carless now, for those keeping score. -Twitter, Wed Jun 08 01:40:16 UTC 2011

Dave and Char - two of the busiest people I know - live about 25 minutes from us, in the opposite direction as the hotel we were staying in. That night, they were in separate cars, on opposite ends of the city from each other, and nowhere near us.

Yet, when these two heard of the bind we were in, they juggled logistics to drive out to us and loan us one of their two cars.

Seriously. Dropped it right off to our hotel.

I swear, the time since #NoMi has been like an extended Nerd/Geek edition "It Gets Better" PSA for us. SO much love for/from our community! / I don't think that I've ever been more proud to be a nerd, or my husband proud to be a geek. Completely at a loss for words. - Twitter, Wed Jun 08 03:38:03 UTC 2011

Luckily (?), Porter noticed that Char's car had severely worn rear shock mounts, and was later able to fix them for her. With the ridiculously huge karmic debt we were racking up, it was great to be able to start returning some of the favor!

Members of the geek community had our backs in so many ways, I'm worried that there is no way I'll be able to do it all justice, with these words. I'm also dreading the possibility of missing anyone! We were dealing with so many acts of kindness, in a time of such stress...

I think a big thing inspiring the geek community to come out for us so spectacularly was their ability to relate to us, in various ways... Peter with his molding basement, Tara with her childhood tornado... I'm guessing that there was a fair amount of "we've been there" and "that could have been us".

162

As people who have been frequently judged and misunderstood for being different, it was amazing to have this support, from people who actually understood us and could relate to us.

One example that stands out in my mind was the "House" issue... and there is no way for me to explain this without sounding really... dumb.

Porter and I have our routines, which are important to us. Things are done in a certain way, on certain days/dates. When something ends up being missed, it feels a bit... discombobulating.

Monday nights are "House" nights, and we plan our schedule around watching it, our favorite serial show. I mean, to the point where I gave up on the idea of training for roller skating, as their adult practices fell on Monday nights.

The day after the tornado was not only a "House" night, but it was the last one of the season, it being the season finale. We were prepared for it to be the last "House Night" for a while, but we hadn't been ready to miss it entirely. Late that afternoon, I realized that we would be missing it, and tweeted disappointment about it.

Tom - a local member of the Convergence community - was able to relate. As the father of a teenage boy with Aspergers, he had a pretty clear idea of what it's like to have routine disrupted. I'm sure he had a pretty good idea of what kind of hell it was for us to have to move between hotels, etc... in a way that many other people probably can't comprehend.

So, Tom - who I only knew through Twitter - not only recorded it for us, he went to the further efforts of editing the commercials out, AND delivering it to us!

It may seem like a small gesture to others, but he was able to restore a bit of normalcy for us - no small feat, given the circumstances.

Just short of two weeks later, another friend took care of us in a similar way.

Shawn Bakken is one of our local Mensan friends - great guy. He was one of the first locals that I met, and has been a friend of ours ever since.

163

If the name sounds familiar, it's because he went really far in the first season of "Beauty and the Geek". I tease him mercilessly about it - and other things - but only because I've come to see him as sort of an adopted older brother. I tease because I care!

Shawn and I share a love of the X-Men franchise. He's more into the comics, I adore the movies, having never cracked a comic book in my life. We'd both very much been looking forward to the fifth X-Men movie, "First Class".

Well, when the tornado hit... going to the movie became demoted on the priority list. Where the tornado had rendered us instantly destitute, going to a movie was a luxury that we just couldn't afford, no matter how long we'd been waiting for it.

Aside from X-Men and little membership cards that "prove" that we're smart, Shawn and I have something else in common - being stupid about sports injuries. He was all gimped up with a recurring knee injury, and was unable to help with the cleanup, as a result. I think he felt bad about that, even though, really... we definitely didn't want anyone hurting themselves on our behalf!

So, a few days after the tornado, he emailed to tell us that he wanted to take us out to watch the new X-Men movie, as his "non-donation" (His words).

The distraction was sorely needed. That night, we were able to forget that we were temporarily homeless tornado victims... we were just two geeks and a nerd, watching a super hero movie.

That is, until one character started up with the tornadoes. What is it with tornadoes in super hero movies, anyway?

Anyway, Shawn was great. Aside from the movie distraction, he also came by several times in the days following the tornado, to keep us company, lend moral support and essentially hold our hands through it. 35 minute drive each way for him to do so!

He wasn't the only Mensan to help us out. Jennifer - another local - came out several times, helping to clear debris, provide moral support, and yell at the occasional vulture.

When the word went out about what happened, Mensan friends from around the country spread the news, sharing links to my cookbooks, and urging their friends to buy copies to help us out. It was kind of amazing to see this network go active like that.

Another far-off Mensan friend contacted me to let me know that her fiancé -another Mensan - worked for FEMA, and could help answer any questions we may have about what to expect, going forward. He was great - offering us "concierge service" - he was just a phone call away, if we had any questions, concerns, or "ran into any bureaucratic walls" along the way.

Additionally, he provided me with some great links about FEMA and the Small Business Association, and the various ways that they may be able to help... which I was able to share with friends, neighbors, and whoever else could use them.

It was a bit strange for us to be in that position - neither one of us has ever been someone that "knows someone". Porter hadn't been in any fraternity, I'd never been in any sort of sorority, and neither of us has ever been well connected, or benefitted from any sort of organized network. We were used to being the people who would never be those who were on the positive end of "It's not what you know, it's WHO you know".

This was sort of... majestic. It was like something out of a movie... or realizing that we had our very own fairy godmother(s). A LOT of them.

There's another category of help that we received, that still blows me away to this day. For the most part, this group can be summed up as "Completely random strangers who found us by way of someone that we'd worked with in the past"

About a year before the tornado, I worked with Paul and Storm - a geeky comedic music duo - to create a Tardis cake for Wil Wheaton when they performed a show together in Minneapolis. The show featured other geek royalty - cast members from Mystery Science Theater 3000, Adam Savage from Myth Busters, Neil Gaiman, and more. The show - Wootstock - traveled to a few cities, and had fans around the country.

The Minneapolis show was a ton of fun, and - as a result of this geek royalty tweeting about me - I ended up meeting a ton of cool people from around the country, on Twitter.

A couple days after the tornado, I decided that it would be best if I just blogged about what had happened, answering a lot of the questions that were being asked repeatedly - what happened, are we ok, and what we need, moving forward.

I suggested that those who wanted to help could buy my cookbooks, letting me earn my way out of this mess. I've never had to accept charity before, and was uncomfortable with the idea.

In addition, added Paypal donation link, as some close friends had been asking how they could help out in a more direct way, already owning my books. I was thinking that the odd friend may chip in $5-10, maybe up to $30. That's what I try to do, when I am directed to such a post. I was thinking that if we could even get one night of cheapo hotel paid for, that would be amazing.

The first donation covered that hotel night - $50... and it was from someone that I didn't know.

We were stunned.

A few more donations came in. $5-10 donations from strangers, some larger donations from friends, and then ... another $50 from a stranger. Then $100 from a stranger... and another $100 from a stranger. One donation came from as far away as England!

By the time the flow of donations ended, we'd raised $1375 - in three days. Enough to pay for about 3 weeks of hotel stays!

Some of the donations had comments attached:

"This isn't charity - because, somehow, I know for sure, you'd be moved to do the same thing for a stranger like me if the situation were reversed. Wishing you and yours a w-a-y- better second half to 2011."

"Hang in there, guys. Hope this helps!"

"Loved seeing the stories about your TARDIS cake last year (via @wilw and @donttrythis); so sorry to hear about your home!"

"Best of luck rebuilding! I was referred by Bill Corbett!"

I cried. We had strangers rooting for us from afar. Given some of the comments, we realized that the strangers were finding the blog by way of the Wootstock stars, some of whom had retweeted my blog entry link.

Just another example of how amazing the geek community is.

I've always donated to things like this ... when they happen to *other* people. I've always thought that my donation - just whatever I could afford - was simply money that would help the person move forward from whatever crisis had fallen upon them.

Never in a million years would I have imagined the power of even the smallest of donations, from a stranger. Beyond the money itself, just the gesture of caring, the little notes rooting for us - I was blown away. It meant so much to us... I just don't even have the words.

When I was growing up, constantly ridiculed for being different... I had no idea that THIS is what being a nerd would eventually mean. My childhood, I was so isolated from other people... I would never have pictured that some day, other people like me - from around the world - would form such a community.

That friends could be made from thousands of miles away, and that one day... all of that hatred and exclusion that I'd been subjected to would be so starkly contrasted with this. With an outpouring of love and support from complete strangers.

I still have no idea how to repay that kindness, short of paying it forward. I hope that we can be the people that these people seem to think that we are, people worthy of their concern and charity.

10 months after the tornado, once the most urgent of repairs and rebuild had been taken care of - and with the next tornado season upon us - we decided to buy a chainsaw. While we are unlikely to need it ourselves, we wanted to be prepared in case this happens to someone else in the community. Armed with this experience - and all of the DIY skills it ended up bringing - we're looking forward to being able to pay it forward.

It seems kind of silly and stupid right now, but when the donations started coming in, I decided that it was of the UTMOST urgency to send customized thank you cards.

I thought that sending generic, stock thank you cards would seem so trite, while I was still super overwhelmed at the kindness of strangers. We may have been temporarily homeless and turning feral, but we couldn't be rude!

So, I decided that the best way to personally thank people would be to take a photo of us in front of the giant debris pile that was building in front of our house. Nothing says "we appreciate you" like a photo of the unidentifiable remains of our deck, porch, and part of our roof, right?

I mean, really... what would Martha Stewart do?

Surreal moment to start the day: "Crap, we forgot to take our picture in front of our debris pile, & it'll probably get taken today" - Tue May 31 12:00:10 UTC 2011

Yes, I was worried about getting the photo for THANK YOU CARDS ... at 7am. - Twitter, Tue May 31 12:01:09 UTC 2011

While I was supposed to be writing, I was more concerned with what color scheme would be most appropriate for tornado donation thank you cards. Blues and greys? Something sunnier and happier? Match the color to one from the photo? It's not really a subject I'd ever come across, either through graphic design & card design or wedding industry etiquette!

What IS the suggested time line for getting thank you cards out, given that situation? It took us about a month to receive the cards, sign them, and mail them out. That felt rude, but I had to balance "Get them out fast" with "we can't afford to pay an expensive printer or for rush shipping".

Should you ever find yourself in the position to make use of post-disaster thank you card etiquette rules that don't exist, here's what we came up with:

- Make the thank you personal.

- Get the cards out to donors and volunteers as soon as possible. People will expect that you have other stuff on your plate, but try to pick away at signing them when you can.

- When it comes to card design, try to offset the destruction in the photo with happy colors, as appropriate. While neon pink may not be appropriate, a nice sky blue can be positive and go well with your newly de-canopied sky. For a trim color, we suggest sampling a color from the photo itself - in our case, green from the grass.

... now you know!

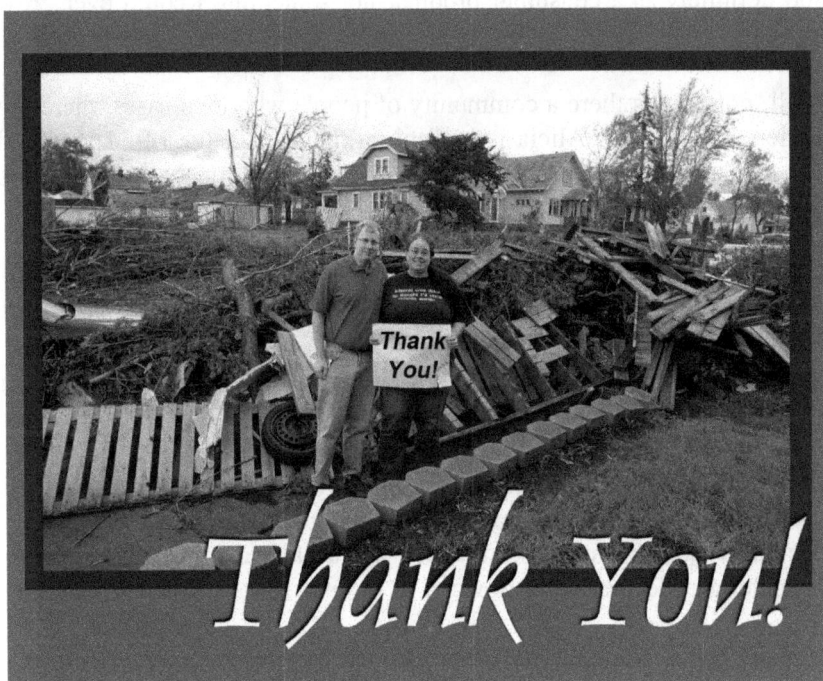

Suck it, Martha Stewart!

This spring, we will have our first glimpse of what will be a beautiful, lasting reminder of the generosity - and diversity - of the geek community.

Just as we were surprised to learn that Peter had previously owned a landscaping company, we were pleasantly surprised to learn that another local Convergence acquaintance - Alicia - was heavily involved in the iris community.

I had no idea that there was an iris community. I liked irises, we had some at my childhood home... but that's about all I knew about them. As quickly as I took to floral design, I've never been lucky with planting flowers. As a result, I kind of look at them as this weird, magical, mysterious thing... and definitely as a consumer product, not something I could ever grow myself.

Well, not only is there a community of people who love irises, there are societies for them! Alicia is not only a member of the Minnesota and American Iris Societies, she's training to be a judge for the American Iris Society.

See, you learn something new every day!

Alicia got a hold of me in August, offering to donate us some iris bulbs. She was participating in an iris dig (Again, who knew?), and had a long list of available varieties.

Porter and I were a little giddy, wading through photos of different iris varieties, deciding what we liked best. After all of the very boring-but-necessary design and rebuild work, it was actually fun to decide on something as decorative as flowers.

It really drove home the idea that we were starting to emerge from this destruction hell, and made us look forward to the following year. Unlike most of our design and construction choices, we wouldn't see the result of this immediately. By the time spring came, we'd have no idea of what varieties we planted, and where they were, so we looked forward to these "surprise" bursts of color.

I'm not sure that I've ever felt like such a noob, as I did when Alicia was patiently explaining how to plant them, and how to care for them. When she handed me the bags of bulbs - plant matter attached - I felt like someone was handing me a newborn baby, and I was afraid of dropping it. As far as the plants go in that analogy, I was dreading the idea that I'd probably end up killing them, per my history with planting flowers.

I have no idea how she put up with me, but she did. Not only was she so kind to think of us in the first place, she was incredibly gracious and patient with my... non-green thumb of death.

With her gift, we were inspired to create new flower beds along out sidewalk, specifically for them. We were further inspired to buy some other flower bulbs, to contrast and compliment the irises - tulips, hyacinths, crocuses... I planted them all, and held my breath.

As I complete this book, getting ready to send it to print, the tulips and hyacinths are in full bloom. I feel like I won some sort of battle against mother nature... or maybe "she" is just being generous, given what nature threw at us last year. Ooooor maybe "she" is tapping out, after what we did to the tree that was thrown at us? I don't know, but the ideas sure make for interesting mental images, huh?

I do know that my little victory is gorgeous. There's no way I would have planted them, without Alicia's encouragement in that area. The iris greenery is coming in now - tall leaves, no flowers yet - but I look forward to their future.

Big thanks to Alicia, not only for the donation, but for the new learning experience, encouragement, and for bringing some color back to our house.

North Minneapolis Post Tornado Watch

While we were being taken care of by our awesome community - and extended "family" - of nerds, geeks, and Mensans, there were many people in north Minneapolis who went without that kind of support.

You know, throughout writing this book, I've usually had a pretty good idea of what needs to be said about any certain issue. I have huge amounts of saved tweets, facebook statuses, and emails that frame the story for me, my own words throughout the whole post-tornado ordeal.

When it comes to the North Minneapolis Post Tornado Watch page, I just don't even know where to start. This grassroots community effort was just so... monumental. I have no idea how they managed to pull it all off, and I have no idea how to do it all justice.

The NMPTW started as a Facebook page with a corresponding Twitter account. It quickly became a hub for those affected by the tornado, those who wanted to find out if loved ones were ok, and those who wanted to help. The page was started the same day as the tornado, and very quickly gained a huge following.

Within a day of the tornado, the page also set up a google info page, keeping track of such vital information as shelter locations, where people could find meals, where people could find a shower, home renter information, and more.

Where - for the entire year following the tornado - any news we heard from the city was filtered through the media, and rife with spin and self-congratulatory nonsense, this Facebook page became THE go-to place for up to the minute information about what was going on.

The google page was such an amazing resource - they had configured a map with various symbols indicating various different resources, with full details about each available when clicked.

To give you an idea about how in depth they got with the resource information, one of them included the message

"North Minneapolis residents without power, you can charge your cell phones, make phone calls, and use some computerss for internet access at the University of Minnesota's Urban Research and Outreach/Engagement Center (UROC) , 2001 Plymouth Ave North (On Plymouth and Penn). Contact number is 612-626-UROC (8762). You can use facilities between 8am and 5pm cst. More venues to be posted as we receive info"

As a logistics nerd myself, I can't tell you how impressed I was with the level of care and detail put into this. I've never seen anything like it in my life!

If you needed clothes, food, information on shelters, how to find transportation to the shelters or disaster center... I honestly can't think of anything that they did NOT cover.

For those on the other side of the disaster, there was a lot of information on various charities and groups locally, how to donate, and what they needed. Certain shelters needed hygiene items, others needed diapers, many needed non-perishable foods... If you had something - or money to donate - the page made it spectacularly easy for people to determine who to approach with that aid. Additionally, there was a long list of volunteer opportunities, along with the information and contact information for each.

Much of this information was compiled onto resource sheets for handing out to affected residents, as not everyone had internet access. Through the Facebook page, they were able to obtain not only the volunteer legwork to blanket the areas with these sheets, but also allow people who were willing to print the sheets themselves, to do so.

As the people helping out reported back with specific needs on certain blocks of the affected area, another map was configured to reflect those, as well. If a certain block needed resource sheets, it was mapped - to help others decide where they should go.

The Facebook page itself was responsible for directing help to individuals, as well. Someone could write to the page, requesting a certain type of help needed, and the page would post it anonymously, on behalf of the tornado victim. Some people needed certain sizes of donated clothes for their kids, having lost everything in the tornado. Others needed personal care items, help with cleanup, or even just contractor referrals.

While the City of Minneapolis had been pretty worthless when it came to any amount of communication or logistics whatsoever, this Facebook page, Twitter account, and resource page were started by one guy... living in New York City.

Let that process for a second. Some Joe Blow on the other side of the country was far more helpful, communicative, and efficient than the city staff in the area affected. To put a finer point on this, he wasn't some professional in any sort of disaster or logistics related career... he was a DJ.

Yes. A DJ on the other side of the country ran circles around the city when it came to disaster communication and resource management/dissemination.

Peter Kerre, you are an amazing, AMAZING person.

He didn't end up doing it alone, soon being joined by other amazing, brilliant, caring, and ridiculously generous people. Mandi Studler, Genesia Williams, Shane Williams, and Anthony Newby soon joined his efforts, and together... well, they worked miracles.

As they tirelessly worked to gather and share resources - employing the best grasp of mass communication skills I think I've ever even heard of - they also planned their own donation drive.

"Super Saturday" occurred on June 11, 2011 - 3 weeks after the tornado.

The people behind the page obtained the use of a warehouse, and invited people to bring donations for the tornado victims - food for both humans and pets, bottled drinks, hygiene items, etc.

Taking the non-perishable food items we rescued from our kitchen to donate to North Minneapolis Post Tornado watch 's big collection today. We're not gonna have a kitchen to use them in for a WHILE, not worth storing them in our limited available space in the meantime. Can do others more good than us! - Facebook, June 11, 2011

In only 12 hours, they received 26,130 donated items, at a total weight of 14,224 lbs, as well as $705 worth of gift cards. Over the 24 hours that followed, the items were picked up by various shelters that were housing tornado victims.

Amazing. It's absolutely amazing what good people can do, when they really put their mind to it.

They followed up with a second "Super Saturday" in October, this one as a fall clothing drive... also very successful.

Amazing work. We were so incredibly lucky to have this small team of people SO invested in looking out for the area.

While I'll get into my issues with the city in a coming chapter, I'd like to point out that while these heroes were doing such wonderful work, the city refused to work with them. When the tornado page group offered to work with the city, and to disseminate any information that the city wanted to put out, they were repeatedly shot down.

Months after the tornado, some city staff agreed to meet with Peter - apparently more as an effort to placate him, than actually come up with solutions. It was disheartening not only for the people working on behalf of the page, but those of us who the North Minneapolis Post Tornado Watch had been working so tirelessly to help.

In the weeks following the tornado, these volunteers barely slept. By contrast, the city crews took a long weekend off from cleanup, just one week after the tornado - before even the most immediate cleanup needs were finished.

Unlike most of the other organizations involved with the recovery efforts, these people had no budget. They volunteered their time, not even being paid salaries - again, unlike the other organizations.

Personally - and I'm sure that many people would agree with me - each and every person involved with running this page deserves some sort of humanitarian award. I've never seen such heart, drive, compassion and tenacity in my life.

The Neighborhood Cookout

Several days following the tornado, I started to hear murmurs of people getting together to host neighborhood cookouts. It was a great idea - we had no kitchen, many people were still without electricity, and the shelters were really being stretched to the limits of their budgets and capabilities.

Beyond that, it was seen as a good way to bring community together, and have a bit of an enjoyable time, amidst all of the... shit. I'm sure that being surrounded by that level of destruction was really wearing on everyone, to say the least. I know that we were pretty much holding on to our own sanity by a thread, by that point.

Fresh off the shock of receiving donations from strangers, we wanted to help out, as well. I was operating under a bizarre mix of stress, hopelessness, shame (at having to accept charity), and pride in our geek community. I also felt guilty at accepting donations, and wanted to get RIGHT on paying it forward.

I may have been fairly useless when it came to lifting, hauling, and repair work... but I could COOK.

Through the North Minneapolis Post Tornado Watch page, I was put into contact with "Aztec" Alex Rodriguez, a guy who was organizing a large cookout.

Alex had been watching the coverage of the tornado, and just felt the need to help in any way he could. He discussed the idea of a cookout with his boss, who he'd grown up with, and who used to live in North Minneapolis, and decided to go ahead with it.

From that point, it snowballed. Other former northsiders from his childhood joined in, one of them donating $200 in burgers and hot dogs. That donation inspired Alex and his boss to do more, so they convinced Sam's Club to donate a bunch of food as well.

While he had originally planned to stand on a street corner and hand out hot dogs, it became a much bigger event, with all of these people coming together to help out their former community. They arranged to use the parking lot of a local funeral home, and set the date and time.

The day before the cookout, I signed on. After tossing around some ideas, we decided that I would make a big pot of jambalaya. It was relatively cheap to make, healthy, filling comfort food - very important. Additionally, it was something that I thought I'd be able to make, given our logistical issues. No kitchen, cooking it in a parking lot...

Add in that I'd never made a huge batch of my jambalaya before, and... yeah. We were in for an adventure. It just felt like something that we HAD to do. So, at 6:30 in the morning, just 6 short days after the tornado, we left our crappy little hotel room, and headed to the store to buy the groceries we'd need - $192 worth, in total.

I had to gasp when we saw the total, and hope that people who had donated to us wouldn't be offended by the expenditure. I tried to put that worry aside, assuring myself that we were acting as good stewards of this donated money.

Soon to become a ridiculous amount of Jambalaya

I prepped the ingredients on a fold out banquet table in our living room, bagging as I went, and putting them into a cooler with ice. I may have been stretching food laws in doing this, but I was definitely safe about everything, rest assured! All told, it took about 2 hours to chop all of the veggies and meat by hand: 15 lbs each of chicken breast & smoked sausage, 5 heads celery, 16 peppers, 10 onions.. Yeah.

We packed the car with the ingredient coolers, the tent we used for selling my books at farmer's markets, and a propane tank. We decided to use our turkey fryer and huge stock pots - 7.5 and 10 gallon - which we used for home brewing. Our brew mash paddle made a pretty badass "wooden spoon", so we sanitized it and brought it along.

We drove the 4 blocks or so to the funeral home, planning to set up about an hour before the cookout began.

As we arrived, we saw the others setting up the largest outdoor grill I've ever seen in my life. I'm talking industrial sized monster of a grill. I have no idea where they got it, or how they transported it to the cookout site.

We set up the tent, table, and turkey fryer, and cranked some Eurodance tunes. I'll tell you this much, there may be no experience more surreal than cooking something like gallons of jambalaya, outdoors, in a funeral home parking lot, surrounded by tornado destruction... to the tune of "Cotton Eyed Joe". Add to that, the fact that I was stirring it with what looked like a canoe oar? I'm sure it was quite the image, haha!

Making jambalaya in a 10 gallon pot, with a brew paddle.

I don't have any experience working in a restaurant or cooking for that many people... or in those kind of conditions... so there was a LOT of finger crossing going on. I was dreading that it wouldn't cook up right.

I was making my tried and true recipe for jambalaya, only 5x the recipe, and with a small tweak. With shrimp allergies being as common as they are, I swapped it out for extra chicken and sausage. Good thing, too – LOADS of shrimp allergies that day! .

Between our tent and the other tents set up, with all of Alex's friends and volunteers - the atmosphere wasn't just pleasant, it was... jovial. Unless you looked beyond the confines of this parking lot, you'd never have guessed the circumstances behind this cookout.

A few friends of ours arrived to help out - Mark & Heather, who had been there for us within hours of the tornado, along with their son.

Three local Mensa friends - Barb, Karen, and Ron - showed up as well. We were so happy to have the moral support and good company, this was shaping up to be a great day.

We were both shocked when we found out that they came bearing gifts. Karen and Barb presented us with envelopes, while Ron... Ron got very "Mensan" about it all!

Ron presented us with a box, saying that he was inspired by a post apocalyptic sci fi novel called "Dies the Fire". Within the box, we found various beverage related items - instant coffee, instant tea, whitener, sugar packets. He explained that in this book, one of the characters came upon an ammo can full of foodstuffs, amidst the destruction detailed in the book.

While neither one of us had heard of the book - much less read it - we were so touched at the thought that he had put into this survival kit for us. So much awesome.

The money that Barb and Karen gave us more than covered our grocery purchases that day, which made us breathe a sigh of relief. Barb mentioned that she wanted us to use the donation to take care of the cats, which we did - more on that in a bit.

Anyway, yes - Jambalaya.

After a bit of drama as the result of a miscalculation - the jambalaya batch did NOT fit in the 10 gallon pot, so we had to use the 7.5 gallon pot as backup - the jambalaya bubbled away, and we prepared for the arrival of our guests.

Well, the jambalaya turned out beyond good, it was my best batch ever – and I make great jambalaya! It went over SO well, and put smiles on an awful lot of faces that day.... it was such a nice change from all of the "non perishable food" and takeout junk that I know we – and most others – had been stuck living with.

Woo! The Jambalaya got a "hallelujah!", and the guy came back for seconds! - Twitter, Sat May 28 18:43:08 UTC 2011

One guy had gone up to Penn to sing praises of the jambalaya, telling people they should come. SO glad it's going over well. In MN!! #NoMi - Twitter, Sat May 28 19:23:19 UTC 2011

"My neighbor told me that I need to get some of this Jambalaya. She's from the south, and said it's the real deal!" "I'm Canadian!" #NoMi - Twitter, Sat May 28 20:32:51 UTC 2011

People were smiling, everyone got a hearty meal, and there was a great feeling of community.

The Jambalaya ended up serving 270 people. 270!!!! The cookout people estimated that about 500 people were served that afternoon, in total.

Afterwards, we were so pumped. We wished that we had the spare money to do it again, but also realized that we would need to be very careful, what with our own tornado bills piling up.

For the day though, we figured that $192 wouldn't make or break us, when we were SO far beyond what our insurance will cover. Given that it'll take us 5 years to pay off the tornado, we look at it as $192 of ... therapy. It was very therapeutic. I hope no one that donated or bought books are upset about the expense – we needed that experience, looking back on it. It really did us a world of good to get away from our own wreck, and help others.

It was fun, too. Definitely boosted our spirits, and I'm sure it boosted a lot more that day. 270 servings! I'm still shocked that we pulled that off!

So very thankful to Alex and his crew, not only for the spirit and generosity that they showed in setting it all up in the first place - and feeding 500 people! - but also for allowing us to participate. They really made us - a couple of complete strangers - feel completely welcome. This chapter may be about the ways that the tornado brought out the best in people like Alex... but he also helped it bring out the best in US.

So, I'd like to share my original recipe, that I based the mega batch off of. Even without multiplying the recipe, this makes a ton of Jambalaya.

With flavoring the stock as I do, and with all of the chopping involved, it is a bit more labor intensive than the average dinner recipe. I like making a huge batch of this on a weekend, then pretty much living on it for a week or two – it makes GREAT leftovers! It freezes fairly well, but never lasts long enough around here to make it to the freezer

Oh, and if you don't trust a jambalaya recipe coming from a Canadian, know this – we got a TON of compliments on us providing "the real deal" that day!

Chicken, Shrimp, & Sausage Jambalaya

2 lbs large raw shrimp. (deveined, shell still on)
8 cups chicken stock
2 lbs Boneless skinless chicken breast, cubed
2 tbsp vegetable oil
2 lbs Andouille sausage (substitute kielbassa if unavailable)
2 large onions, chopped
2 green bell peppers, chopped
1 red bell pepper, chopped
1 jalapeno, chopped
4-6 ribs celery, chopped
1 small can tomato paste
2 28 oz cans diced tomatoes
6-8 cloves garlic, pressed
3 tsp cayenne
2 tsp black pepper
1 tsp each: dried oregano, dried sage, dried thyme, crushed bay leaves
1 tsp salt
2 lb bag rice

Start out by flavoring your chicken stock. (This is optional, but very much worth the effort) Peel all 2 lbs of your shrimp, putting shells and tails in a medium or large pot (not the LARGE pot you'll need to make the jambalaya though!). Cover raw shrimp and keep it in the fridge for later. Cover shrimp shells with the chicken stock.

Optionally, feel free to add any celery you have left after reserving 4-6 ribs, some onion, or whatever else you'd like to flavor the stock with. I like just celery and onion in mine, leaving additional flavors for later! Heat stock on low for 30 minutes to an hour or so, until it smells and tastes amazing. Strain everything out, and reserve the stock.

In the meantime, brown chicken in vegetable oil, set aside.

In LARGE, heavy pot: brown sausage. Add onions, peppers, and sausage. Cook vegetables until soft.

Add tomato paste to vegetables. Cook, stirring frequently, until tomato paste starts to caramelize/ brown a bit. This will add a lot of flavor to the finished jambalaya. Keep a close eye on it, do NOT allow it to burn!

Add diced tomatoes, cooked chicken breast, shrimp stock, and all of the herbs and spices – everything remaining, aside from the rice & raw shrimp. Turn heat down to low, and simmer for 10-20 minutes. Taste, and adjust seasonings if desired.

Add rice to pot. Cover and cook on low for 20 minutes or so, stirring fairly frequently – you don't want it to burn onto the bottom of the pot! Remove lid, allow to cook uncovered for another 5- 10 minutes or so, depending on your rice. When rice is almost cooked through, add shrimp to pot and stir well. Cook until rice is done, and shrimp is cooked through.

Serve hot!

A few days later, we were at the store, picking up some supplies for the cats - cat litter, food, a couple small catnip toys for them to play with - when both sets of our eyes fell upon a series of boxes.

They were different components to a modular cat structure set. You'd buy the pieces you want, and set them together using thin pvc pipes and fittings. There were tubes and little cubbies and corner hideout units... just awesome.

With Barb's request that we use her donation to take care of the cats... we got a little stupid with it. I mean, we spoil our cats rotten, but the purchase that day went far beyond what we would have ever spent, if not for the cicrumstances.

We may not have entirely been in our right minds at the time, and we felt so guilty about the cats being housed away from use for so long, and... we rationalized that we had her permission to.

So on a rainy day a few days later, feeling pretty beaten down about the whole tornado situation - we hauled those boxes out.

It was a lot of fun, assembling these pieces, and planning for this insane, epic cat structure. We planned it to be structurally sound and well balanced. We designed it so that there would be ample perches to look out the patio door, once it was replaced.

We felt like a couple of kids playing with toys, and it was SO nice to be able to focus on creating something, rather than all of the destruction around us. Again with the therapy!

As my husband recalls:

"It was a combination of guilt and excitement. I felt guilty because we spent so much money on it. I am a frugal person, and to spend a lot on the best of days is tough for me ... but in tough times it was even more difficult.

I was excited for the cats. They had spent so much time cooped up in a small room, without us, without much to do. This would be their reward for being so good about it. They took it so well, they didn't destroy my dad's furniture or anything like that. They deserved this, and much more.

I remember designing the structure in my head, and talking to Marie about it. We'd discuss how we thought the sleeping structures should be on different levels, and we talked about how high we should make it, and how we'd have to make it sort of pyramid shaped so they can get up and down. It was GIANT KITTY LEGOS. How awesome is that?

At the end, we were constrained by certain features to making the structure a certain shape, but it's still awesome. It's great, they love it, I love it, we all win!"

We were to embarrassed to tell Barb about what we did with her donation for MONTHS afterwards.

When she attended our pi day party - 10 months after the tornado - we finally told her. We were showing people around the house, showing all of the areas that had been repaired. When she was checking out the repairs in our bedroom upstairs, it was impossible to miss this gigantic structure, which had definitely not been there before the tornado.

So, we told her that this was what her donation paid for. We told her about the guilt we felt about the cats, and wanting them to have something cool to come home to, and about our completely childish afternoon assembling it... and she was completely cool with it.

Awesome.

To this day, the cats love it. Almost every horizontal surface is used as napping platforms. They love perching up high, and they love "hiding" in the enclosed areas. There's usually at least one cat in that thing... sometimes all four!

Also, it's nice to have a permanent reminder of her generosity and concern for our cats. I'm sure that all six of us will always treasure it!

Flower Bombed

Right around the time that Alex and his friends were putting together the cookout, another neighborhood effort was underway.

On the day of the tornado, my twitter name wasn't the only one that was trending. Jennifer Emmert - a popular blogger, for "Prior Fat Girl" - was also hit. I'd never heard of her until that day, but started following her when many of our mutual friends used our names together in tweets about the tornado.

Jen had recently lost her mother, and the tornado had taken the flowers that Jen had planted in her memory. When Jen lamented the loss of those flowers - given their meaning to her - other tweeps and bloggers wanted to help replace the flowers.

Jen mentioned that the rest of the neighborhood could use some good cheer, and suggested spreading floral gifts to the rest of the area. That was the beginning of "Project Flower Bomb".

In the week following the tornado, Jen and a few of her friends raised almost $300 in donated cash and supplies. They got together and potted about 130 flower plants, then distributed them to residents in the area. Each potted flower had a tag attached, explaining why they were doing this, how to take care of it, and requesting the recipient to "share the cheer".

We were one of those "flower bombed" in the tornado zone. One of my tweeps - who I'd never met - was involved with the project, and made a special trip to our house, delivering our flower pot herself. It was great to meet her, and put a face to the name!

While I ended up killing the flower (Again with the non-green thumb of death!), we really appreciated the little bit of color that it brought to us, while we had it.

As our house hadn't been occupied for years before we bought it, there had been no flowers growing when that first spring came. With so much to clean up and repair after the tornado, flowers weren't something we were able to get to until much later that year.

It was really nice to see an organized effort aimed specifically to bring cheer to the area. With so much focus on digging out from the debris, funds, logistics, and the rebuild - I can't say that something as simple as smiling was all that high on many people's priority lists, that first week.

Incompetence in the City

Looking back over the past year, it's hard to pinpoint the very first misstep that the city made. There were just so many, that it feels like it's been a constant battle... from day one. I'm sure that an entire book could be written on the subject, but I only have space - and patience! - to touch on a few of the major ones that we were exposed to.

I've never lived anywhere, where the city would actively work against the residents affected by a natural disaster like this. Hell, I've never HEARD of a city that holds its citizens in such low regard, as to cause more headaches, drama, and problems than the disaster itself.

Until our tornado, that is.

Work Issues

There was a LOT of work to go around, not only the first few days after the tornado, but for the coming weeks as well. A LOT. Trees everywhere, most roads impassable, downed power lines everywhere... the whole area was a mess.

The city set up roadblocks fairly early, but completely dropped the ball on the logistics with them. While the area was inaccessible from certain routes - the main ones - it was still possible to access them from more roundabout routes. It came off as a very half-assed attempt - like they merely wanted to give the appearance of doing something,

So, while this served to delay help from volunteers coming to help their friends and families... it did absolutely nothing to slow the flow of the vultures. I can't tell you how frustrating it is to hear from friends who are being held back - and read the many accounts online of people trying to get in to help - while fending off morally bereft salesmen in droves.

The theme of them delaying help from reaching the area reached a low point with the fining of one of the volunteers in the area, Mike Haege of Hastings, Minnesota.

Mike's sister had lived in the area at one point, so they were familiar with the area and its economic situation. As people who frequently volunteered their time to help others, they felt compelled to come help out in the cleanup efforts. He was the owner of a tree trimming company, and was licensed and insured to do tree work in his area.

The evening of the tornado, Mike posted an ad on Craigslist, offering free tree clearing help to tornado victims.

The next morning, Mike decided that he could probably do more good if he were to volunteer with Urban Homeworks - a local nonprofit that was handling cleanup volunteer efforts. He took down his ad and prepared to drive into the city, over an hour away from him.

Not knowing what he was going to encounter, he brought a variety of his professional tree trimming equipment - a bucket truck, wood chipper, chain saw, etc.

Around 10:30 am, he registered with Urban Homeworks. After signing all their waivers and whatnot - was assigned to a team that was charged with clearing tree debris. Their hands were marked to identify them as volunteers, and they were sent on their way.

Great, right? Amid all of these people who were "Average Joes with chainsaws" was someone with professional experience, who knew what he was doing.

He was armed with just his chainsaw, as it was immediately obvious to him that the area was SUCH a mess, he wouldn't be using the truck or the chipper. Together with his fellow volunteers, he wandered around the area, asking people if they needed help. For those who did, they worked on clearing the downed trees that were blocking sidewalks, driveways, doorways, etc.

While these heroes - yes, heroes - were helping the residents dig out from the many thousands of trees that were tossed about the area, they were approached by a city inspector.

That inspector told them that they were not licensed for tree work, and would have to leave. The volunteers showed their hand markings and papers to prove that they were registered volunteers.

The inspector didn't believe them, saying she'd already kicked out 15 tree companies that day. She once again told them to leave.

As Mike and his crew went to leave their volunteer area, they were approached by people asking for help. People were yelling out to them from houses, asking for help getting out. One family in particular had a large pine tree blocking their door, with kids trying to climb out over it to get out of the house.

Because Mike and his fellow volunteers are HUMAN and had COMPASSION, they pulled over to help.

Well, the police pulled up, reminding them that the inspector had asked them to leave. They blocked the barely-passable street with their squad car for over an hour, waiting for another inspector to show up.

While this was going on, all of the nearby residents were upset, and yelling at the police to tell them that these were people trying to help, that no one was charging money, and that they NEEDED the help. Mike was worried about the street being blocked off, asking the police if they could all move to a side street to wait for the inspector... and they threatened to tow his equipment.

Eventually an inspector showed up, once again kicked them out of the area, telling him to expect a hefty fine for this. They were also told that if they were to stop and help anyone else, the fine would double, and it would double for EACH time it happened.

Let me be perfectly clear here: This is a man who wouldn't even hand out business cards to people who were asking for them. He wasn't there to promote his business, he was there to HELP. Everyone except for the city employees knew this, appreciated it, and WANTED him there. The city, on the other hand, treated him like a criminal.

Mike and the other volunteers complied. Mike left the state to work a month long contract in another state. The story broke, people on the internet lost their shit over it, and there was a HUGE public demand to have this impeding fine waived. I know that I was far from the only person to vent my anger about the situation at both of the area's city councilmen.

Mike came home to a $275 fine. As more than 20 days had passed since it had been issued, he was not able to file an appeal, and he paid it.

The City never did waive or return the fine, and never apologized for treating him like utter shit.

For all of the vultures running around, gumming up our roads, making a nuisance of themselves, and contributing NOTHING positive to the cleanup efforts, the fact that the city not only repeatedly harassed this guy for volunteering blows my mind. Almost a year later, and my hands are shaking, just thinking about it.

The city tried to make him out to be a bad guy in the media. All of their comments revolved around what a danger he was to the area, as an "unlicensed" rogue on a rampage. To read their comments, you'd picture a crazy person on a huge boom truck, running rampant and pulling down power lines with this "dangerous" heavy equipment.

He wasn't unlicensed, though. He wasn't some uneducated schmuck that got his hands on someone's equipment and decided to run wild. This was a licensed, insured tree professional. That he hadn't paid a fee to the city of Minneapolis for a license to work in the city has absolutely no reflection on his competence. Further, contrary to the comments about his equipment - he only ever used a chain saw.

The thing is, with the many trees everywhere, there were MANY chainsaws everywhere. Many, many people who were unlicensed to do tree removal - not just in Minneapolis, but ANYWHERE - used their chainsaws to HELP. To the best of my knowledge, not a single one of these other volunteers were even approached about their use of a chainsaw, much less harassed, kicked out, and fined.

In desperate, emergency times... certain formalities need to be relaxed.

With all of the vouching for and begging to let Mike continue to help the residents get cut out from under the arboreal carnage - both during and after the incident - it disgusts me that this went as far as it did. It disgusts me that the city would so actively and viciously work against someone who was giving his labor and experience so freely, the day after the disaster.

Looking back, almost a year later - this wasn't about safety. This was about money and greed on the city's part. This was about someone doing great work that the area needed - and wanted - that would end up picking away at the man hours that the city would spend in this area, even if on a very small level.

I don't even want to think about how many skilled potential volunteers were scared off by this.

To Mike's credit, the incident is not going to prevent him from helping out the next time something like this happens... EXCEPT if it happens within the city of Minneapolis.

The city of Minneapolis punctuated the incident by giving their clearing crews the long weekend off, just one week after the tornado... when many roads were still impassable. Thanks, assholes.

There's a street and a sidewalk under there, somewhere.

The subject of licensed contractors came up again, just a week after the tornado.

In an effort to discourage people from hiring unlicensed contractors, the city circulated a list of contractors. It was titled "Need Help with Home Repairs?", and included a warning: "Don't be scammed by unlicensed, unscrupulous contractors. Get multiple bids and do your homework."

Great, right?

Well, the list included 22 unlicensed contractors... of 34 companies listed. The list was posted to their website for at least a week before it was noticed and removed.

I have no idea how the companies got listed in the first place. Judging by the money-centric actions of the city over the past year, I'd be willing to bet it was paid advertising. Further, I wholeheartedly believe that the city's public stance on unlicensed contractors has less to do with public safety, than it does with their profits. When you kick out one experienced, licensed, and insured volunteer, citing "licensing" as the reason... it's hard to take any other licensing stance as 100% altruistic.

Just over a month after the tornado, the city ended up drawing a pretty clear picture of what the real, unstated problem with having professional tree workers providing their help to residents - free of charge- could have been. On June 29th, the City of Minneapolis posted the following to their own Facebook page:

"Homeowners who still have fallen trees on their property are responsible for their removal, but that work can be expensive. The City recognizes this, so with a homeowner's permission, the City can finance the removal of the tree, have the work done, and assess the costs to the homeowner's property taxes, spreading out payments over 5 years. "

Sounds great on first read, right? Upon reading the information on their website, I realized that what they were doing was profiteering.

In order to use this financial help - which, unlike most other avenues for financial aid, did not seem to require any sort of qualification beyond owning the property - you had to use the city crews. You had to pay whatever price it was that the city charged, without the ability to use a different contractor, or get competing bids.

Beyond that profit, the city indicated that it would also be charging administrative fees, an inspection fee, AND an annual interest rate of 8%, assessed to the homeowner's property taxes over a period of five years. I found this to be incredibly predatory.

Those of us who had friends with chainsaws only had to pay for pizza and beer.

Those without chainsaw-wielding friends - but who had some money - were able to get competitive bids from several companies... not paying "administrative" fees or interest.

It was the poorest and most disadvantaged people who had to take the city up on this offer, and who were taken advantage of in the process.

Let me be clear... in this emergency situation, I'm not aware of a single person who paid an "inspection fee" to have these fallen trees removed from their property. Everyone did what had to be done, with a lot of hard work. I don't think anyone, anywhere, stopped to wonder if they needed to get any sort of permit, or pay any sort of "inspection fee" to remove this debris from their yard.

Why should the city profit several different ways from this "favor", and then act like it's such a generous thing for them to do? I still don't understand how this was even legal. It seems to me that something in the FTC should forbid this sort of behavior. At the very, very least... it was predatory lending.

Anyway.

Beyond the major tree work the city had some interesting ideas and definitions about "debris removal".

Woo! City is finally clearing the huge piles of debris from our front of our house! Now... we'll have room for MORE debris! #NoMi - Twitter, Tue May 31 15:59:51 UTC 2011

We were all told to haul all of our tornado debris up to the front curb, and that the city would remove it. We all busted our asses to move the debris as quickly as we could, to ensure we could get as much of it hauled away as possible.

Not only that, we wanted the back cleared so that the power lines could be re-strung, and our utilities restored ASAP.

Once the city trucks made their rounds? That was the first indication any of us had that "tornado debris", as far as the city was concerned, was only "valuable large pieces of hardwood".

While I'll be touching on the communication issues in a bit, I'd like to note that we learned of the fact that the city was really only interested in major tree debris AFTER they came by.

The city's newly stated stance on debris removal?

" We are not removing construction or other materials. Additional debris - concrete, sheetrock, wood and shingles can be brought to the North Transfer Station for free. You just need to call 311 to get a voucher."

Yep. In an area where most people's vehicles ended up with trees on them, we were now expected to individually rent pickup trucks to haul the non-valuable debris. Never mind that this was a new task on our plate, adding stress and expense. Yet another burden on those of us already saddled with HUGE burdens. Never mind that this probably should have been specified when they originally told everyone to haul their *debris* out front for the city to remove.

Just found out that the city will NOT be picking up non-tree debris, we have to pay/haul everything ELSE! #NoMi #BULLSHIT - Twitter, Thu Jun 02 03:41:44 UTC 2011

They actually picked through our debris pile, removing the largest of the tree trunk pieces - really nice oak and walnut - leaving the rest of the random debris. We were left with a huge pile of smaller branches, broken wood planks, and random pieces of not only our own house, but other people's homes.

To add insult to injury, the city crews threw large pieces of debris up onto our newly-cleared, raked front lawn! In their rush to pick out the debris that they wanted, they littered out lawn with broken shingles, wood with nails sticking of it, and broken glass - shattering it further, in the process.

193

The amount of debris the city left for US to haul! They even tossed some big pieces on our lawn! #NoMi - Twitter, Thu Jun 02 03:50:52 UTC 2011

I have no idea why they only wanted to move the big wood, after telling us that the *debris* would be picked up. Given their ridiculous focus on money, I'm guessing that they were able to sell it or otherwise profit from it, either as straight up lumber, or as mulch.

After yelling at two city councillor secretaries, they did end up removing our debris pile.

To this day, the city has not responded to my requests for information on the value of the tree debris, and what was done with it.

The Letter of Noncompliance

The afternoon of Saturday June 11th brought the first bit of communication that we received from the City of Minneapolis - and it was a letter that sent me into a screaming rage.

194

According to this notice, the city had sent an inspector to our house the day before, determined that it was not properly "up to code", and that we had til June 24th - less than two weeks later, and only about a month after the tornado - to bring it back up to code, or we would " face civil or criminal charges".

Now, this notice was with regards to the "truth of sale in housing" disclosures, a list of items that we had to take care of within 90 days of buying the house. We had done the little things inside - smoke detectors, outlet covers, etc - but the only item on the list that would be visible from the outside was our deck. You know, the deck we'd purchased the railing material for on the morning of the tornado?

Now, any moron could clearly see that the reason our deck had no railings yet was because had been smashed to bits.

To say that I was livid would be a monumental understatement. I couldn't believe the gall of even sending a building inspector to the area, when many people hadn't received their insurance pay outs yet, etc. We'd been hit by a tornado! Also, less than two weeks to bring our house up to code?

Were these people high on something?

I dropped what I was doing, and called the number on the letter. I really did try to keep calm, but the tornado had screwed with my ability to keep my cool, and I had already exhausted my patience with the city.

I started out cool and collected, I know that much. I don't remember a whole lot of the call, aside from the fact that the whole neighborhood probably heard the last bit of it. I know that I said "Because my house got smashed by a TORNADO" no less than six times, with each instance increasing in volume.

I know that my husband had to leave the room, as he was in hysterics over the message I was leaving. He didn't want his laughter to throw me off.

It's not like we're sitting on our hands and not doing anything!! We don't even HAVE a deck to put siding on anymore!!! I AM SO MAD! - Twitter, Sat Jun 11 15:08:37 UTC 2011

If stop tweeting on the 24th it's cause the city thinks I'm a criminal because I can't get $100k+ worth of damage fixed in less than 1 month - Twitter, Sat Jun 11 15:13:35 UTC 2011

I received a return call right away - which shocked me, given that this was on a Saturday.

The city employee that called sounded mortified, shaky, and was extremely apologetic. I think I may have scared the shit out of him with my voice mail. I know that I sure as hell wouldn't want to have to deal with me, when raging... you wouldn't like me when I'm tornadoed!

He explained that it had been an automatic letter, and that - contrary to what it said - that no inspector had been out to my property. He told me to call the office the next day, and that someone would give us an extension on it.

You would think, given the technology we have these days, that someone would have been able to flag the addresses within the destruction area. You would think that they could have sent a letter that was more in line with... "We see your house got smashed, please let us know when you have time to get it all up to code, we'll extend it DUE TO A TORNADO".

You would also think that a city would have compassion towards its residents, and that its employees would have even two brain cells to rub together. I sure thought so, anyway.

Then again, this is the same city that had major exits to our area barricaded and rerouted for weeks after the tornado, making it difficult for people to get into the area. I think it was for some sort of cleaning, but long stretches of time would go by, with no work being done in the closed off sections.

Also, this is the same city that prompted this tweet:

Not impressed with "no parking on this block" signs with no dates specified, no work being done. Parking space =rare. #NoMi #Logistics - Twitter, Sun May 29 18:36:01 UTC 2011

Logistics are apparently not a concern or priority for our city. This theme has played out over the entire course of the cleanup and rebuild efforts, and it's driven me - a logistics nerd - absolutely insane.

In stark contrast to their zeal in sending us a threatening letter, the city hasn't been as diligent in dealing with more pressing issues.

In the weeks that followed the tornado, absentee landlords were a huge issue - taking rent money from their tenants, then disappearing - leaving those tenants in uninhabitable conditions.

Several months later, my husband and I drove around the tornado damaged zone, photographing all of the gigantic tree stumps that the city had yet to remove. These were on city property - between the sidewalk and the street - and many involved large sections of pavement pulled up at severe angles.

There were sections of sidewalks - on fairly busy streets - standing up at 45 degree angles or worse, with dead tree roots hanging out everywhere. We watched a group of kids carry their bikes up over one of these new embankments - at least 4 feet over where the undamaged sidewalk section ended - rather than walk out onto the street.

This was a safety issue. There was no reason that these huge sections of tree stumps, their roots, and the torn up sidewalk should be out there, 3 months after the tornado. There was no reason that these trees - a fire hazard, given our ridiculously hot summer - should force the kids of the neighborhood into choosing between climbing over them, or walking out in the street. I'd like to share a few of the photos, taken August 15, 2011.

These are just a few of the hundreds of examples we saw, and dozens that we photographed. Absolutely shameful.

3 months. Given the warning letter that we received over our "non compliance", a lot of us think that the city should have sent themselves a citation over the negligence they exhibited here.

Not one to accept responsibility for their own fuck ups, the city tried to throw FEMA under the bus - a theme that would repeat throughout the recovery effort. They claimed that they were waiting for FEMA funds, before they would be "able" to remove the uprooted tree sections, and repair the damaged sidewalks.

The thing is, when tornadoes have hit other, more affluent areas of the city in the past... it didn't take 3 months before the city cleared this sort of hazard.

Money was a huge issue, throughout the recovery process. In general, you'd expect that - there was a huge amount of damage done to not only homes, but to city property, utilities, businesses, etc.

The thing is, the city of Minneapolis handled their finances poorly. They constantly demonstrated bad judgement, greed, and poor prioritization throughout this whole ordeal.

When the city crews took a long weekend off, just 5 days after the tornado, they cited finances. I don't know about you, but in my eyes... when a disaster hits, you do what needs to be done. Roads were still impassable, many people had no electricity, etc. It was still a huge mess, 5 days later, there was still a ton of immediate work that needed to be done. I don't care where the city got the money, they should have made it work.

The Stadium Issue

Absolutely no exaggeration here: those of us affected by the tornado had to hear about all of the money that the city and state were looking to pour into a football stadium that we don't need... on a daily basis.

Now, I was born and raised in Winnipeg. I was there when the Jets were threatening to leave, I watched as my fellow grade school students would be donating the contents of their piggy banks to "keep" them there... and you know what? No one died when the big babies left the city.

In that case, the arena had been built in 1955, the Jets left about 40 years later, and it was demolished around 50 years after it had been built. It was such a shame, as it was a GREAT building.

In the case of the Minnesota Vikings stadium - The Metrodome is only 30 years old. I find it utterly ridiculous that such an expensive building - that is younger than I am! - is deemed to be so totally inadequate for our football team.

Now, as a business owner myself, I've got to say - the idea of the government chipping in ANY money for a business that makes millions upon millions of dollars is completely asinine. This isn't a charity, this is a multimillion dollar business.

If they are in such need of a new stadium, they should be more than capable of paying for it themselves. If they're not capable of paying for it themselves, too bad - save up for it, and live within your means, like the rest of us.

If the team owner is able to buy a 19 million dollar apartment in New York, why do they deserve "welfare" from THIS city and state? Beyond the cost of the apartment, there is the fact that it was money spent *elsewhere*. If he can't invest in the area, why should the area invest in his team?

Up until very recently, the Ontario Teacher's Pension Plan owned 80% of the Toronto Maple Leafs, Raptors, AND the arena they play in. At some point since the tornado, they sold their stake to a couple other businesses.

In Wisconsin, the team raises funds for their stadium by having the fans buy "shares" - and the fans are only TOO happy to do so.

WHY should Minneapolis be kicking in anywhere between hundreds of thousands - to millions! - of dollars for a new stadium - especially given all the times that "lack of money" was cited as to why Minneapolis repeatedly dropped the ball/cut corners with regards to the tornado recovery?

To me, not only is a sports team a business that should be self sufficient, it's a "frill". It should be one of the absolute lowest priorities when it comes to tax money.

If all of the infrastructure in the area is sound, the education system working (it's NOT), and no one was going hungry? Sure, kick some money over to entertainment. I'm sure if all the basic needs - NEEDS - of the city were taken care of, people would have little or no problems with something like a newer stadium.

However, that's not the case. We have a big section of the area smashed by a tornado, bridges falling apart, many homeless people, and kids graduating who are barely able to spell. We have school divisions reducing the school week down to 4 days, due to "lack of funds" It's utterly ridiculous that a stupid sports team comes before community and infrastructure.

The fact that those of us had to hear about the stadium daily was a huge slap in the face. Daily - including on the days that the city decided to take off for "budget reasons".

While the local and state governments held special sessions to endlessly debate this stadium, it took until mid December for the local governments to meet to DISCUSS the possibility of a disaster declaration.

By contrast, our tornado zone was declared a "major disaster" on a federal level on June 6th.

While tornado victims were being sent notices threatening "civil and criminal charges" if their damaged properties were not brought up to code within a few short weeks, the Metrodome was able to keep their roof deflated as long as they wanted, to make a point.

While tornado victims were portrayed in the media and attacked in comments as "waiting for a handout" - whether from FEMA, or from the insurance that they PURCHASED - it's somehow more appropriate that this sports team be given handouts. I guess welfare is more palatable if it's aimed at men who make ridiculous salaries chasing a ball while wearing tights.

Maybe it's a culture difference, but it blows my mind... just how many people are anti-welfare, but completely ok with government money going towards a multimillion dollar sports team. Could you imagine where society would be, if the same sort of effort, attention, and priority were given to education?

Either way, I'm completely disgusted that the city was able to take a weekend off, fight me for months over a sidewalk (more on that in a bit), and wait for four months before starting to fix streets and sidewalks in the area for "monetary reasons", while having to hear about this shit on a daily basis throughout.

At one point, a news story about the tornado zone's damage and needs was followed up immediately with a story about how the city was fighting to keep the new stadium within its borders, rather than let it go to a nearby suburb - and more about the money that this city was looking to throw at it.

It's enough to make someone sick. Have a little respect, and work as hard for your residents, as you do for a football team.

Communication Issues

If I were to sum up all of the communication issues that we encountered with the city, I would have to say that it all stemmed from a wonderful combination of incompetence and pride.

Incompetence is pretty self explanatory. This was a system that was NOT prepared for any sort of a natural disaster, staffed by people who can't grasp basic concepts of communication, efficiency, and logistics.

As far as pride goes... The only time anyone really received information from the city, it was through the media, and in the form of the city patting itself on the back for something. In a few cases, it was something that someone ELSE had done... and in others, they were taking pride in work that hadn't even been done yet.

To this day, the city claims that it sent people door to door to check on tornado victims. Our own councilperson - Barbara Johnson - claims to have gone door to door herself.

Now, the only times that anyone from the city came to our door, it was scheduled and expected - city inspectors with regards to building permit inspections, and an assessor with regards to property damage assessment for property tax purposes. Not once were we "checked in on", and we were there from early morning til late at night. Additionally, I have yet to come across anyone - on my street, or online -who had been contacted by this supposed door to door sweep.

In addition to this "check on people" sweep, the city claims to have distributed 12,000 flyers with resource information. Again, we never received one, and - so far as I can tell - no one that anyone has heard from on the North Minneapolis Tornado Page - a community of over 3,500 people! - has either.

Curious, huh?

Urban Homeworks - a local housing organization - organized a volunteer cleanup day on behalf of the city, which took place 2 weeks after the tornado. This was deemed the "North Side Volunteer Clean-Up Day", June 4th.

I feel sort of bad for having to complain about something that 3000+ people apparently volunteered for, but it was a mess.

The idea was that crews would roam the area, clearing debris from the yards of anyone who needed it. (They would ask permission before doing work). Great idea, so many of us really needed it.

However, for all of the work that went into the publicity campaign for this effort - and for all of the self-back patting that the city did afterwards - very, very little effort went into the actual organization of the event, and in was a massive headache for homeowners in the area.

While we were so thankful for the help, it really would have been great if the city had thought out a plan with regards to where the cleared debris was to be moved to.... as a coordinated effort with those that would be picking it up.

Basically, volunteers on June 4th were told to haul tree debris out to the front boulevard, other debris to the back. The city hadn't announced anything beyond "where it will be picked up later", so... no big deal.

Other crews were told the opposite, and this came after our neighbor had been told to haul his tree debris - from a MASSIVE evergreen - out to the back alley. There was no way that he was going to haul all of it out to the front, after following the first set of instructions that the city had given him.

The crews were fairly indiscriminate with where the debris went, so long as it was in the general area that the city requested of any particular crew. Our garage and driveway out back, for instance, were blocked off with not only debris from our yard, but the neighbor's as well. I guess that the crews figured one pile would be better than two.

"Later" ended up being much later. The debris sat there for 10 days, before anyone was told what was being done with it.

On June 14th, the city posted the following to their facebook page, along with information on how to sign up:

205

"There are two upcoming Clean Sweep days - June 18 and June 25 - in north Minneapolis to help folks get storm debris loaded onto trucks for proper disposal. 200 volunteers are needed for each day"

Given our previous issues with the city crews picking through "storm debris" for TREE debris, I had to ask clarification as to whether this was all debris, or just tree debris. The city replied:

" Volunteers on the Clean Sweep days will be going through alleys and loading trucks with construction and household debris, metal and tires."

Great! Finally! So, two and three weeks after the debris piles were created, the city picked them up. Sort of.

"Construction debris" apparently didn't include all of the broken cement, so we were stuck with the huge pile from not only our house, but at least one neighbor's house. We eventually had to pay to have it all removed from our driveway. It would have been nice to know ahead of time, we could have avoided being saddled with all of that work and expense ourselves.

The tree debris was a bit of a different story.

Really annoyed at debris situation in #NoMi. HORRIBLE communication from city, everyone told it will be removed, looks like it won't / Further, with removal assumed, neighbors are just dumping their crap on OUR pile. I am NOT wanting to get stuck hauling it! #NoMi - Twitter, Mon Jun 13 01:54:19 UTC 2011

4 weeks since the tornado. Why we're all still walking around piles of rubble, I don't know. #NoMi #WouldBeClearedByNowIfMinnetonka - Twitter, Sat Jun 18 18:37:22 UTC 2011

By July 9th I was so fed up with waiting, that I posted the following to the city's official facebook page:

"Is the city finished picking up tree debris? There is a pile out front of my house, it's not even ours. I'm getting sick of the fact that - though we had people here clearing everything out early on - both our front boulevard and back driveway got used as dumping grounds.

Thank you, city people, for finally picking up all of the crap in the back yard... but we came home this morning to find a huge chunk of TREE added to the pile out front. We have enough to worry about - financially and "to do list" to dig out from the tornado without having to take on the hassle and expense of renting a truck to get rid of someone else's debris. That pile was made from the volunteer clean up, never got picked up, and now people are using it as an open invitation to dump there. This is BEYOND aggravating!"

Their reply?

"Marie - the City is done with its regular sweeps to collect tree debris, but you can still call 311 to schedule a tree debris pick up."

Why on earth did they have the volunteers move debris to the front boulevard for pick up, if they weren't planning to do any more "regular sweeps" to collect it? Insane... and something that should have been addressed in the planning of the original "clean sweep".

aaaand the city will pick up the tree debris pile that their volunteers left out front! WOO! Now... I need a cocktail. - Twitter, Mon Jul 11 18:54:27 UTC 2011

Throughout the aftermath fiasco, residents were asked to call 311 for pretty much everything. Report situations, volunteering, for information on resources, to get a hold of different departments of the local government, etc.

311 was woefully unequipped to deal with these inquiries. Some bit of city communication would refer people to 311 for more details, the 311 operators would have no idea what it was about, etc. If calling about a certain issue, half the time they wouldn't know who to refer you to. Monumentally frustrating... and this was supposed to be THE front line for city communication and resources.

The thing is, so many of these communication issues would have been solved if anyone at the city would have taken a good hard look at the situation, assessed the strengths and weaknesses of their abilities, and worked with others. Peter Kerre and the North Minneapolis Tornado Post Tornado Watch people approached them early on - repeatedly - and were brushed off. It's utterly ridiculous to me that a guy - just a regular guy -

living in NY was responsible for the vast majority of tornado updates and resource information that anyone in the area actually received. That the communication from the city was SO horribly inadequate, that this ad hoc online community was the default go-to.

The fact that the city repeatedly brushed them off, then distributed the resource sheet compiled by them? I don't even have the words. Let me quote Mandi, on behalf of the North Minneapolis Post Tornado Watch page:

"Yes. It was quite the shocker. I had been at the disaster recovery center at Farview passing them out to people while they waited in the never ending lines for help; some city staff / volunteers tried to make me leave.. and the next day (I think it was the very next day-,my memory of events can be a bit foggy because of all of the 'WTF' moments...), the city of Mpls FB page shared the resource sheet - which was fine, don't get me wrong - it was in fact very resourceful. I can't recall whether it stopped at sharing online or if they actually had some printed and distributed.. I feel as though they did, but am not sure on that..

The city was too busy patting itself on the back for what a good job it was doing to acknowledge the reality of the situation. The deficiencies in the city's emergency management were painfully obvious. We had people on the ground, in the know, willing and able to help. The city wanted nothing to do with it. Our efforts were treated like a burden to the city, not an asset. I could understand that if the city had things under control.. That was not the case. The communication from the city to news outlets was intentionally falsely optimistic, not realistic. Let's not forget that the city just dedicated a staff member to manning the tornado line in what - January? December? They put on a pretty face for the media, saying that there was money available to help people affected, but no one was returning phone calls to the designated phone line! Run around, run around, run around..

It didn't have to be so hard, but the city chose to not have a disaster plan in place (frightening) and to concern itself more with PR in the media than actually helping the community."

These weren't disaster situation professionals, these were regular people who got together to help the community. Their grasp of logistics and communication far surpassed that of the city, and if it weren't for their efforts, I have no idea how things would have turned out.

The disaster victims would have been FAR worse off.

Oh, and the people behind the tornado page didn't take a long weekend off, either. The city should really be ashamed of themselves.

I've got to give Peter Kerre credit, though. When he gave a talk about "Social Media and Disaster Recovery" at the University of Minnesota", he was VERY diplomatic when it came to the city. I have no idea how he managed that particular dance, but kudos to him.

The NCRT Fiasco

Fairly early on, the city was somehow involved in the establishment of a group called the "Northside Community Response Team". I'm not sure exactly when it was founded, but they set up a Facebook page for it a full month after the tornado, on June 22, 2011.

To the best of my knowledge - NCRT was set up as almost a competitor to the North Minneapolis Tornado Watch page. Their very first post:

"Welcome to the NCRT page! If you have questions, need information or have information, please inbox us!"

... despite the fact that FB pages didn't allow people to message the page itself.

In the beginning, NCRT attempted to be an information hub, but just couldn't compete with the Post Tornado Watch page. In comparison to NMPTW's 3500+ readers, NCRT was able to get only about 80 people to "like" it.

You'll have to pardon me if some of this information seems a bit murky. To be quite honest, I still have no idea if NCRT is an actual entity. If it is, I have no idea if it's a non-profit, or just an ad hoc subdivision of the local government.

Given the communication issues, I'm not sure NCRT knows. Calls to various groups that are a part of NCRT haven't turned up an answer to that, either.

I also have no idea how many people worked there in the months following the tornado, or how many do now. Here is the description on the NCRT Facebook page:

"The Northside Community Response Team was created in direct response to the May 22 tornado that tore through North Minneapolis. We are a collaborative of over 30 community agencies and individuals committed to pooling our resources to provide information, assistance and support to those impacted by the storm. Working with local officials and service providers, we are working dilligently to identify and support those in need."

All I know is that whenever the city has talked of funds available to help tornado victims, they usually directed people to NCRT to apply for said funds. This was the case in the weeks following the tornado, and it was the case in mid November, when the city announced several hundred thousand dollars available to help tornado victims.

What happened when people contacted the NCRT was... lunacy. The vast majority of times reported, the NCRT did not answer the phone, and did not return messages.

Whenever someone was able to get a hold of NCRT, they would be referred elsewhere - another organization or 311 (The City of Minneapolis information line). Once a person followed the NCRT recommendation to call the other party, they would be told that they were supposed to call the NCRT.

The multitude of complaints from people on the Post Tornado Watch page who were not receiving responses from - or just given the runaround by - the NCRT were only ever met with agreement and more complaints, never with so much as one person who had gotten somewhere with them.

It didn't take long for people - tornado victims and otherwise - to start asking questions about NCRT. As this was pretty much the sole agency people were being referred to for financial aid, it was bizarre that no one seemed to be receiving help from them. Apparently they banned the media from their meetings over questions about where the money went.

210

In mid August - with calls from June still unreturned - the NCRT angered a lot of local tornado victims when they threw themselves an ice cream social, advertised as:

"As the summer comes to a close, we want to honor all of those who have contributed to the success and accomplishments of the Northside Community Response Team"

I can only imagine how frustrating and insulting that had to be for people who'd been given the run around for months on end.

In November, city announced more money for tornado victims. Once again they directed people to the NCRT... and once again, the communication issues persisted.

Two weeks after the November announcement, I posted the following to Facebook:

"Where NCRT dropped the ball on communication, did nothing but refer people elsewhere, and spend more time patting themselves on the back than on, say, returning calls the FIRST time around- why were they charged with distributing this latest batch of money to supposedly be earmarked for tornado recovery? It's now been 2 weeks since the big announcement, and yet NO ONE is reporting having gotten a returned call from NCRT."

On a lark, I left a message, to see how long it would take for a reply.

I would wait about two months for that reply. When I finally did get to talk to someone, I was informed that the reason for the communication issues was that they only *just* hired someone to monitor the messages, and to make contact with tornado victims.

... in January. Seven months after the tornado. Seven months of the city referring people to the NCRT. Why was all of this money filtering to a brand new entity with NO communication structure in place?

To this day, I have no idea what role the city played in the formation of the NCRT. Depending on who you ask, they formed it. To other people, they provided the financing to it. Who knows?

211

The thing is, no matter who founded it, I'm blown away that the city "worked" so closely with them, promoted them so heavily... and continued to do so, even after the first several month's worth of no communication.

To this day, I still cannot find any answers as to where the money went. There was SO much money donated to tornado victims, in the name of recovery... yet no one seems to know anyone who received help locally, from these venues.

I could be wrong, but in my observation, it looks like the money that went to NCRT basically funded itself and the partner organizations, paying themselves to "administer" the money.

If I am wrong, I'm far from alone in being so. I think I speak for all of us here when I say that we would love to see some accountability for all of these funds that were intended for disaster assistance.

One news report states that the City of Minneapolis has received 2.2 million dollars for tornado assistance. Where did it go?

The Saga of our Sidewalk

This is going to sound so petty - especially after posting photos of sidewalks FAR more damaged than our own... but it's caused enough headaches for us, I really need to rant about it.

When the tornado ripped thousands of trees out of the ground, the roots of those trees caused a lot of damage to the sidewalks in the area. Our own sidewalk was ripped up as the result of a tree that had been growing on the boulevard between the street and our front yard.

Given the scope of the rest of our damages - needing a whole new roof, for instance - this section of sidewalk wasn't a huge priority for us. The seam between two portions of pavement lay almost exactly in front of where the tree had been, and had pulled up maybe 1" above level, cracking both of the pavement sections that flanked it.

It was pulled up enough to be ugly - and that the city would expect us to fix it - but not bad enough to actually be dangerous. Besides, there was talk that the city was going to receive federal money for sidewalk damage, so we ignored it.

The city had placed several markings on the curb directly in front of the pulled up sidewalk, so it was obvious that they had seen the damage.
Three key points:

1. As property owners, we are responsible for the maintenance and repair of our sidewalks, in normal situations. Had this been caused by anything other than the tornado, the city would make us pay to repair those two sections of sidewalk.

2. Given that the damage was caused by a tree pulling up from underneath it, we had no idea what to expect for years to come. Who knows what moisture, freezing, thawing, and rotting of any existing roots could do to the current state of the sidewalk. Probably nothing good.

3. As it was technically city property, sidewalk damage was NOT something covered by our insurance - even if we'd had enough coverage - and I doubt any insurance company was paying out for it.

As predicted, the city received a federal disaster declaration, and FEMA approved them for something like $300,000 to repair the roads, curbs, and sidewalks. Great! We wouldn't have to worry about this additional expense.

Sidewalk repair didn't begin til the beginning of September. Again, not sure why it should have taken that long, but I digress.

At some point, I saw the city crews working on a sidewalk maybe half a block from our property, and I was happy to know that we would soon follow.

Except, we didn't. They finished up on our street, missing us completely. They didn't come back the next day, either.

I called 311, was bounced around many times, and finally got to speak to someone who sounded like he was the guy to talk to about sidewalks. I expressed concern that my sidewalk seemed to have been missed, he said he would look into it.

The next thing I knew - October 19th - the city was bleating to the media about how they had finished the sidewalk repair in the tornado zone.

Um.. What? No. Looking outside my window told a VERY different story. Not only had our sidewalk not been repaired, the stump of the tree that had pulled it up was still there, as well.

A quick rant online turned up a few other people in the same situation - either their sidewalk had been skipped entirely, or only partially done. One person reported that the sidewalk had been fixed, aside from the part that bridged between the sidewalk and the road - which had been removed by the crew, but not replaced.

I've said it before, I'll say it again: If the city spent half the effort working on the repairs as they did patting themselves on the back, everything WOULD have been done LONG ago.

When I called the city about it, I was first told that they "forgot" me, and then that it was FEMA's fault for not getting me on a list, and/or not paying for my sidewalk section specifically.

Further, I was essentially told that I was out of luck... that whatever happened the city was done in the area, that next summer they'd be working in another part of the city, and I'd have to deal with it myself. I was told that it doesn't even matter if I were to produce photos of the damage including the tree stump that is still there - we were on our own.

I called my city councilor to discuss it, but it didn't get me very far. We basically had two separate one-sided "conversations". Her monologue about how great the city had handled the tornado, exalting the virtues of the local government wasn't going to go far with me, given the months of frustration leading up to this call. I felt like I was listening to a pre-recorded PR speech. It was gross.

On the other side of it, my concerns were falling on deaf ears. The only time I was able to pull her out of this plastic, polished "spin doctor" mode was when I dropped the words "idiots" and "incompetence". THEN she got upset.

Well, guess what, Barb Johnson? I have a huge vocabulary, and I'm at a complete loss for better words to describe the city's actions following the tornado. How about negligent? Greed? There are so many words that accurately represent the various facets of the city's ineptitude and failures, but "idiots" and "incompetence" are FAR from inaccurate or inappropriate.

As a result of that conversation, her office had a sidewalk inspector call me about the sidewalk, who had some interesting ideas about what caused that crack, and why the city would not have to pay for it.

First he told me that it had not been pulled up, that the sidewalk was level. Let's have a look at that:

There's about 1.5" space between left side of the level and the sidewalk below it.

Then he told me that the tornado didn't cause the crack. Depending on what part of the conversation we look at (he flip flopped a few times), either it was an existing crack that I hadn't noticed before, it that there was a tiny crack in the sidewalk that hadn't been visible yet, but that the forestry people had "made it worse" in removing the tree.

First of all - and I told him this - I'm an Aspie. This sidewalk section was immediately in front of the spot where I parked my car every single day. TRUST ME, I would notice a crack in the sidewalk section I walked over multiple times daily. Hell, I think ANYONE would, but someone with Aspergers? That's a sensory issue, both the sight of it and the feel of it under my feet as I pass over it. There is absolutely NO way that I would miss two big sections of cracked sidewalk. That's something that I would have been ACUTELY aware of, thanks.

215

Secondly, had the city's forestry people caused a microscopic crack to enlarge to THAT degree, in removing the stump of a tree damaged in the tornado... again, why am I on the hook for this?

Lastly, this completely ignores the fact that at the time I first started complaining of them missing my sidewalk, the stump was still there. Also, nothing that they did when removing the stump would have caused the crack anyways - I had watched.

Replacement Tree
The crack
X —— Where previous tree had been
Marks made by city crews

Side note: I feel bad that the photos aren't doing it justice, and I know it looks petty. The big thing to us is that - as benign as this looks - it IS something that we will be forced to pay to replace in the next year or two, due to the city's ordinances.

Another one of his theories was that the cracks were caused by freezing and thawing. WHAT?! I had walked on that sidewalk the MORNING of the tornado, there was no crack. Then, later that day - cracked. May 22... sure, freezing and thawing sounds completely reasonable. Ugh.

Finally, he told me that it was essentially my own fault for not calling the city before they left my street, for reporting the damage. What the hell? If the curb directly in front of it is marked with several different markings, why would I assume that it means ANYTHING other than "the people who know what they're doing have been here and seen the damage", until it's apparent that we've been skipped over?

Ridiculous.

I flipped out. Angry message on the city's official facebook page, irate call to my city councilor's office, rants on Twitter, Facebook, etc... I was mad. Yes, this was fairly piddly in the grand scheme of our tornado repairs and expenses to date - probably a couple thousand dollars - but it was the principle. I was sick to death of the city screwing everything up, repeatedly trying to profit from the tornado, etc.

To be fair, I was sick of a lot of things that had nothing to do with the city, but... this was it. The straw that broke the camel's back.

So I asked questions on the city's Facebook page. Any of their posts that were financial or even remotely tornado related, I pressed for answers about my sidewalk. If there was any way anything could be TWISTED to be remotely financial related, I brought it up. I was *mad*!

I pointed out things like the fact that not only are they saving money by not repairing it now, that they stood to profit from this tornado damage when they assess our property for in it a year or to.

I pointed out that they received FEMA money to fix these sidewalks.

I pointed out that we have paid out over $2000 in building permits as a result of the tornado. I pointed out that thousands of houses had done the same. The fact that - with this being a lower income area, that this was an unexpected influx of income that would not have happened without the tornado, and therefor a BOON to their budget, a surplus.

Having paid $2000+ in permits ourselves, I was PISSED that we were being told that we were being stuck with this. Also, I took pretty much everything that the sidewalk inspector had said to me as a huge insult to my intelligence.

Eventually - December 15th - I received a call from Dan Bauer - someone else at the city. Apparently my Facebook nagging had finally irritated the right person, and they had asked him to call me. Two things from that conversation stuck out enough for me to rant about it online.

1. He said that the sidewalk inspector had determined that our sidewalk had not only been damaged long before the tornado, but that it had been filled in by a homeowner at least a year ago.

2. He had the gall to say that they have to give me THIS much difficulty, because they wouldn't want to "misappropriate funds".

Now, I'm all for due diligence, but this was ridiculous.

He told me that he was going to forward me an email from Jim Glenn, the sidewalk inspector.

Well, he forwarded me much more than that. He forwarded me an entire chain of emails about not only my sidewalk specifically, but about my Facebook posts. The first email in the chain was dated October 6th, and he sent it to me on December 15th.

Over 2 months, 4 different city employees involved. This isn't "due diligence", this is sitting around with thumbs up asses, making a tornado victim fight tooth and nail for something the city should be covering.

The email string was... spectacular. My favorites:

1. *"The panels at (my address redacted) appear to have old clay cracks that were filled in by the owner with caulking material probably in years past. I don't see any defects caused by the tornado in May"* - Jim Glenn, Sidewalk Inspector (November 30)

Here's the thing: My husband put caulking material in the cracks in October, after we were told that we were "out of luck". He thought that this would be a good way to try and prevent further damage, as winter was coming. The silicone caulking was so fresh, that some leaves had blown into it while it was curing overnight, and were stuck into the fresh material. I mean.. stuck. There's no way that he could have missed that... and no way that anyone would assume that these fresh leaves were from prior years. Come on.

Secondly, sidewalks cracked "in years past" would look very different from relatively fresh ones. Hell, silicone caulking that is over a year old would look very different from fresh. Shouldn't a sidewalk inspector be able to know the difference?

Additionally, this is the same person who inspected the crack BEFORE we put the caulking in. Again, a fresh crack looks very different from an old crack. Did he manage to miss the fact that there was no vegetation growing in there, prior to our repair?

Where do we buy the caulk that this city inspector is apparently used to? Bet using THAT, if it looks like new "years" later... would be FAR cheaper than actually repairing this, huh?

Ridiculous. If you work in public works, can look at silicone caulking that was applied within a week before you get there, and can mistake it for being several years old... you're either a total moron - and working in the WRONG department! - or a crook.

2. "... *this resident's complaints continue to be an issue on our Facebook page*" and   "*We brought it up because she kept commenting on our Facebook page almost on a weekly basis*" - Matthew Lindstrom, Communications Department.

Yep. My complaints are an "issue", but the fact that a tree pulled up my sidewalk is... what, exactly?

Also, yeah - Don't bother bringing it up because there is a tornado victim that was even POSSIBLY passed over. Bring it up because you're tired of my commenting on it. Awesome, guys. Overall, the entire email thread wasn't "Hey, let's look into this and see if we can help out", it's "Hey, can we get more information from you about why it's NOT our problem".

Here's a hint, Matt in communications... when a city is hit by a natural disaster, communicating information about resources, etc to the residents should be a higher priority than communication with the media to pat yourself on the back.

Only initiating communication because complaints are becoming an "issue" on your Facebook page? Seriously? Where do I even start with this? Are you sane/compassionate/honorable enough to at least be embarrassed to sign your emails "City of Minneapolis Communications Department"?

Since this email, we've had no progress on this, and we'll be stuck dealing with this ourselves. I am very frustrated at the demonstration that having geometry, physics, facts, photographs,& logic on our side means nothing.

It may just be a few thousand dollars to repair, but it's a few thousand that we don't have laying around... and we shouldn't have to. Even if we do it ourselves, we're still hauling the broken concrete, paying for THAT disposal.... this is utter garbage that the city walked right past it without bothering to fix it.

Throughout the entire post-tornado recovery process, it's really become apparent to me that the city is concerned more about money than anything, in the wake of the tornado. It's too bad - I've always wanted to assume the best, and haven't paid a lot of attention to the anti-government people... but damned if they aren't right on how awful the city has been on this.

I really don't like being negative. When you're a person that thrives on a diet of Eurodance and energy drinks.. You're a person that thrives on *positivity*. I am, anyway!

I may have almost nothing but bile and vitriol to spew about the City of Minneapolis (The political entity, not the land mass and it people)... but after a year of dealing with their crap after the tornado... there really is little else to say about them. I do think it's important for our experiences to get out there.

Perhaps the city officials can take a long hard look at themselves and their priorities, and learn for the next time.

Perhaps the residents of Minneapolis can take a good hard look at the people they've elected - and who they are yet to elect - and decide if this is the kind of nonsense they want to deal with, if they were in our shoes... or if they want better, more principled people in power next time around.

Or maybe this chapter can just serve as a "how NOT to handle a natural disaster" manual for others cities.
Either way... this has been a whole lot of "needed to be said", and I don't think you'll find a single person in the area who would disagree with me.

These were just the most major of problems we dealt with, personally. I just don't have the space to detail every last conversation and dropped ball that happened, in our experience. To write anything that fully explained the many ways that the city dropped the ball on our whole area would take at LEAST a whole book.

FEMA

Going back to the last section for a second - when the city claimed that it was somehow FEMA's fault for "not having us on a list" for sidewalk repairs, I have two things to point out:

1. At the point FEMA came though, our sidewalk was still completely obscured by fallen trees.

2. In that forwarded email string, it was indicated that the city were the ones who did the initial inspection and came up with the list of affected addresses.

This was not the first or the only time that the city lied about FEMA. I'd like to discuss that.

First of all, the reason that the city was able to get away with lying about FEMA was because the general public has some weird ideas about FEMA. I'm in a unique position, as someone who not only was affected by a tornado, but as someone with a friend who works for FEMA. I'm also someone who researches everything.

So let me clarify what FEMA is, and is not.

FEMA is, as one friend puts it, "a checkbook on wheels". They exist solely to make up the difference between what a disaster actually costs, and what insurance, city, and state will pay for. They are NOT a magical lottery for disaster victims to get rich off, they are the very last line of defense against complete financial ruin in the wake of a disaster.

To put that even more clearly: A disaster victim - whether individual or municipal - must exhaust all other major financial aid streams before FEMA will kick in. That is, insurance money, then state and city aid. If that comes up short of what is needed, FEMA kicks in.

I like to relate it to losing a job. When you lose a job, your first line of defense is your unemployment insurance. This is your homeowners insurance, in the case of a tornado.

When your unemployment runs out, and things get desperate... then you may end up looking to welfare. In the case of tornado aid, this would be your city and state disaster money.

When you are at your absolute most desperate, when things are as bad as they can get, and you are living on the street... the person that gives you a blanket? That's FEMA.

Don't take this as any judgment on FEMA. Unlike the city of Minneapolis, whose actions were governed by greed and incompetence, being the entity that gives you that "blanket" is their actual purpose. Their availability to aid any particular disaster is dictated by the numbers - the amount of public and private damage that occurred, and the amount of front line - insurance/city/state money available to deal with it.

FEMA's not supposed to buy you a whole new house, or make tornado victims rich. They're supposed to step in when you are fucked beyond belief, to put it simply. You don't WANT to qualify for individual FEMA aid.

It seems to me like the public view on FEMA is that they are more like... a Publisher's Clearing House Prize Team waiting for them as they leave their former job, presenting them with a big check.

In Minneapolis, we were lucky. The tornado didn't flatten us, like many tornadoes do in other areas. Yes, there was mass destruction, but it was destruction that was relatively easy to recover from. Relatively.

So, we didn't qualify for individual aid from FEMA, though we did qualify for some infrastructure funding for street and sidewalk repairs.

I can see why people in the area were upset. We would hear about all the money that the city and/or state was putting into tornado repairs, and hear "to help victims of the tornado" all the time - but no one seems to know anyone who actually received that help. (I know that some people were able to get help from the Small Business Association several months later, but that's it.)

When anger was directed at the city - with good reason, in my opinion - the city decided that it would be easier to throw FEMA under the bus, than to admit that the city is run by a bunch of incompetent fuck ups. They're not big on the whole "take responsibility for your own actions" thing.

So, playing on the public's fuzzy knowledge of FEMA, the city blamed FEMA. They made it seem like a personal slight, not that we simply didn't meet the requirements for individual FEMA aid.

At one point, the city elaborated on the "Blame FEMA" song, by fudging some numbers. They claimed that FEMA had put a figure on the amount of volunteer hours that were contributed to the cleanup effort, used it to decrease the value of the actual damage, and that FEMA was using it against the city. That we did not receive FEMA aid because of the volunteering.

The thing is, FEMA did put a dollar figure on that volunteering - but they used it in favor of the city, to boost the actual value of "funding" that the city contributed. They counted that "cost" of volunteer work against the 25% that the local has to pay to meet the 75/25 share of the cost of the disaster.

The city is supposed to pay for 25% of the tornado damage cost. FEMA counted volunteer labor as partial payment for that. Essentially, Minneapolis leveraged labor as part of their financial obligation.

Say we had 1 million in damage. The city would be required to pay $250k. If the volunteer labor was valued at, say, $100k... then the city would only be on the hook for $150k in ACTUAL money.

I pulled those numbers out of my ass, just to illustrate. I don't know the actual values of the damage or volunteer "value". The point is, it's a far cry from "FEMA is screwing us over because they reduced the damage value because of the volunteers, and NOW we don't qualify as a result".

I'm all for being angry over how this was handled, but the anger should be directed at those who ACTUALLY dropped the ball.

From my view, FEMA did absolutely nothing wrong.

While FEMA was able to have people from other regions on the ground here within days... even a year later, no one from the city has come by to check on things, other than the inspectors with regard to permits. The FEMA people who came to our door seemed genuinely concerned with what had happened, and actually seemed like they were working FOR us. That was in stark contrast to constantly having to fight the city for anything.

FEMA has to sit back and be thrown under the bus by a crooked, greedy, and incompetent city that is more than happy to use FEMA funds to repair (some) sidewalks and roads.

Truly, I have to wonder how often FEMA offices have to replace their desks. I'm sure they end up with many head-shaped dents from dealing with all of this idiocy.

In researching publicly available FEMA documents, I learned some interesting things about the city, mostly in regard to another recent disaster, the 35W bridge collapse in 2007.

In a document named "I-35W Bridge Collapse and Response", I learned that our city apparently has an "Office of Emergency Preparedness, *"separate from both the fire and police agencies."* I'm guessing that this will be a shock to anyone that had been affected by our tornado.

I'm just wondering how it fits together with my city councilor excusing the communication issues I had brought up to her with - let me quote her here - *"it was an emergency, and we didn't expect it...."*

We have a whole office dedicated to emergency preparedness, but they didn't "expect" the possibility that our city - a large spread of land, in the state that had the most tornadoes in 2010 - MIGHT just be hit by a tornado at some point.

Geniuses.

"By city ordinance, OEP has responsibility and authority for overseeing the city's response under a Declaration of Emergency. The OEP is also responsible for preparedness, mitigation, recovery, training, and grant administration involving emergency preparedness. OEP operates under an all-hazards approach, and conforms with the Department of Homeland Security (DHS) National Incident Management System (NIMS) standards."

All hazards. All.

Apparently, the city Communications Director gets designated as a "Public Information Officer" for the office, in the event of an emergency.

Again, given that those of us in the area pretty much had to take to social media for any information, and received that information from everyone BUT the city... I'm sure this will be *news* to a lot of people.

Then again, the city seems to have some bizarre definitions so far, maybe by "Public Information Officer", they mean "Publicist for the City". By "Information", they probably mean "Obtain positive press for the city, using whatever means necessary. Facts not important".

A few other things that stood out to me in this document:

- Apparently someone in Public Works has *"had extensive training in NIMS and MnNIMS"*, and acts as "Logistics Section Chief" during a major event, and has *"participated in several practical exercises prior to the incident and preparedness planning for contingencies like debris management"*

... So, why was it so difficult to coordinate debris removal even months after the tornado, when this department mobilized for the bridge collapse in only 20 minutes?

Also, how is it that the left hand never had any idea what the right hand was doing at ANY point throughout the aftermath and cleanup... if ANYONE at the city has "logistics" in their title?

"The EOC (Emergency Operations Center" was of insufficient size to manage a major event."

Awesome.

Also, I learned that FEMA has online courses that anyone can take, free of charge. Independent study courses that teach the principles of emergency management - the same courses that FEMA makes the cities take. Most classes take about an hour, and you can even get a certificate at the end of each.

In other words, if you have an hour, you can have a better understanding of emergency management than our city apparently does.

If you're interested, visit training.fema.gov.

Mental Health
& Creative Coping

Tornado Claus

The first Friday after the tornado - May 27 - Porter decided to go to work for the day.

I guess we were at a point where we couldn't really be effective, without something else being in place - probably either insurance or contractor related. Looking back, I don't remember. Maybe he just needed a break from the mess.

Down to one car, I dropped him off at work. I dreaded the idea of going to the house, in the state it was in, in the state the neighborhood was in. I really wasn't ready to be alone in that.

On the other hand, hanging out in the hotel all day didn't sound like such a great plan either. The helplessness of the situation began to sink in.

I CANNOT tell you how much I hate feeling helpless. I am mega "Type A", and this was... ridiculous. All of it. I really started to wonder if I was losing my mind. I sat in my car in the hotel parking lot, and took to twitter for ... I don't know what. Consolation?

Seriously starting to wonder if I'm mentally ill. Haven't freaked out about #Nomi as much as I probably should. 1 big "lose my shit", 1 mild. - Twitter, Fri May 27 13:15:22 UTC 2011

Is it the aspergers? Am I just stronger than I thought? Full out mental illness? What would Elvis Stojko do? The stuff I think about...#NoMi - Twitter, Fri May 27 13:16:56 UTC 2011

Do crazy people wonder if they are crazy? Does wondering if you're crazy preclude the possibility somehow? Am I losing it right now? #NoMi - Twitter, Fri May 27 13:17:56 UTC 2011

In the midst of questioning my own mental health, I had an idea. I would pick up some supplies - nothing expensive, just little necessities - and hand them out in our neighborhood.

The idea started out as just bottled water, and cheap baseball caps, but sort of morphed from there. I stopped at a dollar store, and came across mini tubes of sunscreen and spf lip balm. Perfect!

As I was about to check out, mentally patting myself on the back for how useful all of this stuff would be - there were an awful lot of sunburned people in the neighborhood! - another display caught my eye. Inspiration hit, and my mood instantly brightened.

Now armed with a ton of bubble kits & lollipops from dollar store. Gonna get a couple cases of water, drive around as "Tornado Claus". #NoMi - Twitter, Fri May 27 14:33:26 UTC 2011

Once I was loaded up with my supplies, I got everything organized - price tags off the hats, lip balms removed from their outer packaging (so I could hand them out individually), etc. I cut a slit into one of the cases of water, and hit the road.

Also decided to put Aspergers and misanthropy aside for the day and offer up hugs, if needed. #NoMi - Twitter, Fri May 27 15:24:04 UTC 2011

I went on twitter, described my husband's car, what I wearing, and let people know to flag me down if they needed anything. I hooked my phone up to the car radio, happy to be able to listen to my favorite radio station's internet feed as my "Tornado Claus" soundtrack.

Wearing white hat, Thundercats t-shirt, driving Burgundy Malibu. See me and need anything, let me know! #NoMi - Twitter, Fri May 27 15:21:07 UTC 2011

Then, I just drove up and down the streets, offering up water and supplies to whoever looked like they needed it. I am NOT a social person, and I've never been good with approaching strangers, but this felt... right.

Some people seemed a little suspicious of my intentions at first, but quickly warmed up when I mentioned that I live in the area, had my house smashed, and was trying to do SOMETHING. Some people needed the water, hadn't considered sun protection, or were glad to give the kids something to do. Others just wanted conversation and someone to tell them that everything was going to be ok.

I wasn't in a big hurry - it was this, or try to get some writing done at home, alone. With no air conditioner... with the sound of chainsaws and construction work all around me. I'm capable of a lot of different things, but that day... I just wasn't capable of that.

What I can't do? Be at my house, alone. Went back to pee. Yeah, just not ready for being alone there! This will be therapy! #NoMi - Twitter, Fri May 27 15:18:11 UTC 2011

At some point, I recognized this feeling I was having - being able to put the realities of the situation aside, being able to get over my social issues, and just help. I'd experienced it before, during another crisis.

When the flights were grounded on 09/11/01, it was the same sort of thing. Everyone - including me! - felt helpless. I went to help at my friend's church, assembling bedding for the 100+ people that would be housed there while the planes were grounded.

I spent the next few days making trips to local restaurants for donated food, driving the passengers to stores for supplies, taking people to the bar (the church was "Dry"), and taking groups sightseeing. I felt like I was on some sort of... other setting. I managed to set aside all of my awkwardness with dealing with strangers, I managed to not freak out at being in an enclosed space with that many people, and THAT much over stimulation, and just get things done.

While I was "Tornado Clausing", I felt that same sort of... autopilot. It felt good, like I actually had control over something, and that I wasn't as helpless as I felt when surrounded by our own destruction.

I left my "Claus" stuff in the car, so I could go out whenever necessary. When things got to be too overwhelming for me at the house, I'd Tornado Claus. It definitely helped me get through things.

Once repairs started happening, and families were either back in their own homes or situated elsewhere, there was far less need for the supplies I was offering. I gave the remaining bubble kits to my neighbor Sarah, who worked with kids. She was thrilled, and able to put them to good use.

Surreality

It's kind of amazing how an event like a tornado can skew a person's perceptions on certain things. It really alters a person's reality.

On May 29 - one week after the tornado - I was finally starting to accept what had happened. I was feeling better after the cookout the day before, and things were starting to calm down a little.

I was sitting on the front steps with my friend Shawn, basket of water balloons on hand, ready to take out some vultures. I'm sure I was talking some pretty big smack about it.

Then a Red Cross truck came up the road, and it freaked me RIGHT out. I'm sure that there is no way to describe the scene without sounding completely idiotic...

The truck was slowly driving up the road, announcing - via loudspeaker - that they had water and sandwiches for anyone who wanted them, inviting people to come out for them. I'm sure it's a perfectly normal occurrence, given the situation.

My absolute favorite movie of all time is "Outbreak". The way this truck was slowly going up the road, with the loudspeaker going... it ... how do I put this?

There's a scene in outbreak where the army is going through a town that was infected with "Motaba" - essentially Ebola Zaire. Everyone's bleeding out and dying, the army guys are in full hazard suits and masks, etc... Anyway, the army is driving their tanks and other huge vehicles through the town, directing people with a loudspeaker. Rounding up the sick to go off to quarantine and die.

Anyway, my brain decided to make this HUGE, strong association between the movie scene, and this Red Cross truck with the sandwiches. I have no idea what I'd been processing everything as, up to that point... but in that second, I was finally hit with the realization that "Holy fuck, this is a DISASTER".

Don't get me wrong, I knew it was a disaster-with-a-small-d when we were running from our car to the house, right after it hit. I knew it was a big deal. I can't describe what the difference was between my understanding of it up til that point, and the "Big D Disaster" realization I had at that moment, but it upset me greatly.

I have no idea why that stupid loudspeaker affected me SO dramatically, when things like discussing shelter options and talking to people from FEMA did not. The brain is a weird thing. Also, Dustin Hoffman never came to save US, haha!

A couple days later, we were at Half Price Books when another weird freakout happened. I LOVE Half Price Books. I love anything to do with books - major books stores, used places, libraries. I wanted to be a librarian when I was in elementary school!

So, we're looking through books about building decks, landscaping, etc. We had a LOT of decisions to make before we could get projects started, and neither one of us had done this before.

There were so many books on decks, and so many different ways to do it all.. I felt like the walls were closing in on me. All I knew was that I had to get out of there RIGHT THEN. A book store! That was a first for me.

Aside from reacting weirdly to such seemingly innocuous things, I found myself saying things that were... off. Things that no sane person would say with a straight face, or things that I should have thought twice about.

For instance, when we'd have inspectors, contractors, etc come to our house, I was embarrassed at what a mess our house was. Beyond the actual damage, the "liveable" areas of the house had become emergency storage and staging areas, and it looked awful.

So, as always, I'd apologize for it. Specifically, I apologized for our house "looking like a tornado hit it".

Oh wait. One did.

I think I'm going to have to stop using that colloquialism, once we get our repairs and cleanup finished. I had no idea how casually I used to toss around the term! I'll be more judicious with it in the future.

For now though... Gotta say, the dark humor of using it kind of amuses me!

Another one was "There was a tree laying on my car". I never could have imagined ever having to see/say anything like that in my life. The fact that I just pop it off like it's nothing, now? SO bizarre.

Also, the surreality of it all permeated my dreams on more than one occasion. In my favorite, I was dressed up as Marg Delahunty, Warrior Princess... and was going after Vultures and scam artist contractors!

My Birthday

The tornado happened just one week before my birthday. We hadn't made huge plans for it - all I had wanted was for Porter to make me a pavlova, and for us to just spend the day in bed, lazing around and watching superhero movies.

We managed to forget all about my birthday until a couple days before. At first, we were just going to skip it. We were still living in a hotel, and there was still a lot of work to be done.

Well, after another day of stress and labor, we decided that a day in bed with superhero movies could do us both some good. We'd gotten our bedroom mostly cleaned up at that point - the debris and broken glass were gone, even if the patio door was just a tarp duct taped onto out walls, and there was still a tree sticking out of a wall.

We had to play both the tornado card AND the birthday card to get our local video rental shop to rent us more than their 4 movie limit, but we were soon on our way "home" with an armload of superhero movies - many rented specifically for being bad.

Supergirl was our first movie, we'd heard it was awful. What we hadn't heard was the fact that there was a big red tornado in it.

Oh awesome. There's an evil magic windstorm, throwing shit around and knocking trees over. Cause I SO wanna see that right now :/ #SuperGirl - Twitter, Mon May 30 14:29:54 UTC 2011

The weather outside made it hard to forget about the tornado for the day. We were still terrified about the possibility of water/mold damage, and the rain was coming down HARD. I'm not sure if there's any noise more unsettling than listening to rain coming down on the tarp that's covering the spots where your roof is missing.

Is that HAIL?! Or is that just what rain sounds like when chunks of your roof are missing? God this sucks. Maybe this was a bad idea. - Twitter, Mon May 30 14:53:56 UTC 2011

My husband decided to be a COMPLETE jackass and go up on the rood to add more tarp. (He may have had a different definition for his actions)

Awesome. Hubby wants to go up on our compromised AND wet roof to try and add more tarp. Cause I need more stress like that :/ #NoMi / Jesus. It's raining like crazy, and he's still going up there. It's not REALLY assault if I knock him out for his own protection, right? If he falls off after ignoring my protestations, you ALL are my witnesses that the homicide was justified. Cool? - Twitter, Mon May 30 15:49:10 UTC 2011

... I could have killed him. I was SO scared and angry. That roof wasn't safe to be on, even if it had been sunny and dry out. Heavy rains, extreme wind, and him not being a roofer? Yeah. I was freaking out.

He survived, I didn't murder him, and we continued our birthday movie marathon.

Having recently watched Superman 1 & 2, we watched Superman 3 as our second movie of the day. Turned out to be another movie with a tornado!

ARE YOU FUCKING KIDDING ME!? Tornadoes in Superman 3!? Second movie, both with a tornado! #WorstBdayEver #TornadoesAreBullshit - Mon May 30 19:12:56 UTC 2011

I don't remember what other movies we watched that day - there was copious drinking involved. I think the final total was something like 4 superhero movies that had either a tornado or some sort of wind storm and/or flying trees involved.

Yeah, good choices there. Who knew that superhero movies were so tornadic?

The "Worst Birthday Ever" comment was meant facetiously. While I've definitely had birthdays that happened under more stable circumstances, I'll never forget this one. Even with a storm threatening to rip our tarp off, and a tree sticking out of our wall... we had fun.

Another big reminder of how well I married - I have no idea how I would have gotten through this without Porter. The weather may have made it harder to forget the tornado for the day, per our original plans... But snuggled up and watching the movies with him was a great change of pace.

Music

Apologies in advance. While many auties and aspies obsess over intellectual things like math equations, patterns, etc... my obsession is music. Specifically, Eurodance.

I love it, can't get enough, and can pop off all kinds of trivia about various groups, their members, time lines, singles, countries of origins, etc. Every random phrase that I know in a foreign language - German, Romanian, Italian, Finnish, Swedish, Croatian, etc - I learned from dance music.

Given my obsession, it's no wonder that music factored so heavily in getting through this whole thing. In getting ready to write this book, and going through thousands of my own tweets - I was kinda surprised at how often music came up.

A couple days after the tornado, I jokingly started tweeting songs that I was calling my "Tornado Playlist". You know, there are a LOT of songs that fit. Of the ones I actually listen to, I came up with:

Herbie - Pick it Up
DaRude - Calm Before The Storm / Sandstorm
Annie Lennox - Walking on Broken Glass
Dead or Alive - You Spin me Round
Culture Beat - Crying in the Rain
Ice MC - It's a Rainy Day
Sash - Mysterious Times
Green Day - Basketcase
Ozzy Osbourne - Crazy Train
Barenaked Ladies- Alcohol

... the last four obviously relating more to our states of mind, than tornadoes or the cleanup afterwards!

Other suggestions were made by my Twitter followers, including "She's Like the Wind", "The Thunder Rolls", "Rainbow Connection" and "Twist and Shout". I know Twist and Shout (It's been mega-mixed, duh!), but I'm not familiar with the others.

Cracking really awful, sometimes dark jokes may not have been the most appropriate thing to be at, in the days following the tornado.. but making ridiculous comments and laughing at it is sort of therapeutic. I don't want to think what kind of basket case I'd be if I didn't have at least a few laughs at the ridiculousness of the whole thing. I'm just surprised that I didn't really get told off for it!

Well, about a week and a half after the tornado, I changed my tune. (Ha!) Porter and I were driving, I'd hooked up my phone to his car stereo, and we were listening to some tunes. I realized that, all joking aside, Unique II's "Break My Stride" would definitely have to make it to my "Tornado Soundtrack". Also, Eiffel 65's "Lucky (In My Life)".

As I thought about it, I realized that there are a LOT of great songs that come to mind, as I tried to feel more upbeat about this whole thing. Some came to mind as friends gathered to help. Some came to mind at times that I've been wrestling with the worry that I was just a hair's breadth away from losing my mind completely. I think that all of them are good to listen to if you're feeling down, and all provide a "pick me up"

I compiled a second, much more positively-themed playlist, and shared it with my readers. It was my hope that some of these songs could bring some of the same cheer that they brought - and continue to bring - to me, to others affected by the disaster.

Edwin - Alive
Unique II - Break My Stride
Two Brothers on the 4th Floor - Dreams
E-Type - Last Day Alive
Ace of Base - It's a Beautiful Life
Amadin - Take Me Up
Chumbawamba - Tubthumping
Eiffel 65 - Lucky (In My Life)
E-Type - Life
Robert Miles - One and One
Lohen & Lomax - Live On
Joee - Feel it in the Air

Throughout the recovery process, individual songs that had never had a huge effect on me before, we suddenly having a huge impact on my mental state.

Four days after the tornado, I was beat to shit and went to the chiropractor to undo what the stress and everything had done to my muscles and fascia. As I was hooked up to the TENS unit, I was mentally going over everything I could think of that would need to be done, and when.

I was upset and stressed out, and I think getting a hug from my chiropractor - a complete sadist, but the sweetest guy - almost made it worse. Like it was undoing the bit of "numb" that was holding me together at that point.

All of a sudden, "Footloose" came on over their office radio, and I immediately cheered up. It's hard to be in a bad mood while getting zapped to THAT song! As few days after that....

Dropped hubby at work, went home alone. Turned on computer, put on @z1035toronto. They played 'Lean on Me'. I cried. #NoMi - Twitter, Tue May 31 13:04:58 UTC 2011

A couple weeks later, it was Spirit of the West's "Home for a Rest" that brought me to tears. We were sitting in a pub, grabbing a quick meal while we were in the area on errands. The waterworks started within the first few notes... first time I've ever cried over it. It grabbed me on a couple of levels.

First and foremost, we wouldn't be able to move back into our own house for a while, and I was raw at the idea of staying in hotels any longer.

Secondly... I'd never lived anywhere with tornadoes. I'd never lived anywhere were a city would be so greedy and incompetent, with such little regard for the residents. This song - a Canadian staple - was a bright, flashing reminder of the fact that I was a LONG way from home, physically and ... culturally?

I longed to be back in my "home and native land", where people looked after each other, and where - in the areas I've lived in - tornadoes were not a worry.

Yep. The first few notes brought all of THAT out. What can I say, I seem to have a strong sensory-memory-emotion link!

Shortly after that, we adopted Eiffel 65's "Lucky (In My Life)" as "our" song. Sappy, yes... but with the outpouring of support, love, and labor from our friends and extended geek/nerd community, it seemed appropriate.

One the first "monthiversary" of the tornado, A fellow tornado victim and I were discussing PTSD triggers on Twitter. I'd mentioned that in my past experience with PTSD - car accident - certain songs had been powerful triggers.

For instance, I had the misfortune of getting into that accident *right* around the time that Pearl Jam had covered "The Last Kiss", and that song was EVERYWHERE. That's a horrible song to be subjected to while recovering from car accident injuries!

"Careless Whisper" probably seemed like a weird one to send me over the edge, but I figured it out eventually. When I was in elementary school, entire grades from all over the city would be bussed to attend certain events.

236

One was ... I don't know. I want to say it was about drunk driving, but that wouldn't make a lot of sense, given our ages. Whatever it was, it involved scenes of car crashes, people being pulled out, ending up in wheelchairs, etc... with that song as a backdrop to it all. Apparently my subconscious remembered it better than I did, because hearing that song after my accident screwed me up LONG before I figured out why!

Anyway, I'd mentioned that it was interesting that - this time around - I didn't have a song associated with the trauma. That IF I ended up with PTSD, at least I wouldn't have weird random triggers happen when I was, say, shopping.

One of my tweeps changed that, soon enough. One mention of a phoenix rising from the ashes got the Firebird Suite stuck in my head, and .. Yeah. Association made!

It didn't end up amounting to much. I didn't end up with PTSD, and even if I had - I think I'd associate it more with recovery, than with the actual trauma / tornado itself.

On another occasion:

"So we're looking at tree auctions for our now-barren yard. I come across one for a linden tree, and first reaction is "OMG WE NEED ONE". Then I realize that the only reason I think that is because of "Dragostea Din Tei", which is - by this point - stuck in my head. I have some weird trains of thought sometimes..." - Facebook, June 24, 2011 at 9:54am

Beyond all of that, just a couple more music related observations from the year following the tornado:

1. I listened to Lucenzo's "Vem Dancar Kuduro" several thousand times over the course of tornado recovery. Various versions and mixes, many times daily. Yep, I got THAT obsessed.

2. 2 Unlimited's "No Limit" is one of the greatest pieces of inspirational music ever written.

The New War Measures Act

My Canadianism (Canadianosity?) came out fairly frequently in the months that followed the tornado, in a few different ways. The weirdest way? Rewriting the War Measures Act. I blame my tweep & friend, Lyndsay Peters / @GeekyLyndsay. Here is basically how it went down:

I hashtagged something about our recovery efforts with "Like a Baller".

She mentioned imagining me with a big pimp necklace with a cake on it.

We both smack talked Mother Nature for a bit

She joked that I should stick a copy of the War Measures act on my tree.

We both decided that the idea was so completely badass, it was like - let me quote here - *"like Pierre Trudeau himself is guiding our hands from beyond the grave! #WWPETD"*

Next thing I knew, I had completely bastardized the document.

Know what happens when I lose my routine, & stop taking Ritalin? I re-write the war measures act to adorn my downed walnut tree. - Twitter, Mon Jun 27 14:20:02 UTC 2011

Yep. Starts out:

The War Measures Act
(Proclamation of the War Measures Act, June 27, 2011)

Whereas the War Measures Act provides that the issue of a proclamation under the authority of the homeowner shall be conclusive evidence that insurrection, real or apprehended exists or has existed for any period of time therein stated and its continuance, until by the issue of a further proclamation it is declared that the insurrection no longer exists.

And whereas there is in the atmosphere an element or group known as the Mother Fucking Tornadoes who resort to the use of force and the commission of destructive offences, including smashing, crushing, and puncturing, as a means of pissing off the Homeowner, and whose activities has given rise to a state of increased stress within the Home.

... and continues from there. There was an awful lot of cursing in my version. I mean, I know I have the mouth (fingers?) of a sailor, but... damn. I don't know if I should be impressed, or horrified at myself!

The whole thing continued to make me laugh, online. When I mentioned redoing the War Measures act, one friend asked me what I planned to do with the tree. Lyndsay's response? *"Temporarily suspending its rights."*

I referred the person section 3. (a) of my war measures act of 2011 - *" (a) seizure, dismantling, and re-appropriation of any tools or weapons used by Mother Fucking Tornadoes"*

Lyndsay followed up with: *"The front de Liberation du Arbore is not an aggressive movement, but rather a response to the aggression perpetrated by low pressure cyclonic systems through contact with the Porter House."*

Love her! The laughs were definitely appreciated, and it felt good to post a printout on that downed tree.

Shortly after posting it on the tree, I decided to slap a label on my tornado damaged car, also for a laugh.

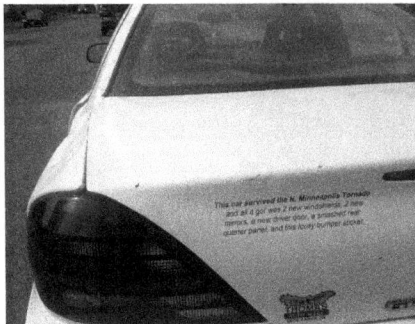

"This car survived the N. Minneapolis Tornado ... and all it got was 2 new windshields, 2 new mirrors, a new driver door, a smashed rear quarter panel, and this lousy bumper sticker".

I love it. I may have to have a car that's still a bit smashed up from the tornado, but at least people won't just assume that I'm a bad driver!

Now, all I really need is a cross stitch sampler that says "Just Watch Me" to hang in the kitchen!

Demolishing the Bathroom

At the end of June, we had already blown way past not only our insurance coverage, but our patience for everything. My husband was back at work full time, and I could NOT focus on writing. Also, not having a kitchen definitely tied my hands on how much I could even do, with regards to writing a cookbook.

I needed progress... so I decided to demolish the bathroom by myself. We had already picked out the tile and new cabinetry, but there was a lot that had to be pulled out before we could start rebuilding it

LOL! Menards carries a tile in color: "Dorian Grey". I'd buy it on name alone, had we not already picked/purchased ours! - Twitter, Tue Jun 28 21:03:03 UTC 2011

We hadn't caught the fact that the bathroom was damaged until long after the insurance adjuster had already left. It was easy to miss - whoever had built our house hadn't done the best job with framing the bathroom window, which dislodged in the tornado.

With a 1" gap in the top corner of the window, water had seeped in and caused damage to the sill under the window, and the surrounding area. The smell of mold was horrible.

Because we already blew past the ceiling of our insurance coverage, it really didn't matter as far as that went - but it had to be dealt with. We decided to use the opportunity to correct a few issues we didn't like - such as the awful, brass-trimmed mirror shower door. Ick. Also, the bathroom tiles were awful.

My husband armed me with a power drill, screwdriver set, chisel and a crowbar, and headed to work. I turned up some music, and set about dismantling the bathroom.

It felt great to finally be in charge of part of the repair. We'd had our kitchen renovations bumped several times at this point, and the feeling that nothing was progressing was driving me INSANE. Armed with tools that I'd rarely- if ever - had the opportunity to use, I felt like I had some power over my surroundings!

I started small: removing the toilet paper holder, taking the small medicine cabinet off the wall, and pulling out the baseboards. I felt almost like I was doing something bad, it was sort of weird. Like I was "getting away" with something, or vandalizing the bathroom - I wonder if that's a common feeling when taking apart a room?

Medicine cabinet is apparently glued on as WELL as screwed on! I get to use a pry bar! Unsupervised! (Yes, I may be coming unhinged) - Twitter, Tue Jun 28 13:16:02 UTC 2011

From there, I got more adventurous. I investigated the shower door, figured out how it was attached, and removed it. I felt sort of victorious as I carried it out the front door, and threw it in our dumpster. Yes, it really was that ugly.

I was sure to take frequent breaks, and I was kept my Tweeps up to date on my progress. I'm sure that they thought I was nuts.

I totally took off a shower door AND frame by myself! With an IMPACT DRIVER!. Pardon me while I grunt a few times. - Twitter, Tue Jun 28 13:31:48 UTC 2011

DISASSEMBLE!!! - Twitter, Tue Jun 28 14:05:19 UTC 2011

Listening to "Danza Kuduro" and improvising Kuduro (as someone who CANNOT dance) in a dinky bathroom while destroying it may not be smart.- Twitter, Tue Jun 28 14:45:35 UTC 2011

After I pulled down all that I thought I could, I really started to get ambitious - I decided to pull off the shower tiles. A quick search on google gave me the information I needed, and I set about my new task.

I felt SO. COMPLETELY. BADASS. Mostly.

My newfound badassery is dulled a bit by needing my husband to be here when I pull the built in cabinet down, because I'm afraid of bugs! - Tue Jun 28 17:45:46 UTC 2011

It felt good. I chipped away at the tiles, marveling at the thought of how big my delts were going to end up, especially after the overhead work. I was able to remove all of the tile that same day, and was so proud of myself. I had to smile when a friend deemed me "wrecking ball", and I couldn't wait for my husband to see my work. I'm not a priss or anything, but I've never really had to do any "handyman" stuff since.. Grade 7 shop class.

Another thing learned today: Sandals and Short sleeves for removing tile? Maybe not my smartest move. BUT.. telling myself cuts = badass.- Twitter, Wed Jun 29 02:59:55 UTC 2011

That night, he supervised while I pulled the decorative header out all by myself.

Upon his inspection, he determined that the drywall - and probably the insulation behind it - would also have to come out. I looked forward to having even more new skills to figure out.

The next day, I pulled out all of the shower drywall, as well as the insulation behind it. The wet, moldy smell was awful, but hey - even more accomplishment for me!

Done. Debris hauled. Bath, floor, surfaces swept. ALL BY MYSELF! So proud. Wed Jun 29 18:22:47 UTC 2011

It was a great feeling of accomplishment to have not only pulled it all down and ripped everything out by myself, but to also have hauled it out AND swept everything up, providing a blank canvas for the rebuild to happen. That little bit of control and progress did wonders for my mental state.

... I'm sure that swinging around a sledgehammer didn't hurt, though!

Aspergers

So much about the tornado was affected by both of us having Aspergers. I don't often think that things would be better if one or both of us were more neurotypical, but the thought crossed my mind more than once since the tornado. I've touched on this with regards to people, and why we couldn't handle going to a shelter, but I'd like to elaborate on the subject.

I find that - with all of the hysteria about autism, Aspergers, vaccines, etc... people don't really have a good idea about what it's like to be an adult aspie. We're just like everyone else, just a bit more sensitive about certain things - especially with regards to sensory issues.

Running the 3 blocks from our car to our house was the most traumatic experience of my life. I really need things to be where they're supposed to be, and running/jumping/climbing over downed power lines, trees everywhere, and seeing a ROOF laying on the ground... I just don't even have the words.

Compounding that problem, the police and EVERY news station in the cities had helicopters up in the air. I'd never had a problem with helicopters, but that MANY, in that situation? Totally overwhelming. Ever since, even the sound of one helicopter really frays my nerves.

Helicopters, trees on the ground everywhere, my house destroyed, not knowing where our 4 cats are, chainsaws going off in all directions, and people everywhere? Yeah. What a nightmare. On the upside, as far as overstimulation goes... I think I've seen the worst. I don't think I'll ever have to face anything THAT crazy ever again.

The first several months after the tornado were hard to deal with, on a daily basis. Months of chainsaws (especially bad for the first 2 weeks!).. The sounds of roof construction... constant banging, nailing, people everywhere... so much NOISE. There were contractors in and out of the house every day for months. I REALLY don't like strangers in the house, or people "messing with my stuff"... and we had absolutely NO routine whatsoever.

To make matters worse, in an effort to save as much money as we could... we were in and out of different hotels for 6 weeks. Our insurance didn't cover hotel while the house was unlivable, so we had to find the best price online... which was only ever applicable for only a few days. Then find another. We had absolutely no stability to "come home to", while our own home was unlivable.

At the end of 6 weeks, we just gave up and stayed in the house anyway. It may have been messed up, but at least it was OURS, and we could establish a little bit of a routine. We still had a LONG way to go, but at least the worst of it was behind us by then. It sucked to live with a non-completely-functional bathroom, and kitchen, but at least it was familiar to us, and we didn't have to keep uprooting from our surroundings.

As I put it on June 8th: *"Too much more time in awful cheapo hotels, and my tornado memoir won't be published, it'll be unearthed, "Blair Witch" style."*

As we slowly adapted to new surroundings and new "routines" - mostly not HAVING a routine - things would continue to change around us.

We eventually started to get used to nothing being where it was supposed to be. There were the kitchen issues - not having one, then having a skeleton of one, then slowly gaining functionality back. All the while, using disposable plates and cutlery. All the while, the locations of all of our kitchen basics would change.

There was the issue of the front entryway, living room, and dining room becoming staging areas for repair – tools and building materials and random stuff EVERYWHERE. It would drive me insane to go to use the washroom ... and have to step carefully over a power cord, and then move a power drill, or whatever. In the spot where a medicine cabinet should be, there would be several wood stain samples, sandpaper, drill bits etc. My tooth brush and tooth paste were kept upstairs by the Jacuzzi, because it was just easier to brush my teeth into the tub drain, than to deal with the bathroom issues. Plus, I didn't want sawdust in my toothbrush!

Our two offices had basically become dumping grounds for whatever didn't fit / needs to be easier access than the living & dining rooms. It was extremely difficult to concentrate with boxes of random crap everywhere.

It's hard to really describe why it made things difficult, it was just that everything was WRONG.

My husband was a complete saint throughout this whole thing. Not only am I more sensitive with sensory issues than he is, I was at home during all the says he was at work, throughout most of the repair process (as far as outside contractors go). He was good about getting me out of there when I needed it - even when I didn't realize it.

244

On another occasion, I - tearfully - asked him to bring me an energy drink when he came home. He brought home an entire bag of my favorite flavor!

Once we were able to start clearing the "staging" areas, I had more issues. I wrote the following for an Aspie audience, as it happened:

"I had to take a few small breaks, but I was making good progress. At one point, NKOTB's "Hangin Tough" came on the radio, and I felt like I was in an 80s movie montage. Had to giggle at the feeling.

But then, it started. The first few, familiar strains of the crescendo of a meltdown. You know, I really have way more to worry about than to have to try and control myself through this. Here's one of the few times I wished I was a bit more neurotypical.

I don't like thinking about the tornado, and all of the mess it's caused the past 7 months... so I wasn't starting out on the best foot. Having to deal with THAT much random mess, piled that deep? Didn't help.

Then, there's just a bunch of little things that don't help. Dust everywhere, which NOW gives me allergies – a new, post-tornado thing. Never mind the feel of it.. ugh. The skin on my hands feels like it's crawling.

Then, there's the issue of not knowing what's down there, but having a keen knowledge of the possibilities. We've had a mouse in the house since the tornado. We've had ever manner of creepy crawly awful, disgusting bug in here. That's just what happens when you have holes through your walls, and are missing a good chunk of roof for a couple of weeks.

Doesn't make it any better for me, of course. I don't mind mice so much, WHEN they are in a cage. It's the random popping-out of places they should not be that freaks me out. I'm really sensitive to sudden movement, which is why bugs and mice bother me so much. I wouldn't say I'm skittish overall, but yeah – that kind of sudden movement freaks me out. So, with every piece of material or equipment I move, I'm sort of steeling myself for something to jump out at me. It's not good on the nerves to be on that kind of guard!

Then, there is the texture thing. This may be the worst part of all, for me. Man, I wish we had workers gloves here – we tore through them all when doing the patio.

I CANNOT handle certain textures. As a kid, I couldn't touch chalk. I had to endure all sorts of ridicule for it, for having to wrap a paper towel around chalk if I was forced to use it.. a new one each time, because it would invariably pick up chalk dust from the ledge. Ugh.

As an adult, we had to be very careful picking out our bathroom tiles, for the same reason. There were a few that I just couldn't even touch, to put them in the cart. I'm not the BEST with the ones we picked out, as far as the sides/backs go – but my husband handled them for the most part, I used gloves when setting them, and now they're fine.

Well, now I have to touch the leftover tiles, along with other textures that skeeve me right out. Stuff with dust and dried dirt on them are bad enough.. but there are a bunch of leftover pieces of "Cement board" that we used for behind the shower tiles. HOLY SHIT, that stuff is just as bad as chalk. I pick up a piece, and I can feel my skin crawl. It starts at the tips, and radiates out to almost my wrists. It's a slow, creepy crawl... and it feels like the moisture just drains out, as it crawls. It's the most disgusting, nerve wracking feeling I can even imagine. By the time the "crawl" reaches my wrist, it usually sends me into a full-body shudder.

Even now, 20 minutes after lifting a few pieces, the skin on my hands doesn't feel "right". I can't explain it. I know there's absolutely NO reason for it. I'm not OCD, I don't have any kind of mental illness, and I certainly don't have any weird traumatic experiences with chalk in my childhood. It just feels AWFUL.

So, I managed to carry out 3 pieces of this cement board, and then felt the meltdown coming on pretty strong. I figured I'd rant out a post to distract myself. It seems to be working – I think I'll go back to it now."

I'm sure someone could write an entire book on the Aspie response to a natural disaster, but I just wanted to touch on some of the issues we had. Basically? Tornadoes and Aspergers do NOT mix.

Tornado Smashed Gingerbread House

I don't really remember what spawned the idea.

I have no idea why we thought it would be a good idea to make a gingerbread house representation of our what our house looked like on the day after the tornado. No clue. It seemed like a good idea at the time, and hey – I'd never made a gingerbread house before. If it turned out looking horrible, I had the ultimate excuse: It being "tornado smashed", it's SUPPOSED to look awful/be falling apart. At the very least, we found the idea hilarious, and figured it would make an awesome blog entry.

So I set about making my first gingerbread house. My husband took photos of the house from all angles, while I took measurements and poured over photos from the day after.

It was weird to look at those photos. I mean... what a mess, completely surreal.

I was trying to think of how I'd do this: "What should I make the downed power lines out of?" and "Wow, the debris in the side yard, that's gonna be a lot of work", etc. So then I get to this picture with the trees sticking out of the side of our bedroom wall, and I find it hilarious. I mean, laughed-out-loud, tears in my eyes hilarious.

If we'd seen it coming, we probably would have done the cat litter
BEFORE running errands that morning!

Before that point, I'd just been kind of numb when looking at them. While looking through them as gingerbread house research, though... I don't know if I was just fucked up, or if I'd healed, or what.

It all started out well. I used the measurements together with photos to design a to-scale template in photoshop. I cut everything out, baked the gingerbread, and made a complete mess of pouring sugar "windows". On the upside, I broke my habit of burning myself with sugar work, coming out of this project completely unscathed!

As I started to pipe the stucco and bricks – leaving "holes" untouched, for where the trees shot through the wall – I did start creeping myself out a little. It was really weird to see this house taking shape in front of me, the house we haven't seen in some time.

The ugly purple-red trim work that was replaced with nice, new blue trim.

The red bricks. Well, overall they looked red, but were really a bizarre, random mash up of red, orange, and brown.. With pink mortar. I couldn't bring myself to use pink frosting for the "mortar lines". It was so, so ugly. The house now looks nothing like it did, even before the tornado. Freshly painted stucco – light blue, rather than the aged white. The bricks painted a medium blue – mortar and all – with dark blue sponged over the actual brick parts.

We were so, SO happy when all the painting was done, and we could sit back and admire our newly-adorable house. I don't know. It was weird to assemble a representation of the old version.

The stucco. By popular vote, I didn't add the "skid marks" that trees left on the side of our house. Skid marks. Can you imagine?

I had to shudder as I attached 2 pretzel sticks to the side of the house. There is something insanely surreal about going up the stairs to the bedroom, and seeing a tree sticking in the wall. Like the wall was just... nothing. I can't even imagine the force that took... I can't believe only one person died in the tornado. There had to have been – from the appearance when it was all over – thousands of trees flying around, with similar force.

The real thing, and the sugar version

Kinda takes the breath away to think about it.

I'd poured extra melted sugar in a pan, to be shattered and used for "broken glass". It was sort of fun at first, very carefully placing the shards in the "doorway" for the upstairs mini deck. It looked really good! Well, as good as a candy version of a smashed door can look...

It didn't really shake me up until I walked upstairs a little while later, past the door that I'd just represented with sugar. I just vividly remembered ALL. THAT. BROKEN. GLASS. I never thought we'd get it out, it was everywhere... along with plant matter, and broken chunks of vinyl tiles from someone elses' house. I can't even imagine what the cats went through, that day.

Extremely vivid memory... and now, we walk around on that same carpet in our bare feet. Surreal.

Placing the Chex "shingles" and Fruit Roll-up "tarp" was a lot of fun. You know, though… creating "destruction" is actually really difficult. When you're doing straight lines of shingles, it's easy.. but skipping some, leaving room for the "hole in the roof", etc? It's a lot to think about! Once the Chex was placed, the roof was airbrushed with a combination of black and silver food coloring, thinned with vodka.

The deck and porch were also a little difficult to set up. I was trying to get a fairly accurate representation at first, but the logistics got in the way. Some debris was holding up parts of the remaining deck, blah blah. So much stuff EVERYWHERE. I eventually just set up my gingerbread "planks" in the general shape that our deck was left in, and called it "good enough".

It wasn't until I started to sculpt the 100+ year old black walnut tree (modeling chocolate), that I started to lose it.

I remember how excited I was last spring. It was a month or so after we'd moved in, the snow was melting… and I found these weird, wrinkly objects on the ground. I quickly realized that they were black walnuts, and – OMG THEY CAME FROM OUR TREE. I was so excited. I'd never had a walnut tree, never had access to one. We excitedly researched what to do with the walnuts, and we made plans for all sorts of stuff we'd make with those walnuts.

As I was shopping for my Christmas baking that weekend, I felt a little bitter as I reached to pick up a pack of walnut pieces. I shouldn't have been buying walnuts, I should have been using OUR walnuts. We never had a chance.

That tree was huge, and gorgeous. I couldn't wait to see it with summer – and fall – foliage. Not only will I not get that chance, the tree is completely irreplaceable. Ripped out of the ground like it was nothing, leaving a huge diameter of toxic soil behind as a twisted "memorial" ground.

Did you know that black walnut trees render the soil below them toxic? I didn't either, till we lost ours. I started tearing up as I carefully wrapped floral wire with chocolate clay, watching this representation of our beloved tree take shape in front of me. I gently placed it over the house and deck, and then just lost it for a few minutes.

When I started this project, I had NO idea that just the act of placing a chocolate tree on my gingerbread house would cause me to just break down. It was just so... I don't know. It just really hit me, right then, just how fucked up this whole thing was.

Beyond the gingerbread house, even... losing what will end up being an entire year of our lives to this, that such an old, healthy, HUGE tree could just be ripped up like that.. like it was NOTHING... all of it. Just surreal.

In the end, I quit working on it earlier than I had planned. I wanted to make the 3 arborvitae trees that used to stand just a couple feet in front of our house. We lost all 3 in the tornado, with one almost blocking the door, leaning up against the house. I wanted to more accurately represent the waist-deep-and-deeper debris in our side yards. I just... couldn't. When I placed that tree on the house, I knew I'd done all I had the strength to.

Man, I've always had a twisted sense of humor, but I never in a million years expected that it would hit me as hard as this gingerbread house project has. I may not have ever made one before, but I'm *pretty* sure it's not supposed to make you sad!

Next year, we'll be making our second gingerbread house ever. It will be the "after" picture, and it will be a celebration of FINALLY being all the way done with the tornado damage – I HOPE!

PTSD

PTSD is an interesting thing... because the human brain is one COMPLICATED dance. I learned this as a result of my first bout with it.

Like I'd mentioned earlier, I had PTSD as the result of a car accident I'd been in, 14 years before the tornado. While it was pretty vicious for the first few years, it had died down in severity over the years, mostly due to a LOT of hard work on my part.

By the day of the tornado, I was to the point where I'd only get upset if exposed to a car accident that I wasn't expecting... I'd usually be fine if warned to expect a crash scene, whether in person or on TV. It was manageable, but still there.

In the days - and weeks - following the tornado, I was dreading the idea of getting hit with PTSD again. Even just the run from the car to the house, right after the tornado... that was so much more traumatic than my car accident had been. I was sure that it was a given that I'd be facing that demon once again.

Early on, it really looked like that was going to happen. I would be VERY on edge upon hearing anything that sounded even remotely like a storm siren.

That had better not be a motherfucking tornado siren.Sat May 28 21:10:37 UTC 2011

False alarm. So much noise around here, brain is playing tricks with me. If I end up with ptsd I am gonna be PISSED. #NoMi - Twitter, Sat May 28 21:12:15 UTC 2011

So many things would set me on edge - the squeal of some of the chainsaws mimicked the sound of those blasted sirens, as did the odd plane, far off police siren, etc. On top of that, our area seems to set off the tornado sirens at the first sign of RAIN, so... I was on edge often.

In other news, was visited by an old adversary for 1st time since #NoMi, today. Oh PTSD. I beat you before. I'll do it again. #NoTimeForBS - Twitter, Sat Jun 18 19:19:02 UTC 2011

Was a very brief meeting, but enough to let me know I should work to head it off at the pass, not let it run wild 10 years like last time - Twitter, Sat Jun 18 19:22:24 UTC 2011

Around a month after the tornado, curiosity finally got the better of me, and I looked up the photos and video from our tornado, to finally put a "face" to what had happened. I'd hoped it would give me some sort of closure on the PTSD front - either that it would finally bring it out, once and for all - so I could stop worrying about when it may hit - or somehow prove that I wouldn't end up with PTSD at all.

It didn't really do either. The photos - and video - were fascinating. I'd always pictured tornadoes as a fairly skinny cone of grey... I don't know, dust?. Pale grey and skinny, that's about it.

What we had was nothing like that. It was a very wide column of very dark grey - maybe even black. Not a skinny, clearly defined funnel, but a wide swath of slowly-moving destruction, sections lighting up every once in awhile from ... I don't know what. I don't know if the storm had electricity of its own, or if those were some of the transformers that had been exploding in the area, sucked upward.

As I looked at the photos and video, the area was put under the first tornado warning since our tornado, as far as I could tell. Hell of a emotional strength test, huh?

It didn't trigger any sort of PTSD. I was sad, looking at the photos... but it would have been far more fucked up to look at them and NOT be sad. SO much destruction. Such a waste.

A few days later, we attended a neighborhood meeting. As this was for our block, and the surrounding blocks... pretty much everyone had went through serious damage. It was a weird evening for us - it was the first time we met any of these people and it felt more like a trauma support group.

Everyone was sharing their stories of when the tornado happened, the event we'd actually missed. I was a little TOO good with the visualizing, and found the evening to be very difficult, but necessary. We felt like we weren't alone, and everyone seemed to be handling everything SO well.

By mid July, I wasn't getting traumatized by storms at all - but I was getting pissed off. As I told myself: "On the upside, at least we don't have to worry about having trees thrown into the house - there really aren't any trees left", I got mad about there being no more trees.

Also, I used to love thunderstorms, wind, and the sound of rain. I was pissed off at the realization that these were essentially ruined for me now. The storm had taken SO much from us, I was pissed off at the idea that it was still taking things from me, even such simple joys.

Most of all, I was pissed off that the storms were upsetting the cats. Soon after we moved them home- after 6 weeks stuck in a bedroom at my father in law's house - bad rain/wind storm made it quite apparent that they remembered the tornado. As the wind picked up, they were all obviously spooked and hid - a first for them.

It wasn't normal "pets that don't like the sound of thunder", either. It was sheer terror. 3 of our 4 cats seemed to have PTSD over the tornado, and were all but inconsolable when it would rain, or when the wind would get loud.

We both felt so guilty to see the cats upset. We ended up deciding to buy some "Cat Sitter" DVDs - tons of footage of birds, gerbils, squirrels, etc. Our line of thinking had to do with distraction, especially if we weren't around when the storm happened.

I couldn't even wait for my husband to come home, the day the package arrived. The weather was miserable, and I was so excited to see if the DVDs would help calm the cats down.

The very first scene started with gerbils onscreen, along with the sound of birds chirping. As soon as the chirping sounded, 3 of the cats BEELINED for the windows to try and find the birds that they were hearing, while one stayed back, completely enthralled with the video. It was hilarious to watch, the three of them wildly searching for non existant birds, and Rat just STARING at the TV.

At one point, Turbo - the smart one - came back to the TV, looked at it for a minute, and then went behind it to find the gerbils. SO cute... and 2 others followed suit.

3 cats are now BEHIND the tv. Um..? #MissingThePoint - Twitter, Thu Jul 28 19:35:21 UTC 2011

An hour and a half later, Turbo was still interested... and while Rat was still in exactly the same place she started in, eye bugged out as she was staring at the activity on the screen. None of them seemed to notice the rain and wind.

In the coming weeks, we'd put the DVDs on when the weather got bad, or if we were going to be gone for a while. It really seemed to help. At the very least, it probably sort of made up for the fact that their "TV" was gone. You see, we have 2 garden windows up front, which used to have two trees right there - complete with tons of squirrels and birds. The cats loved to watch them. When the trees were gone, so were the small animals.

As I write this, it's ten months since the tornado. They still get upset about storms, but are slowly getting better about it - they'll let us try to comfort them, etc. I think they have a long road ahead, but - with them back in the house, and most of our repairs done - we're also more available to help them out with it.

While the cats seem to have ended up with some sort of feline PTSD, I never did end up with it. Interestingly enough, not only did I NOT end up with PTSD, but it seems to have cured my existing, accident-related PTSD.

I have no idea how it happened, but I started noticing it shortly after the tornado. With the reduced lane size, and horrible visibility around corners in the area, there were a few car accidents... and none of them affected me in the way that they normally would have.

At first, I thought maybe the immediate trauma of the tornado had just switched off the ability to go into accident-related PTSD - like prioritizing stressors. I liked the mental image of my brain telling part of itself to shut up, that we had more important things to worry about.

The thing is... it never did come back. Over the 11 months since the tornado, I've seen rollovers, horrible crashes... been told about crashed, had people describe crashes they were in, seen movies with spectacular crash scenes... and not a single instance has set me off.

I think tornadoes will always have me on edge, to a degree... but I'm so glad it didn't cross THAT line.

In the past few months, we've seen coverage of horrible tornadoes, semi trailers flying through the air, etc. To me, it's upsetting in that it's so relatable now. Now, I know what these people are going through.

Before our tornado, I never really gave it much thought. I'd see coverage of whatever disaster, and I'd think "Wow, that sucks"... and it ended there. I guess I kind of assumed that if you house was destroyed, you'd get your insurance check, and just... start fresh.

Man, that really sounds callous. It's just that... I don't know. Several times in my life, I've just packed my car up with whatever I could fit in it, and move somewhere unknown. I've started over so many times, that I guess that sort of colored my view of these things.

Now... I know how horrible it is. I know that it's not as simple as coming out of the basement, seeing a bunch of destruction, and just shrugging it off. As much of a logistics person as I am, I never gave any thought to what all would be involved with something like this.

I was never exposed to tornadoes, I never knew anyone who'd experienced them, it was an extremely foreign concept. It was something that happened to OTHER people, in another country. It wasn't a whole lot different than, say, giving serious consideration to what logistical concerns would come up if "War of the Worlds" were to happen in real life, after watching the movie.

Not only do I now have experience with tornadoes, but I have friends in areas that have been hit by natural disasters in the past - and continue to be.

In early March this year, when a bunch of tornadoes hit Ohio and surrounding areas - 91 tornadoes in one day, when the MONTHLY record for March was 180! - one of my friends gave us a hell of a scare.

She'd indicated on her Facebook status that tornadoes were coming, and she was holed up in her basement... and then went quiet for 3 hours, as the reports of the damage tornadoes did in her area started popping up on the news and across social media platforms.

I wasn't sure if I should call, if that would unnecessarily tie up phone lines or whatever. Finally, my nerves got the better of me, and I called. She was fine. Contrary to what I was picturing, she was happily eating cheesecake, unharmed and in an undamaged house. Whew!

I see mentions of tornado warnings from my friends all over the states, and yeah, it worries me. I don't want anyone to have to go through this... tornadoes are absolute bullshit.

Mourning

I'm finding that most of the sadness that has happened since the tornado - even a year later - seems to be tree related. I'm NOT a tree hugger by any means, but there's something about the tree loss here that has been unbearable.

In August, when most of the debris had been cleared... the huge stumps that remained were hard to take. They were HUGE reminders of what had happened, and there were just SO many of them.

As the trees started to change color for the fall, it was depressing that our street was now bare. In order to get to and from our house, we have to drive down streets that are lined and canopied with huge, very old trees. As those trees are started to turn for the fall, it was just such a stark change as we approached our house. All this gorgeous, brightly colored foliage, to... nothing.

That theme continued through in the winter, when we missed out on glistening ice-covered branches, or trees covered with a layer of snow after a new snowfall. When the holiday season hit, there were no trees with Christmas lights - partially because there were no trees, partially because people in our area had more pressing concerns than stringing decorative lights. It just felt wrong.

Of all of the physical damage the tornado caused to property, the trees were the least replaceable. Sure, we may have gotten new trees to plant in the spots the lost the original ones... but a 1-2" diameter tree doesn't fill the void - physically or emotionally - left by the loss of the original ones. These trees were over 100 years old! In my lifetime, the new ones won't grow to canopy the street the way that the original ones did.

It sounds like a silly thing to be upset about, but I know that I'm far from alone in this. This is an old neighborhood - my house was built in 1928, and it feels like we lost part of our history. Between all of the repairs, and the barren sky overhead, it feels like a new development on my street... just weird.

The loss of the trees mean different things to different people. Some families in the area have owned their houses for several generations, and had sentimental value of various types attached to those trees.

As I've mentioned, the loss of ours hit us pretty hard. Aside from the beauty of it and the shade it provided, it represented... I don't know how to put it. I guess.. It was a potential that went unrealized. We'd made so many plans for that tree, and as a result of it.

Logistically, we planned garden around it, planning to build a raised one. We discussed the logistics at length, planning not only how to work around the toxic soil, but how to prevent the new walnuts from rendering the raised garden toxic as well. We planned around the shade it provided... now, it's gone. All of the work and planning.

As far as the actual walnuts went, we planned for those as well. We had excitedly looked up harvesting them, learning how process them, tips on when, and how to do it without injuring ourselves or staining things that we didn't want to stain. We were so excited for that first harvest - as a fun activity to do together, and how we would reap the benefits of our expected bounty. Then, it never happened.

My first cookbook - The Spirited Baker - was all about baking desserts flavored with alcohol. As a result, I'm on a lot of email lists concerning "liquid culture" - bartending news, booze industry news, etc.

Just 3 weeks after the tornado, one of those emails happened to be all about making Nocino - a walnut liqueur from Italy, and one of our planned uses for our walnuts. It kind of felt like twisting the knife in a wound, to receive that email so soon after the tornado.

Back when we had first realized that it was a walnut tree, Nocino was one of the first ideas we'd had for the walnuts. As neither of us had tried it before, we decided to hold off on doing so - that our own nocino would be the first we would have.

8 months after the tornado, we came across a bottle of it while browsing through a new liquor store. It sort of stung to see it - a reminder of what we'd missed out on. We bought it.

That first taste of Nocino was bittersweet , in more than one way.

Physical Health

One thing I've learned throughout this whole experience is just how easy it is to forget about certain basic needs, being so entirely focused on others. In our quest to secure our house - our shelter - we had a habit of ignoring our health.

From day one, it was easy to ignore things like meals and keeping hydrated. When trying to process that level of trauma, it's almost like our brains were incapable of noticing when we were supposed to be hungry, or supposed to eat something.

Losing any sense of time probably didn't help. The days really seemed to flow together - many times, we couldn't tell what day of the week it was, or whether we were in weekday/weekend. While we tend to eat lunch right around noon, sometimes it would be 3pm before anyone noticed that we hadn't eaten anything - usually because someone started getting shaky.

Nutrition became a challenge for us, for several months after the tornado.

I have a non-celiac, auto immune allergy to gluten. I don't think it'll ever kill me, but eating wheat hurts. When I eat gluten, I develop severe fibromyalgia and various other inflammatory pain issues. The fascia over my muscles seizes up, my muscles develop bizarre ridges, my joints hurt, and life is basically miserable.

Without a kitchen, eating gluten free is a huge challenge. There are basically no gluten free options locally, so eating gluten free usually requires driving outside of the area and purchasing food from a specialty restaurant - and costs a fortune.

With time, logistics, and money working against us, I decided that it would just be easier to go off gluten free, until we were able to use our kitchen again. Not the smartest decision, health wise... but trying to be gluten free and occasionally "getting glutened" was far more painful and nasty than just maintaining a "dirty" diet.

Beyond my own dietary/allergy issues, Porter was feeling negative effects from our new diet as well. While we were both used to healthy, home cooked foods, every meal now came down to a choice between Wendy's, Taco Bell, Burger King, or McDonald's. While he wanted to eat healthy, a salad at any of these places wouldn't provide the calories he'd need for long days of hauling debris and construction work.

An added challenge was the fact that I don't sweat properly. No matter what I do, no matter how hard I work out - it's a rare occasion that I sweat at all. When I do, it'll be a couple square inches on my lower back, and just a bit of a glisten.

While not sweating tends to sound like a good thing to people, it makes it impossible to regulate my body heat - which became dangerous during the summer heat wave we experienced. I'm ridiculously susceptible to heat exhaustion and heat stroke, so I tend to stay inside all summer, every summer.

No electricity, then our air conditioner being damaged even when we DID get electricity back... toiling outside in 100+ degree heat - it was bad. Heat sickness was a frequent occurrence for me, in the months following the tornado.

NOT going outside and working is not a huge problem, under normal circumstances. My husband does the lawn work, and I do more of the chores inside. When your house gets hit by a tornado, though - remaining inside while friends and strangers are volunteering their time and labor is DIFFICULT.

I couldn't handle feeling guilty - on top of all the other emotions at the time - so I'd go out, push myself too far, and pay for it. At one point, I got heat sick, threw up, fought to keep conscious for 20 minutes... cooled myself down and went right back out to get back at it.

I figured I could afford to lose some brain cells, but my actions may have shown otherwise!

Ugh. Cooled down, now forced to wear far less clothing than I'm comfortable in and work under an umbrella. #TooFatAndHairyForShorts - Twitter, Sun Jul 24 19:39:01 UTC 2011

The next day, I pushed it too far and ended up with a full on heat stroke. I was awake for an hour and a half, then passed out for 3 hours. When I was conscious, I was completely out of it. I was confined to bed rest for a few days.

Bed rest is complete bullshit, by the way. As exhausted as I was, I was bored out of my mind and wanted to do something helpful. I hated being up in bed with my ice packs and water, while friends and family had been busting their asses for us outside. I wanted to go lay bricks, and contribute to the rebuild... but I was too weak to even lift those bricks.

At least that prevented me from doing something REALLY stupid, I guess.

Mercifully (?), my heat stroke had happened such that bed rest occurred on week days, and NOT when we actually had people over, helping out. With my husband at work, I was on my own.

Me being left alone with my thoughts tends to lead to weird ideas. By the end of my first day of bedrest, I had it in my head that I REALLY needed to buy a pair of Zubaz pants. Don't ask me why, I have no idea. I have no idea why the thought even crossed my mind in the first place, much less why it stuck, and became an obsession.

#ThisIsMyBrainOnHeatStroke #GuessINeededThat2BilBrainCells seemed to be appropriate hashtags when I told Twitter about my new obsession with the ugliest pants in the world. Luckily, my friends online talked me out of it

The second day of bed rest, I was beyond fed up, and got it in my head that I should make spanakopita. Never mind that I'd never made it before, all of a sudden, it was a URGENT that I do this.

This is what happens when you fry a few billion brain cells, I guess. Spanakopita and Zubaz. Does it GET more random?

By the time I got out of bed, got dressed, and got down to the car, I was second guessing my ability to pull off the "feat" of actually shopping for the ingredients. It was hot out, and I was still SUPER weak. I was vaguely aware of the fact that this was a STUPID idea, but pushed the thought aside. I had a MISSION.

I turned my car on, and Despina Vandi's "Come Along Now" started playing - Vandi being a famous Greek singer. I decided that this was some sort of cosmic message that I was doing the right thing, and powered through. With a rough idea of what should be in Spanakopita, I bought what I needed and headed home.

The kitchen was nowhere near ready to cook in - no cabinets or counters. As we hadn't even grouted the floor yet, I shouldn't have been doing anything messy in there yet. More accurately, it was an unfinished room with a fridge and a stove randomly tossed in it, rather than an actual kitchen.

I didn't bother following a recipe, even though it was my first time making it. This wasn't really a "Heat stroke delirium" thing, gleaning a basic idea and winging it from there is just my style. I don't know that I had the reading comprehension skills to follow a recipe at the time, anyway...

I didn't have any measuring utensils, as they were all packed. I eyeballed everything and took notes, deciding that this would, at the very least, make a good blog entry.

I was SO exhausted afterwards, even though it's an incredibly easy thing to make... but it was SO worth it

For the first time since the tornado, the house was filled with the smell of good, PROPER food cooking in our "kitchen"... not just the smell of whatever takeout we brought home to survive on.

The look on my husband's face when he came home to the final few minutes of wilting the spinach, the grin on his face at the aroma – THAT made all the effort worth it, before we even tasted it.

Oh, they tasted fabulous. Home cooked food! By my hand! Only the second time I'd actually cooked something in the two months since the tornado ripped our house – and lives – apart! (The first time being the jambalaya). They were crispy, hot, savory, and just so good... so needed. I think it did us a world of cook to eat real food, at HOME again. 2 months is far too long.

Spanakopita

4 cloves garlic, minced
1 large onion, finely chopped
1 bunch green onion, finely chopped
1.5 lbs baby spinach, ripped up
1 small bunch parsley, chopped
1 handful of dried or freeze dried dill
8 oz feta cheese, crumbled
1 cup ricotta cheese
2 eggs, beaten
1 package fillo (phyllo) sheets, thawed.
1 cup butter, melted

In a large pot, saute garlic, onion, and green onion together over medium heat until soft and translucent. Add spinach and parsley, continue to cook until wilted down to almost nothing. Drain well, cool to room temperature.

Add dill, feta, ricotta, and eggs, stir until everything is well incorporated.

Preheat oven to 375

Unroll one tube of fillo sheets carefully. If the sheets break, it's not a big deal – just quicker and easier to use if they don't!

Lay one sheet out on your work surface (In my case, the back of a cookie sheet! Lightly but completely brush with melted butter, lay another sheet on top. Repeat one more time for a total of 3 sheets, cover the remaining sheets with plastic wrap and a towel to keep them from drying out.

Cut the sheet pile lengthwise into 3 long strips.

Place about 2 Tbsp of spinach filling at one end of each strip. Fold one of the end corners over the filling, meeting the short end up with the long side of the strip. (IE: That end of the strip will now have one point, with a covered triangle shaped "dumpling".)

Fold the triangle "dumpling" up along the length of the strip, "flag style", until reaching the end. Tuck under any remaining overhang of fillo sheet, place on lightly greased baking sheet.

Continue with remaining dough and filling, until you run out of one, the other, or both.

Lightly brush the tops of each spanakopita with melted butter, bake for 17-20 minutes. Pastries should be golden brown.

Serve warm, preferably with some tzatziki to dip them in!

On the subject of tornado recipes, we never did come up with a finalized "tornado" cocktail recipe, for all of the times that the idea came up.

Although there's a "Hurricane" cocktail, there's no popular equivalent for "Tornado". We wanted to rectify that, as there were many times where an good drink was called for - and to have a thematic one would have given us a laugh.

I've got it! "Tornado", the cocktail. Get a bottle of absinthe. Pour a shot, give it to your contractor. Drink the rest, you need it! #NoMi - Twitter, Mon May 30 15:16:18 UTC 2011

... that may not actually qualify as a cocktail, but it's the best I can come up with now, short of including sawdust/broken glass! #NoMi - Twitter, Mon May 30 15:18:01 UTC 2011

Another suggestion was that it should be something made in a blender - I like it!

Light at the End of the Tunnel

As our repairs progressed, our life slowly started to normalize. Obvious, right? I guess I just never knew how much of a marathon the whole process would be, back when the tornado hit. Maybe it was totally naive, but I thought that we were looking at maybe 2-3 months to get everything fixed up and back to normal.

As each job finished up, we were able to relax a bit more, having another reason to celebrate, and another bit of evidence that things would go back to normal.

After a long summer of work, our entire backyard was functional. On August 27th, we invited people over to simply enjoy the weather and drink some wine with us. It was great to finally be able to enjoy the fruits of all of that labor, and it was nice to be able to do so with friends. It also felt incredibly good to be able to extend a social invite that didn't have any mention of the day's workload included!

After all of the HUGE projects, insane deadlines ... fussing around with little things like assembling end tables and flameless mosquito candles for the new deck and patio felt pretty good.

So, we relaxed. We grilled some brats and cracked open some bottles of wine, and we chatted about things that had absolutely nothing to do with tornadoes, home repair, or any of the other subjects that had consumed the 3 months prior to that day. We felt NORMAL.

That day marked the beginning of us being able to take some time off from the tornado. From that point forward, we would take a day - or whole weekend - off, here and there. Having that time away from working on tornado cleanup/rebuild did wonders for our mental health, I'm sure.

We soon had our first brew day, finally getting around to all of the wines we started before the tornado. We had a bunch of wines that we were supposed to transfer over to fresh fermenting vessels the week after the tornado, and had been forced to ignore them for a few months. Luckily none were adversely affected, and all of them tasted wonderful. Our brew days were a fun way that we'd spend time together, and we were so happy to be able to go back to it.

With the back yard construction finished up for the time being - it was time to move the cleanup indoors. With Tara's help, we made a huge dent on the mass of crap that was our first floor - organizing tools to go to the basement, tossing out garbage, sorting random items to go where they were supposed to.

Although the cleanup still left us with piles of items in each room, they were now passable. We went from having a narrow path to navigate through, to having wide open rooms, with organized piles of boxes towards the edges. It was a HUGE improvement - it no longer felt like a dumping ground.

By mid October, we were able to haul away most of the remaining debris, allowing us to finally plant our little apple tree. That poor thing had suffered so much abuse - being hit with a tornado not even an hour after we brought it home, months of neglect, left in the same pot that we got it in... constantly getting knocked over - it's a wonder it was still alive. Resilient little guy!

A month later, we decided that we would actually go ahead and celebrate Thanksgiving with a proper meal. We still had only the skeleton of our kitchen - Fridge, stove, temporary sink, and plastic shelving units - but somehow we made it work.

Due to the ridiculous heat wave, we ate our Thanksgiving dinner outside on our new deck. I'd gone all out on the cooking - turkey, stuffing, homemade cranberry sauce, pie - doing so felt like I was thumbing my nose at all of the crap we'd been through since the tornado.

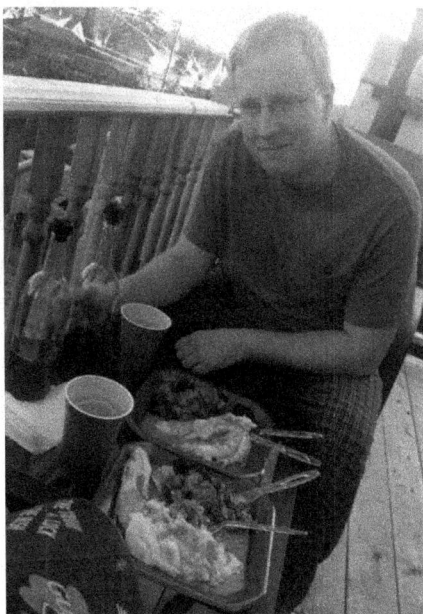

Thanksgiving dinner. Outside, paper plates, wine out of plastic cups. Wearing PJs. #SuckItMarthaStewart - Twitter, Thu Nov 24 21:47 UTC 2011

While we celebrated Thanksgiving our own way, we decided to use the Christmas break to get a bunch of work done on our house. While we had organized the rooms to the point where they were open enough to get through without tripping on anything, there was a lot of work to be done.

The new goal? Room by room, get each one looking like the tornado had never happened. No more tools. No sawdust. Clean the windows and walls, sweep the floor, nothing left where it shouldn't be. Our front entry would be a front entry - the 7 months worth of building equipment and supplies were out of there!

Front entry, before and after

Our livingroom would be a LIVING room again... The thick layer of sawdust on the couch would be painstakingly removed, the TV would finally be installed, and we would actually be able to use the room as it was intended.

We went through a lot of caffeine that week, but when we emerged, it all looked great. The bathroom, hallway, front entry, and living room were all pristine. The only thing "off" about the dining room was that we had to use it to store the food shelving until our kitchen cabinets were installed.

It was such a relief to feel like our house was actually our house again. We dubbed the week's efforts "Operation 'It Never Happened'". SO much happened that week - all of the little finishing touches in the washroom, trimming the last deck beam, re hanging curtain rods, preparing the kitchen for the cabinet building, hanging the new storm door - it was a productive week. Not much of a holiday, though!

January 8th was a huge day for us. With the cleanup done, and the whole first floor in livable shape- we were finally able to let the cats come downstairs. They had been sequestered up in our bedroom for 6 months, after 6 weeks away.

Investigating their "new" surroundings

January 19th was another huge milestone for us. With enough of the kitchen shelves finished to be useful, we were able to dig out our actual plates, cutlery, and glasses. I'm pretty sure that I heard the Hallelujah Chorus when I opened the box that contained the cutlery.

I swear, after this... I will never, ever take plates, glasses, and cutlery for granted again. Eight months of disposable dinnerware can do weird things to a person! It was unbelievably great to have a feeling of permanence again, if that makes sense.

A few days later, I was able to graduate from my "post-tornado, emergency survival, essentials only"' spice bin - literally a small plastic tub with random packets of spices and dried herbs... mostly unlabelled. It felt downright luxurious to use an actual spice rack!

I can definitely say that the tornado has given me a huge appreciation for the little things. Spice rack, plates... yeah. Getting them back really went a long way to making us feel fully human again.

The glassware had been stored in the dishwasher ever since we had packed up the kitchen after the tornado. Amazingly, NOTHING broke! Beyond actually being able to use real dishes again, being able to wash them in the dishwasher was a huge milestone for us. The small victories were coming fairly often by this point, and it felt wonderful!

By mid-March, all of the shelves for the upper cabinetry in the kitchen were created and installed. We were finally able to move all of the kitchen stuff from the dining room to the living room for the last time!

As the lower cabinets had no drawers or shelves yet, I disassembled the temporary shelving, using one shelf/risers in each lower cabinet, dividing each space into 2 storage surfaces. They fit perfectly, and we were able to neatly store it all in the kitchen. We cleaned up the dining room, which now looked as it had before the tornado.

At this point, we were finally in a better spot than we were before the tornado!

I wish that we could say the same for other casualties of the same tornado. It felt a bit weird to be celebrating all of our little victories, as there were many homes still tarped up, having had no work done yet.

It sounds like a lot of these properties were bought as "investments", with the owners just walking out on them, rather than repair the damage. Just two doors down from us - and in plain view of our bedroom deck - there's a house that lost most of its roof. That owner didn't even bother to put tarp up until weeks after the tornado - shameful. Such a beautiful house, probably completely full of mold after all of the rain we received before it was covered with tarp.

It's depressing to have this constant reminder of what happened, just because the buyer couldn't be bothered. It would have been nice if the city had pursued these investment buyers, the same way they went after people who actually were working to fix their homes.

Ugh. On a brighter note..

As spring arrived, our little apple tree started blossoming! It had survived its first winter in the ground, and it was beautiful. Additionally, the flowers that we had planted in the fall started blooming - the first real signs of life in our yard since this ordeal had begun.

We were shocked that the flowers came up as bright purples and fuchsias. We'd tried to plant flowers- specifically the tulips - in shades of blue and off-blue purples. Whoops! So much for our monochromatic blue house!

My amazing ability to kill/otherwise stunt the growth of flowers has apparently lifted! The brightly colored tulips and hyacinths inspired us to buy a bunch of vivid spring bulbs to plant: caladium, calls lilies, gladiolas, stargazer lilies, bleeding hearts, and more.

Success is a great encouragement to try again, and my hopes are high for these new plants. Who knows, maybe gardening is another skill that I gained as a result of this? I think it makes a great addition to home design, painting, ceramic tiling, grouting, staining, brick laying, and everything else that I've learned in the past 11 months!

We have come so incredibly far since May 22, 2011. Aside from all of the DIY skills we picked up, we learned a lot about ourselves, had our resilience tested, and I think we're stronger people for it - emotionally AND physically.

We learned a lot about our friends - both friends we knew before the tornado, as well as those we made as a result of the tornado. It was great that we came to know some awesome people who had been either acquaintances or even strangers up til that point.

On the emotional front, we're heading into storm season once again, with a clear view that yes... it can happen here. I wouldn't say that I'm worried about getting hit again - I know that the odds are extremely slim.

Also, if we were to get hit again, I know that it would be the last time ever - I did make Porter promise that if we get hit again, we move somewhere that does not GET tornadoes. If it happens again, it would suck - but at least it would be an end to hearing those awful sirens all the time.

We're still mourning the loss of our walnut tree, but it's more of a "That really sucks", than the emotional upheaval that it was even a few months ago. Looking forward to finally receiving the lumber from that tree, we're just glad that it wasn't a complete waste.

Professionally, I still regret the impact that this had on my second book, "Evil Cake Overlord". It's a great book, I'm incredibly proud of it... but it came out immediately before the tornado. I lost an entire year of promoting it, as the tornado damage definitely took priority. Who knows what kind of success it could have met with, had I been able to devote my time to it, as planned?

I'm still very angry at all of the crap that the city put us through. I don't know if I'll ever get past that level of... betrayal? I am still disgusted that the lives of city residents were of little importance.

We still have to hear about the football stadium on a daily basis - a daily slap in the face. Special sessions of the government, all the talk of the millions upon millions of dollars that is being thrown at it. I can't help but wonder what state the tornado zone would be in, if the city and state gave that sort of consideration, priority, and urgency to dealing with the disaster.

Right now, all we have left to do is to finish the kitchen, fix the landscaping, and repair our fence. We are at least a few months away from finally being finished all of the repairs, but at least we have full functionality back. From here on out, the work is basically all cosmetic in nature... which can be done at a far more reasonable pace. I can't wait for the day for our work days to end with NO to do list. I can't wait til our weekends are completely open, to do with as we please.

Still, it's such a great feeling to have some sort of normal life back. We can kick back and watch a movie on week nights, we can go out and see friends on the weekend. We can sleep. We can relax. We're no longer the harried, beat up tornado victims that we were for months on end - we're just us.

After stress, heat sickness, nutrition issues, sunburns, scrapes, pulled muscles, dehydration, literally wearing our fingertips raw.. Overall, I think we made out well after the tornado. We didn't have anywhere near enough money to have professionals do it, but I've learned that labor and sanity are perfectly valid "alternate currencies", under desperate circumstances!

It's nice to no longer be picking mortar out of my hair.

Aside from mortar, my hair has undergone a drastic change since the tornado happened - it started out brown, and now it's bright teal. I like it, and I'll be keeping it for the foreseeable future. It may seem silly, but it's definitely tied in to the tornado, and our journey ever since that day.

I had bright turquoise hair when I was in my teens. I loved it, and it suited me. As I aged (I hesitate to say "grew up"!), I learned to conform, to try and fit in. I kept a natural color of hair, I wore clothes that other people wore, and ... I lost a bit of myself.

After the tornado, I just came to realize that life is too short to worry about what people think of my hair color. That's actually a point far more significant than that one sentence can possibly cover... but still. Life is too short, period. I'm going to enjoy it.

I really, really enjoy our house, and so does Porter. We worked hard for it, and now it's completely customized to US. We're completely in love with our "new" house.

When we bought it just before the tornado, we knew it needed work, and that we'd get to it eventually. Now that we've seen what everything cost, and how much work was involved... I have no idea if we would have actually done anywhere NEAR this, had we not been forced to.

We may not have had enough insurance money to cover it all, but hey... it covered a lot of what we wanted to replace anyway. I still can't believe how lucky we were, with the damage pretty much being isolated to those areas. With the exception of the damage to our bedroom... I mean, what are the odds?

Overall, we're incredibly grateful for all that has come as a result of the experience. We have friendships that we will cherish for a lifetime, myriad new skills, and a gorgeous new house.

Going forward, I like to think of the past 11 months as sort of an inoculation against adversity. We've seen some pretty awful times as the result of our tornado, but emerged as better people for it. Should something major like this happen to us - or anyone close to us - again, I think we've gained the "immunity" necessary to handle it a LOT better the next time.

Going forward, the things that would have stressed us out before... don't seem so major. It's given us a much better perspective on life.

The cats are doing much better, especially now that they've gotten back full access to the main floor.

They still get upset during major storms, but are perfectly fine during regular rain, wind, and storms. We've actually decided to use the cats as a good way to discern when bad weather is coming. While the news stations will carry on like the apocalypse is upon us during even a small amount of rain, the cats are less sensationalistic. If they're calm, we're calm - I think it works well.

Though they may have lost their "tv" when the trees came down out front, they love their new show - courtesy of the new deck.

You see, the new design is far more welcoming to visits from squirrels. We make sure to keep an ample supply of sunflower seeds out there to encourage this "reality TV", and the cats love it.

As I prepare to send this book to the printer - at the last possible minute - we are currently under a tornado watch, with a thunderstorm raging outside. I can't help but feel like everything has come full circle.. It just kind of feels appropriate.

Before the tornado, I loved to listen to thunderstorms. With the tornado, that simple pleasure was taken away from me - along with so much else. For months following the tornado, even the idea of a storm had me on edge.

Now I listen to the heavy rain on our new roof, and it feels like a greeting from an old friend.

Random Thoughts
Thoughts from our year as tornado victims

The tornado destroyed blocks around my house. I lost my car. The rooster? Still fucking crowing. - Twitter, Sun May 22 22:07:11 UTC 2011

Tornadoes are complete bullshit. So badly wanting to run for the border right now. - Twitter, Sun May 22 22:58:30 UTC 2011

The vultures and helicopters are getting to me. Enough of a warzone as is. - Twitter, Mon May 23 19:19:41 UTC 2011

Tornadoes and fibro do NOT mix. Ow! I could use a whole vat of extra strength A535 right now. Of COURSE it's not available here. Of course.- Twitter, Tue May 24 00:47:14 UTC 2011

Realizing that I am a messed up person. Normally FAR more surly and misanthropic than I have been, post-tornado. #Backwards #NoMi - Twitter, Wed May 25 15:26:08 UTC 2011

Driving through the war zone, hoping our new favorite burrito place still exists. Surreal. - Twitter, Wed May 25 19:35:03 UTC 2011

Woo! El Burrito Cubano is SAFE!! Didn't get hit! - Twitter, Wed May 25 19:51:52 UTC 2011

Always fun: screeching "OMG YOU HAVE SYPHILUS NOW!" when someone drinks from your used water bottle. #AmusementAnyWayICanGetIt - Twitter, Thu May 26 01:20:04 UTC 2011

RT @bnsheehan: @Celebr8nGenr8n You know, tweets like that don't convince me that I shouldn't view you as a role model.Thu May 26 01:53:38 UTC 2011

Maybe this massive sunburn will clear up the stress-acne the tornado left me with? #NoMi #AlwaysLookOnBrightSideOfLife - Twitter, Thu May 26 23:10:01 UTC 2011

Just realized what getting to our #NoMi house reminded me of. There was a Red Hot Chili Peppers video that was themed like a video game / When we were rushing to save the cats, and trees were blocking every path. That's what it reminded me of! #NoMi - Twitter, Thu May 26 23:43:44 UTC 2011

Would it be really wrong if I started praying to Morgan Freeman for the roof repairs to be speedy and as drama free as possible?- Twitter, Tue May 31 00:33:09 UTC 2011

Hearing the wind flap around the tarp over the missing chunks of our roof on the next floor up is really disconcerting. Hope it holds! #NoMi - Twitter, Tue May 31 16:13:12 UTC 2011

It's amazing, the good that listening to "Summer of '69" can do for the soul.- Twitter, Tue May 31 19:21:39 UTC 2011

Haha... UPS delivered my book mailers to my back door. Bet that was a bit of an adventure for em! - Twitter, Tue May 31 21:41:27 UTC 2011

I'm an intelligent, ANGRY Irish Canadian w/ an internet connection who just got tornadoed. You do NOT want to fuck with me right now. #NoMi - Twitter, Thu Jun 02 14:21:20 UTC 2011

You know what I probably look like right now? Brad Pitt in 12 Monkeys. Well, except fat and female.- Twitter, Thu Jun 02 14:48:23 UTC 2011

Discovered another tornado casualty in my kitchen:My FAVORITE blush brush ever. Got wet, is moldy. Sigh. That sucks. NO idea how to replace! / That seems so lame and petty of me, I'm sorry. I'm not a big makeup person, and that's the first one I ever liked, didn't make me look 80s!- Twitter, Fri Jun 03 22:54:16 UTC 2011

Big volunteer day in #NoMi today! Going back to the house to yell at people to get off our lawn. Lol. Cause we're old like that!- Twitter, Sat Jun 04 12:31:56 UTC 2011

For #Nomi. I will try to keep this in mind: RT @exceptionalfood: A scar simply means you were stronger than whatever tried to hurt you.- Twitter, Sat Jun 04 20:35:49 UTC 2011

I don't think I've been so focused on one thing in my life. Tornadoes seem to be cure for my ADD. Temporarily so, I hope! #NoMi - Twitter, Sun Jun 05 12:45:58 UTC 2011

I think that being half crazy Pre- tornado is helping me cope. Like a live culture immunization against going complete BatShit nuts.- Twitter, Mon Jun 06 13:40:31 UTC 2011

You know what? It's probably better to have gone through a disaster early in life, and we did get off fairly easy - $ aside. #NoMi - Twitter, Mon Jun 06 21:51:37 UTC 2011

#DND friends: how many experience points do we earn for getting through the #NoMi tornado without injury/killing each other? / RT @introvertedwife: @Celebr8nGenr8n You've at least got a good 25% wind resistance now. / Come to think of it, the house is getting its armor class boosted with the new roof, etc, huh? #NoMi #LifesDMIsSadistic / What would my car be, #DND friends? She has a Mega tree of doom land on her, and still runs! That's pretty badass. Warrior?

I like it! Now she needs a name! RT @timboerger White Chariot of Might, +2 resistance to Nature based attacks. +3 save vs. deity.- Twitter, Mon Jun 06 22:17:01 UTC 2011

Apparently I have to be REALLY careful when typing "roofers" and "roofing" now. All of those roofie jokes are coming back to haunt me!- Twitter, Tue Jun 07 15:10:11 UTC 2011

"Two Aspies in a Cheap Hotel" is the name of our 2 Brothers on the Fourth Floor cover band.- Twitter, Thu Jun 09 01:21:08 UTC 2011

Cleaning the "livable" rooms today-where all the tools and crap were dumped/stored during tornado cleanup. I'd say "what a disaster", but..- Twitter, Sat Jun 11 14:26:21 UTC 2011

OMG. Did you guys know there is such a thing as "multiple vortex tornadoes"? Just read about em. I may never sleep soundly again!- Twitter, Tue Jun 14 19:53:23 UTC 2011

Listening to @Iamknaan's "Waving Flag", losing it. I've lost ability/strength to deal with tornado aftermath.- Twitter, Thu Jun 16 15:07:20 UTC 2011

Can't wait for all of the rebuild around here to be done. The whine from the power tools sometimes sounds like tornado sirens. Screws w/ me - Twitter, Tue Jun 21 19:13:55 UTC 2011

I've lost track of how many times I've almost typed "tornado" as "Toronto". #WhatsItMean #ItMeansTorontoDoesntHaveFuckingTornadoes - Twitter, Fri Jun 24 18:41:44 UTC 2011

Seriously, all the giant creepy bugs - the likes of which I'd never seen before losing our roof - it's getting old FAST. This is so gross!- Twitter, Sat Jun 25 05:27:03 UTC 2011

Know what tornado renovation PROGRESS feels like? It feels like Ricky Martin's "Copa de Vida"/"Cup of Life"... Awesome through and through!- Twitter, Tue Jul 12 23:13:35 UTC 2011

Tipped the painter with bottle of wine. Now receiving hilarious, not entirely coherent text msgs from him. LOL! (He loves it!) #HomeBrew - Twitter, Wed Jul 13 03:29:33 UTC 2011

For all my energy drink abuse lately, I should have approached @MonsterEnergy about sponsoring our Tornado Recovery! -Twitter, Fri Jul 15 14:15:57 UTC 2011

Had screaming meltdown before 8am. Now making flower reproductive organs out of Tootsie Rolls while tornado repair work continues around me.- Twitter, Tue Jul 19 14:32:52 UTC 2011

Still love how this was supposed to be my first summer of "not a lot of physical labor" & "being able to have weekends", by not doing cake.- Twitter, Sun Jul 24 21:13:17 UTC 2011

Thai food and Captain America! I'm just excited to get out of my grubbies for an evening... as hawt as pants covered in mortar may be! / I were to analyze the crust layers on my pants, I would find mortar, grout, landscape adhesive, dust from plaster... #BringingSexyBack / RT @introvertedwife: @Celebr8nGenr8n Hey, mortar covered pants are all the rage in France.- Twitter, Thu Jul 28 16:25:10 UTC 2011

I need like a vat of A535 and a big muscular massage therapist. Named "Sven". Yes. Also a dirty big rum cocktail. #Tornadoista #RepairPain - Twitter, Fri Jul 29 00:27:20 UTC 2011

Is Sears pretty much Mecca to most guys, or did I marry a weird one? I mean, I KNOW he's weird already, but... :D - Twitter, Fri Jul 29 22:15:16 UTC 2011

Serious discussion: building a Tardis outhouse or toolshed in the back yard next year. #Tornadoista #LosingIt - Twitter, Sat Jul 30 01:08:07 UTC 2011

Well, THAT was interesting. Under the mass (I mean MASS) of deadly nightshade, there was a cherry tomato plant. We had no idea. #WTF - Twitter, Sun Oct 9 20:33:04 UTC 2011

Fun new tornado-house challenge: Dying my hair without a mirror. I'm sure I'll end up with green stains ALL over my neck, shoulders, & face / However, given that it's a week before Halloween, I think I can pull off the stained-green-skin look. I'll say it's my 'V' costume. LOL - Twitter, Thur Nov 10 17:00:35 UTC 2011

Getting ready to be interviewed about the tornado. Considering how ridiculous I was with my @cbc interviews (radio).... oh boy... #nervous / It's hard to strike a balance between 'get the point across' and 'don't swear-you're on TV, dummy!' when talking about such a sore subject!- Twitter, Mon Nov 21 23:43:34 UTC 2011

Ok, the '6 months since the tornado' coverage is starting to get to me. So many pictures of mass destruction. :(/ I can't believe it's been half a year already. I never imagined that the aftermath would stretch out for this long - and no end in sight!- Twitter, Tue Nov 22 23:15:37 UTC 2011

So I had a dream last night that I themed my tornado memoir around Dante's Inferno. Uhm. I've never read that. Wtf?- Twitter, Wed Nov 23 15:23:07 UTC 2011

Shit. Wanted to go make snow angels, realized there is still broken glass and repair debris under the snow. #TornadoesAreBullshit - Twitter, Sun Dec 04 13:35 UTC 2011

Hope the 'My house only looks like a tornado hit it, because one did!' excuse will hold up long enough to get everything rebuilt/sorted!- Twitter, Thur Dec 15 16:02:08 UTC 2011

It doesn't feel very Christmassy around here. Not much decoration in the neighborhood - most people have bigger fish to fry w/ cleanup. / That and... almost no trees anywhere. I thought fall would be the worst for the 'OMG the trees are gone', but ... still feels weird. - Twitter, Thur Dec 22 22:47:07 UTC 2011

Bizarre dream last night: Was picking up our milled lumber, Scott Bakula AND Dean Stockwell were at the mill, separately. WTF? /   I'd turned around to see Stockwell using a calculator, laughed at the image, then explained why it was funny to Bakula. In the dream, it / didn't register that Bakula was IN Quantum Leap for some reason, and I didn't realize why he looked at me like I had two heads til I woke up - Twitter, Sun Jan 1 13:22:45 UTC 2012

Holy crap. You know you're out of touch when you find out that someone you KNOW is in a TV show, by seeing the commercial.- Twitter, Sun Jan 1 17:21:07 UTC 2012

Dear God-of-kitchen-renovation: If you let this finish quickly/easily, I will create a #GlutenFree buttertart & make tons of people happy" / ... and it will be a GLORIOUS butter tart, that will not suck in the slightest - EVEN being gluten free. - Twitter, Sun Jan 21 00:21:52 UTC 2012

He's making mortar... guys, I'm about to get a counter! My last one! I'm gonna have a kitchen this week! 8+ months without is TOO LONG!!- Twitter, Sun Jan 29 20:49:30 UTC 2012

*Can't wait til I no longer have to play the 'Where the hell is my _____ '
game with regards to the kitchen.- Twitter, Wed Feb 1 15:36:06 UTC 2012*

*Getting sawdust & random tornado/construction debris out of a couch with
a faux suede texture is a PAIN.. but feels good to be this far - Twitter, Sun
Feb 12 19:35:49 UTC 2012*

*-Procrastinating on going through boxes of kitchen stuff we packed up after
the tornado. After 8.5 months of cleanup/repair, I'm EXHAUSTED. Twitter,
Sun Feb 12 16:52:40 UTC 2012*

*After 8+ months of plastic cups, *glasses* feel like an amazing luxury. 1
more week til real plates and cutlery!! - Twitter, Sun Feb 12 17:24:50 UTC
2012*

*The tornado made us go kind of feral. Got a little 'Lord of the Flies' there,
for a while. Re-domestication feels GOOD.- Twitter, Sun Feb 12 17:25:30
UTC 2012*

*I've never been so excited to do a load of dishes in my LIFE. Being reamed
by a tornado sure screws with ones priorities & views! - Twitter, Sun Feb
19 21:58:25 UTC 2012*

*Just read that we're about a month away from the start of tornado season.
Oh boy... - Twitter, Tue Feb 21 23:02:36 UTC 2012*

*Just saw coverage of last night's tornadoes. I had NO idea that the could
hit in the middle of the night... I can't even imagine. - Twitter, Wed Feb 29
17:39:52 UTC 2012*

*Just read that in all of Newfoundland, they average 1 tornado every 2-3
years... usually an F0. Hrmmmm... - Twitter, Sat Mar 3 03:26:16 UTC
2012*

*Kentucky can declare a state of emergency the same day, and Minnesota
waited MONTHS? Wtf? Way to go, MN.. but hey, let's get a new STADIUM
- Twitter, Sat Mar 3 03:32:06 UTC 2012*

Tornadoes are complete bullshit. - Twitter, Sat Mar 3 03:35:32 UTC 2012

Well, shit. Wind picked up all of a sudden, kinda pulled at the roof, all 4 cats RAN downstairs. They remember. :(/ Oh yay, a minute after sounded like the wind was going to rip our roof off, read tweets re: other roofs being torn off. I START DRINKING NOW.- Twitter, Tues Mar 20 00:43:01 UTC 2012

First signs of new life after the tornado! So excited!- Twitter, Tues Mar 20 13:18:48 UTC 2012

Marie Porter

Marie is an award winning cake artist based in Minnesota's Twin Cities. Known as much for her delicious and diverse flavor menu as for her sugar artistry, Marie's work has graced magazines and blogs around the world.

As a trained mixologist, Marie has combined her bartending knowledge with her aptitudes for baking and experimentation, culminating in her first cookbook - The Spirited Baker - for beginner and experienced home cooks alike. Having baked and designed for brides, celebrities, and even Klingons, Marie was proud to share her wealth of cake knowledge in her second book, "Evil Cake Overlord".

Marie also maintains a food / lifestyle blog, "Celebration Generation".

Michael Porter

Michael Porter works in medical manufacturing, and is a food and commercial photographer. His work has appeared in local, national, and international magazines, in catalogs, corporate websites, and as well as in many online media outlets.

In addition to being an awesome husband and photographer, Michael is Celebration Generation's "Chief Engineering Officer", responsible for all custom builds, equipment repairs, and warp engine emergencies.

Books by Marie Porter

The Spirited Baker
Intoxicating Desserts & Potent Potables
Marie Porter

Combining liqueurs with more traditional baking ingredients can yield spectacular results. Try Mango Mojito Upside Down Cake, Candy Apple Flan, Jalapeno Beer Peanut Brittle, Lynchburg Lemonade Cupcakes, Pina Colada Rum Cake, Strawberry Daiquiri Chiffon Pie, and so much more.

To further add to your creative possibilities, the first chapter teaches how to infuse spirits to make both basic and cream liqueurs, as well as home made flavor extracts! This book contains over 160 easy to make recipes, with variation suggestions to help create hundreds more!

Evil Cake Overlord
Ridiculously Delicious Cakes
Marie Porter

Celebration Generation has been known for our "ridiculously delicious" moist cakes and tasty, unique flavors since the genesis of our custom cake business. Now, you can have recipes for all of the amazing flavors on our former custom cake menu, as well as many more!

Once you have baked your moist work of gastronomic art, fill and frost your cake with any number of tasty possibilities. Milk chocolate cardamom pear, mango mojito.. even our famous Chai cake - the flavor that got us into "Every Day with Rachel Ray" magazine!

Feeling creative? Use our easy to follow recipe to make our yummy fondant. Forget everything you've heard about fondant - ours is made from marshmallows and powdered sugar, and is essentially candy - you can even flavor it to bring a whole new level of "yum!" to every cake you make!

For wholesale inquiries or to purchase directly, visit

www.celebrationgeneration.com

www.ingramcontent.com/pod-product-compliance
Lightning Source LLC
Chambersburg PA
CBHW071410090426
42737CB00011B/1412